JUNK MEDICINE

Dr. Tom Gray

"All art aspires to the condition of music…"—Walter Pater

For TJ & Tyson…

I

Texas Panhandle

Cannabis Prohibition Era

"Please..."

It's involuntary, it just comes out, like a prayer, as soon as I see the police car appear in my rear view mirror. They shouldn't be back there. When I'd passed them going the opposite direction several miles ago, I'd been expecting them. Here in west Texas, people are friendly, and I'd been given the universal "cops ahead" signal of quickly flashed daytime headlights by an oncoming pick up truck just as I was leaving the city limits. I'd debated whether to even take this route. Better to make for Amarillo and the anonymity of I-40? Or stick to the small towns and sleepier highways that connect them further north in the Texas panhandle. I chose whichever was fastest. I always did.

That's how I found myself headed east on this desolate stretch of highway 152 just a few miles outside of Pampa, Texas. I checked my speed after passing the pick up—sixty-two and safe. The radar detector was silent. I'm convinced I'm invisible, that I have utterly nothing to be concerned about. Just another silver sedan going wherever people go at 11:20 in the morning on a Tuesday. Nothing to see here. Nothing to see at all. I'll be back before anyone even knows I've been gone.

I was about to decide that the pick-up truck was mistaken when I finally saw them coming around the next curve, two Texas State Troopers clearly visible in the cab of their patrolling SUV. I almost…waved. And I smiled a little bit to myself as I sometimes do when I know I have a secret I'm not supposed to have, that I think nobody else could ever imagine. But the smile slowly faded, the sentiment replaced with the gnawing sensation that something doesn't quite feel right. I double checked my speed. Still cruise-controlled at sixty-two. I wanted to press the accelerator, to put some distance between myself and those policemen. But I knew this would be both foolish and unnecessary. Wouldn't it? I mean, for what possible reason could those troopers have taken enough interest in me to turn around out here in the middle of nowhere and follow me? They wouldn't. They couldn't. And I've almost convinced myself this is true, when I see them top the hill behind me as I check the rear view mirror for the tenth time in the last five minutes.

"Please…"

Ok, Ok, Ok…their lights aren't on. They're not after me. Maybe it's not even the same car. But as they settle in just a few lengths behind me, I can see them again clearly in their black SUV, the driver— skinny faced, serious. And the John Goodman-looking motherfucker next to him in the passenger seat. It's them. And they are, in fact, after me.

It's cool, I tell myself. You've been through this before. Like that time in Clayton, New Mexico, a year or so before, when I'd stupidly sped out of town, only to be immediately pulled over by the local police. I was fortunate to have been on the far side of town, after the highways leading towards Trinidad (where I'd actually been) and Taos, (where I claimed to have been) merged. And that time the officer bought it. My mouth was so full of skittles and solidified saliva that I wouldn't have been able to speak if he'd said anything other than "Slow it down, Mr. Gray" as he handed me a warning and sent me off into the night.

This time will be the same, it has to be. But as I glance back and forth between the rear view mirror and the seat next to me, that gnawing sensation in my gut that something has gone permanently wrong, grows. My car is a mess. Wrappers from convenience store snacks litter the floorboard. Bottles, half full of soda and half full of spit, fill the cupholders. And more important than what's here, is what isn't. No luggage. No skis. No trappings of any sort to explain what I, Tom Gray, am doing 350 miles from home in the middle of the staked plains.

After what feels like an eternity, Officer Serious does what I knew he inevitably would—he lights me up. At the same time, my radar detector finally chirps, almost certainly telling the troopers that I am traveling precisely sixty-two miles per hour. But they already knew this. And knowing that they did, makes what is about to happen next feel almost like fate.

I had my alibi ready, I always did, though I hoped I'd never have to use it again. So I'm ready when officer John Goodman approaches my sedan from the passenger side, in the sweeping grass between where I've stopped and the fence separating us from the corn fields beyond. I've lowered both driver and passenger side windows, and the west Texas wind is howling through my car as the officer leans in cautiously, most of his bulk still towards the back of my car. He's younger than I'd thought. Large-joweled, baby-faced, and he's trying to grow a beard but can't, not really. Officer Goodman is almost apologetic, like he doesn't at all want to be doing what he's about to do.

"Hey there, Sir, uh, we got you, uh, we got you going a little fast back there a few miles ago. Going sixty-eight. Speed limit was fifty-five." he says.

I'm not about to argue, not even knowing for a fact that I was traveling precisely sixty-two miles per hour, and the speed limit had increased to sixty-five at least a mile before I'd ever crossed paths with Officer Goodman and his stone faced friend. Speaking of, where exactly is he? I can't see him.

"Ah, I'm so sorry officer, I could've sworn the speed limit was up to sixty-five back there. I guess I just didn't notice." I shrug, innocent.

Officer Goodman asks me no more questions, doesn't so much as glance into the backseat of my car. Just inspects my license and insurance, and with the same apologetic tone, says, "I tell you what, uh Mr. Gray is it? Lot of people make that mistake on this highway. If you'll slow it down, I'm just going to go write you a warning and get you on your way."

I hardly have time to thank him before he's disappeared from view, back to his SUV. To write me a warning. A warning! John Goodman is not a motherfucker at all! Never mind the fact that so far as these fine officers should be concerned, I've done nothing whatsoever to merit said warning, but I do not care. I'll take my warning, and be on my way, just as Officer Goodman has promised. I almost relax.

"Ok if I roll my windows back up?" I shout behind him. He doesn't seem to hear but doesn't seem to care either. So I raise them.

But no sooner has my passenger window sealed, than Officer Serious appears outside of it. And knocks. Motions for me to lower it back down with that rotating wrist motion that no one has had to actually use since last century. I swallow, hard, and press the button. I'm starting to see it now.

"What'd you put your window up for?" Officer Serious asks. Cunningham is his name, says so right there on his uniform. He's aiming for casual, but failing.

"The wind. It's…too windy."

"Hmm…where'd you say you were going again?"

I hadn't. "Oklahoma City, Sir."

Cunningham nods like he's not surprised. "And where you coming from?" His inflection is up. Like he doesn't believe my answer before I even say it.

"Coming from Taos."

"Oh really?" Again, the nod. "Where'd you stay?"

I know the answer. But it comes slower than it should. "Condos…um." I might've snapped my fingers. "Snow Bear."

I am unable to see behind Cunningham's mirrored sunglasses, but I know that his eyes must be piercing, measuring me. He's better at this than I am. I've never seen him before, but he's seen me a thousand times.

"Where's your luggage?"

I curse myself for my carelessness. I'd left my house at 2AM that morning, no longer cautious enough to put on the costume of the skier/hiker I'm pretending to be. I look more like a hobo. My suitcase could be in the trunk, there *is* one in the trunk. But I can't invite him to look there.

"Nope. I own the condo. Everything I need is there. Just jump in the car, and go." I'm ad libbing now, but it sounds reasonable enough. Or at least I hope it does.

"Why you wearing shorts?" Cunningham wonders. "Not cold up there?"

He's right. It is still cold up there, though it's April. I look down at my legs, then slowly back at his sunglasses and the reflection of myself, but I don't answer right away. It is a moment of recognition in which we both acknowledge we are playing a game. I'm pretending to tell the truth, and he's pretending to believe me.

Finally I say, "I dressed for where I'm going, not for where I'm coming from." Like it's professional advice or something.

After another long pause, Officer Cunningham shrugs, "Fair enough…" He ambles to the front of my car, looks down. Satisfied, he heads back to join his partner. "What kind of car is this anyway?"

"Mazda 6," I say. What I want to say is "does this mean I'm not getting my warning?" But he's gone, and I already know the answer anyway.

Minutes go by like hours. I convince myself a six-year-old could've been smoother than I've just been. I feel simultaneous relief and horror as Officer Cunningham again approaches my car, this time on the drivers side. I'm praying he hands me a warning or a ticket, I don't care which. But instead, he asks, "Mr. Gray, you mind joining us out here for just a sec?" The sound of my name in his mouth makes me sick.

But I'm eager to please. I say sure, hop out, join them at the trunk of my car, catch my cap as it whips off my head in the wind, smiling like I just did a magic trick. Tada! We all three chuckle. I am so fucked.

"Now where'd you say you were again? Taos?" Officer Cunningham is in charge here.

"Yep. Yes sir. Taos. Just like it says on my cap."

"And you were doing…what exactly?"

"Closing up my condo. Ski resort shut down for the season a couple weeks ago."

"I see." The officers glance at each other briefly. Both of them stand with most of their weight on one leg, hip jutted out, with a thumb hooked in a belt loop. The wind whips between us making it slightly hard to hear. Cunningham again, "Now, you wouldn't be up to anything you wouldn't want us to know about now would you?"

I feign surprise, which is kinda easy when you're already on the verge of panic.

"Me? No! No, nah. Like…what?"

"Oh you know, don't have any drugs in your car or anything do you? No cocaine, no Heroin, none of them pills, no…marijuana?"

"No, no, nothing like that. Just headed home ya see. Just like I said, I…"

"Well you wouldn't have any objection to us taking a look around then? Inside your car?"

And here we are. The moment these officers have been building towards since they first passed me twenty minutes ago. They want inside my car. I know exactly what I'm supposed to do here, exactly what I'm supposed to say. Or not say. I've rehearsed it. But never under these conditions.

"You know officer, in all my years of driving, never once has a police officer ever asked me if he could take a look inside my car. I can't imagine why you're asking me now," like I'm offended or something.

Cunningham chuckles, "Ya see, it's always the same story. You guys are all nice and polite and everybody's friends, right up until the point where we ask for your permission to search your vehicle. Then all of a sudden we're not such good friends anymore are we. Why's that you reckon?"

The old "if you've got nothing to hide, then why not let us violate your rights" routine.

"Sir, I'm not trying to be rude, I just don't see any reason why you'd feel the need to search through my car?"

"You want to know *why*?" Cunningham kicks it up a notch. "Because you act suspicious, that's why. What'd you roll your windows back up for, huh? See, to me and him, that's suspicious." He gestures towards John Goodman, who once again is a motherfucker. Goodman nods like it's just occurred to him. "In fact, in all our years in law enforcement, we don't recall anyone doing that like you did."

Now I really am incredulous, and offended. "What?!? I did it because it's windy! I even asked you if I could put them back up. This isn't probable cause, this is, this is…this is *bullshit*!"

Cunningham knows it's bullshit. He also knows it doesn't matter. "Do we have your permission to search your car or not," like it doesn't really matter which way I answer.

I'm spinning out here. I know it's not supposed to, but my refusal will only serve to confirm my guilt. Of course, so will allowing these two to open the trunk of my car. Like I said, I'm fucked. So I go with the only choice I've got. I refuse.

"No. You do not have my permission to search my car."

"Fine. Have it your way. We need you to stand right over there." Cunningham gestures towards the fence and the cornfields beyond. "And wait. We have reason to believe that your automobile is being used in the commission of a crime. We're gonna radio back for someone to bring the dog out from Pampa and we'll go over your car that way. Stay right there."

This. Cannot. Be happening. I'm an expert at denial, but only when it's this obvious do I recognize it. I want to run into the cornfield, and I try to calculate how long it might take them to find me. I don't realize it, but I am in no way "standing right there" as Officer Cunningham instructed me to. I'm pacing in circles, hands on my head, then on my hips, then gesturing why, why, why. I don't stop to consider that perhaps this is exactly why the troopers have left me out here alone with my thoughts. Calling for a dog? There's probably not a drug-sniffing dog within three hours of us. They're not calling for any dog. No, Cunningham is teaching his younger partner exactly how you let that fish wear himself out on the line, before you start reeling him in. He's been teaching him since the moment we first drove by each other on the highway and he said, "Lookie there. No front license plate. Car's not from Texas. Why don't we see what he's up to?"

I move quickly through denial, skip anger (although I'll come back to it later), and go straight to bargaining. I know what I've got, and it's not cocaine, not even close. I've got cannabis. And a lot of it. But maybe, just maybe, these cops know what I already know. What EVERYbody should know. Hell, cannabis shouldn't be illegal. It already IS legal in Colorado. And that's exactly where I've been. The fact that these officers clearly suspect that, and thus know exactly what it is I'm hiding in the trunk of my car, escapes me. No, these officers are looking for cocaine. And Heroin. They're saving lives! They're not looking for cannabis. C'mon!

I gesture for Officer Cunningham to come back out. I'm ready to chat. And this, is precisely what he's been waiting for.

"Listen, officer. I want to be reasonable here with you. Now I'm not saying I do or don't have anything in my car that I would or wouldn't want you to find. Or not find." I am doing an imitation of the world's worst lawyer. "But just hypothetically speaking, puuuurely hypothetically speaking, let's say a fella did happen to have a small quantity of something, you know, just for medicinal purposes. You know, for sleep, or, or something like that."

I sound ridiculous. I sound desperate. I sound so, so stupid. But Officer Cunningham, he doesn't let me know that. He seems interested. I swear he almost puts his arm around me. "Well, now, that depends on exactly what we're talkin' about here. Are we just talkin' about a little weed? Or...what?" He's gently reeling me in.

"Weed. Yes. I mean, if that's what I had." I smile, we both smile. Now we're playing a game where I pretend not to be telling the truth, and he pretends not to believe me. "How...would you feel about that?" I'm sheepish.

"Now we're talkin' about weed here, right? Not THC products?" This distinction seems important to him. And it concerns me. I didn't drive all the way to Trinidad, Colorado to the closest dispensary north of the border for the 19th time to buy bud. No sir. I came for that shit you can't smell. What can I say? Vapes, gummies, candies, all of it. I think that's what he means by "THC products." And there's a felonious amount of it in my trunk, right now.

"I'm not sure what you mean, sir. I'm talking about...marijuana."

"None of that hash oil?" he asks. "Nothing like that?"

"Oh no, of course not. I don't have anything like that." Do I? Hell, I don't even know. "Hash" makes me think of the Rolling Stones lounging decadently in some Moroccan drug den, lazing away the summer of '67. I wish.

I'm not sure what I'm expecting here. That these fine red-necked West Texas Troopers are going to take a quantum leap with me ten years into the future to a time and place where cannabis is just…legal? Just like that? And I realize that, yeah…that's exactly my plan. And it's awful.

I gesture openly. "Sooooo…"

"Well we're not gonna just take your word on that, son. Are you giving us permission to search your car?"

It's like all of that west Texas wind just…stops. I suddenly don't care anymore. I know that the only answer to his question is always, always, always supposed to be no. It's a complete sentence. No. But I'm just too fucking tired. I have been for as long as I can remember. I'm tired of this bullshit drive. I'm tired of the lies I tell myself and everyone else. I am simply tired of fighting. And I want to give up.

"Son? What's it gonna be?"

I hand Officer Cunningham the keys without looking at him. "Just open it. It's in the trunk."

"Is that a yes? You're giving us permission to search your vehicle." It's a statement, not a question.

"Well, you know what Willie Nelson said—'If you're gonna be an outlaw, you gotta be honest'".

"That wasn't Willie Nelson. And I don't think that's what he meant. We're good Jimmy! Open it…"

———————————

Now, to someone who's never been in handcuffs, what happens next seems simple. Just put your hands behind your back, keep your mouth shut, do as the officers say, and there will be no problems. Except right now, my mind does not remember this. And it's telling me that what seems to be happening, can't be. And it's telling my body to run. Run into the corn field. Run into the road. Just run. Officer Cunningham breathing behind me might as well be a bear. That's how badly I want to run from him.

The wind which had earlier seemed to stop has now funneled itself inside of my head and I am tossed inside a tornado of terror, anger, and regret. I am emotionally concussed. And instead of running, I collapse to my knees. I want to slither into the ground, to simply disappear. I'm depersonalized to the extent that I only become aware again as the officers are finishing up my Miranda rights, opening the passenger door of their SUV to stuff me into the front seat. I sit there stunned, arms handcuffed behind me, as they quickly comb through the rest of my car looking for anything else of interest. Cunningham returns to the opened door to my right and shows me a zip locked baggie full of some cheap clear capsules full of a brown powdery substance.

"What's this stuff?" he asks.

I shake my head. "It's just an herbal powder. It's nothing." This is a lie, and he knows it, bags it up as further evidence against me. His

15

finding the capsules doesn't really concern me in any way, beyond the fact that they won't be in my car whenever I finally get back to it. By that time I will sorely need them, but they're perfectly legal. But there is a lot more truth yet to be discovered besides what's been poorly hidden inside my trunk. And these Kratom capsules he's just uncovered are a clue.

By the time we are headed back towards Pampa and the county jail, the disorienting emotional whirlwind has passed. All that remains is a simmering but fragile resentment. It's all that prevents me from tumbling into what appears to be a bottomless pit of fear. So I stoke the anger in the only direction I know how—towards officer Cunningham driving beside me, and Jimmy, who sits directly behind me.

"You guys are just wasting your time. You're like a couple of prohibition officers from the 20's. I can't believe you're going to ruin my life over some pot. You have to know this is all going to be legal in a few years. You *have* to know it." I actually scoff.

A decade of attempting to rationalize and justify increasingly uncontrollable behavior has made me fairly knowledgeable (though highly biased) about America's legal history with various intoxicants. But I'm the one in handcuffs here, not these officers.

And they have no trouble making my self-righteousness look like stupidity and selfishness.

Cunningham just shrugs. "You think you can just get high whenever you want, don't you. I don't give a shit what you think is gonna happen. You're breaking the law."

He's right. And any further arguments or excuses I could make would only be complicated by the fact that I'm guilty.

After five silent minutes, Cunningham glances my way. "You ok?"

I don't bother looking at him.

"No." And it is a complete fucking sentence.

"Little Tim, what are the styrofoam cups for?"

Little Tim has three of them, seemed to already know he'd need them.

"Milk. Coffee. Juice" he says, as he holds each cup towards my face. "For in the morning."

Little Tim and I share a holding cell. We're the only two guests in the small county jail, and Little Tim had begged them not to put him in a cell by himself, had to have someone to talk to, he said. Otherwise he'd go crazy. Well that's a relief. But for a guy who is evidently just a few hours of solitude away from insanity, Little Tim's not such a bad guy. He's been pretty helpful. Like now, letting me know that I'll be here until…

"In the morning!?! We're gonna be in here all friggin' night? Why? How do you know? Can't we get bail? I can't be in here all night!"

My jailers aren't such bad guys either. I didn't get one phone call, I got two. I used the first one to call my estranged wife. I was supposed to pick our boys up after school at three. All I had to say was that I'd gone to Colorado, and this time I'd been arrested. That let her know that in the year we'd been separated, almost nothing was as she thought it was. Except that I was still full of shit. That she could count on. My second call was to work. I had a shift that was supposed to start at 7pm. I left a message that I was stuck in Texas and I'd explain later. Somehow.

So technically speaking, there is no reason I can't be here all night. But will I? Little Tim explains.

"They booked us after noon. You see a judge out there? He's always gone by noon. Gotta have the judge here to set your bail. And that's the only way you're gettin' outta here. So might as well get comfortable."

The holding cell is tiny, maybe ten feet by ten, with a stainless steel shitter and sink exposed in one corner, which I'm hoping to hell neither I nor Little Tim will have to use. Along the left wall is a long narrow bench, and an identical one lines the back wall. Little Tim claims the one on the left. Hairs from previous prisoners' body parts have been swept into the corner where my bench meets the wall. Basically where my head will go should I decide to lie down.

Little Tim shows me how to "get comfortable". We've each been issued an inch thick gray canvas mattress which is too wide for the bench but not nearly long enough.

"You do it like this," says Little Tim, as he folds one end of his mattress over to make a sort of pillow. "Your feet are gonna hang off the end. But it ain't so bad."

"Thanks, Little Tim." I feel oddly grateful.

"So...what're you in for?" Little Tim says it, not me, so I figure the cliche must be ok.

"Marijuana. I went to Colorado to bring a bunch of it back home to Oklahoma. And I guess they frown on that sort of thing." I gesture, like what can you do?

"They got you for pot?!? Shit. That stuff's all over the place. The fuck you go all the way to Colorado for?"

I'm too exhausted to explain. "Well what they get you for then?"

"Tint on my damn car windows. Said it was illegal, but it ain't. Fuckin' cop knew it but he pulled me over anyway. But I got a warrant 'cos of a ticket I ain't paid. Hauled my ass in for that. So here I am." Little Tim gestures, like what can you do.

I nod. What can you do, indeed.

I suspect Little Tim got his name because he's, well, little. He's barely over five feet tall, and maybe a hundred twenty pounds, though it's hard to tell in the orange jumpsuit. He's half Hispanic and his head is shaved but the hair has grown out just enough to reveal a few crooked scars where there will never be hair again. I'd guess his age at about thirty, but it's hard to tell. Reminds me a little of Charles Manson, without the menace.

"So what's going to happen in the morning, Little Tim?"

"The judge will be here by nine or ten. You'll have to go before him, he'll tell you what you're gonna be charged with, set your bail, all that shit."

"So what time you think we'll be out of here?"

"Well YOU might be out of here by noon. I ain't going nowhere."

"You're not?" I feel a pang of fear, and wonder if Little Tim wasn't being entirely transparent about why he's here.

"Nope." He looks rueful. "My outstanding fines are like five hundred bucks. Ain't got no way to pay it. Except to sit in here for thirty goddam days. That make any sense to you? Only if I work, I get two for one days. Can get out in just two weeks."

"That's a pretty good deal then, huh."

Little Tim looks at me like are you stupid or something?

"My kid's turning four on the 20th. That's in nine days." He shows me how many on his fingers. "I wanna be at his birthday so bad except I can't, even if I work. So I'm just gonna sit in here the full thirty. It's a lot better once we get outta this holding cell over into population. They got cards, shit to do, people to talk to, stuff like that."

I suppose that just paying the $500 fine is a reach beyond his grasp, so I don't mention it.

Three hours later, or is it fifteen minutes, I can't tell, I say to Little Tim "I'm bored." I need something to do.

Anywhere but here. Any time but now. Anything but this. Anyone…but me. That's basically boredom. Funny how it's also panic. Opposite cliffs of the same chasm.

"Well they got books out there if you wanna read."

20

"You shitting me Little Tim?"

Little Tim is not shitting me, tells me to just bang on the door and the guys at the desk will come see what I want. So I do. The guard who gave me the two phone calls comes over, peeks in the tiny window, opens up and says "Yeah"?

"Little Tim here says you guys got books."

"We do."

"Could I read one?"

"Yeah. Over here."

I follow him out of the holding cell over to a shelf near where they'd taken my mugshot earlier.

"You can take one," the guard says. "But hurry."

I try to but it's all just too surreal. I'm checking out a library book. In jail. My brain is either two seconds ahead of my body or vice versa and I can't figure out what in the hell is going on. I see a title I recognize called *The Corrections* by Jonathan Franzen and I grab it. The guard follows me back to the cell and locks me back inside.

Little Tim hasn't moved.

"I can never read in here," he says. "Over on the main side they got checkers and chess and shit. But books I can't do."

I'm about to find out why. *The Corrections*. I have no idea if the title is meant to be ironic, considering my present environment. I'd never read it before, still haven't, except for the first page which I read about thirty times. Every time I reach the bottom of it I realize I have no idea what I've just read and I have to start all over again.

"Fuck it." I stuff the book underneath my folded up mattress to bolster my pillow and stare at the ceiling. So much for books.

Little Tim grins. "See?"

Eventually they bring us baloney sandwiches and black-eyed peas for dinner. Baloney disgusts me, always has since I was a kid unless it's fried, so Little Tim eats mine. I don't eat the peas either. I never have to eat unless I want to, haven't felt actual hunger in seven years, and right now I don't want to.

"This one here's from a bar fight in Dumas where I broke my pinky, and this'ns where this girl's boyfriend tried to stick me with a busted Bud Light bottle…and…"

Little Tim is showing me his hands, and all the scars, fifty-six of them supposedly, each one attached to various assault charges, although I suspect he's exaggerating. His hands are big for his frame, almost as big as mine, and indeed scarred. He's not bragging, exactly. Just sort of reflecting, maybe on how he got here and where he's going to go.

"You know where Dumas is don't ya?" He asks.

I do. I've traveled through it many times, even spent the night in a motel there once back when I had to drive past Trinidad to Pueblo and this trip took me two days instead of one. But I don't tell any of this to Little Tim. I just nod.

He was right, by the way. About going crazy. The last thing I'd wanted was a cellmate. I'd been afraid, not just of him, but of everything, my thoughts especially.

"Your brain is kinda like a dangerous neighborhood in here," Little Tim tells me. "You don't wanna go there alone." He grins.

I estimate that it must be about 7pm. There's a clock on the wall outside that I can see if I look out the window just right, but I'm too afraid to look. Not that it matters. Whatever minute it is, that's the one I can't bear to be in. To avoid it I'm fantasizing about both a past I can somehow change and a future I hope to avoid. It hasn't crossed my mind to pray, though I don't know how to do the kind of praying that would help, not yet. And just like with the wife, God and I, we're separated anyway.

Little Tim stares at me. "You should try to sleep. You won't be able to but you should try. They'll turn the lights down pretty soon. You look…tired."

"Ok, Little Tim. Maybe so. And…thanks."

"For what?"

"For everything."

"Naw man, thank you. I'dve went fuckin crazy if you wasn't in here."

"Me too, Little Tim. Me too."

"G'night Holmes"

"Night Little Tim. Sleep tight."

For once Little Tim was wrong. Because I sleep. I've no idea how because I haven't been able to sleep without some form of chemical inducement in over a decade. Maybe it's the adage about the guilty sleeping good in prison. Or maybe it's pure exhaustion. But I sleep. It's not for long though, because I awaken to the sound of the cell door squeaking open, and the silhouette of a stranger carrying the familiar gray mattress. We have a new roommate.

"Shit, that you Little Tim?" It's dark except for the emergency lights overhead that stay on always, but it's bright enough for my cell mates to recognize each other. The stranger ignores me other than to subtly size me up without being obvious about it. Unlike Little Tim and me, our new cellie gets to keep his civilian clothes, blue jeans and a dirty white T-shirt. One of the benefits of late check-ins I guess. I half expect Blue Jeans to kick me off my bench, or try, but he just lays his mattress right down on the floor and plops down, one leg flexed with his other ankle resting atop his bent knee. He tells Little Tim about his latest escapades beginning with "Oh Man!", and ending some way that I don't know because I don't listen.

I sneak a furtive glance at the clock through the window, as if maybe I can look away quickly enough if I don't like what I see. I don't and I can't. It's 10:00. As in 10pm. As in this day just will. Not. End. I think maybe I can go back to sleep, but I'm wrong.

For the rest of the night I try to stay as comfortable as I can on top of the canvas and my unread copy of *The Corrections*. It's more crowded in here now, but I'm much more alone, and either because of that or despite it, the urge to explore the dangerous alleyways in my mind becomes overwhelming. Little Tim's admonition be damned.

It's probably 4am, I'm too afraid to check, when it hits me. I know what I'm going to do. And I feel immediately better. I'm going to get out of this. Out of this jail and this jumpsuit, yes, soon enough. But also out of this dead end journey that I've decided ends now, out on that stretch of highway 152 where everything changed. Maybe, just maybe, I got saved there. I'm quitting. The pot and those pills yeah, but I'm quitting everything. It's the only way, and I see it now. I need to make those same two phone calls from yesterday, they're the only ones that matter. My lost wife, she'll see it too, though she won't believe it all at first. And my job? Well, that's what else I'm quitting.

———————————

The lights don't come back on until seven. The effect of having night and day determined by a light switch is disorienting, but the fact that it's actually morning, that I've survived is mildly invigorating. Little Tim has his styrofoam cups stacked and at the ready for the milk/juice/coffee he knows is coming and soon enough it does, along with a flavorless oatmeal and toast. I skip everything but the coffee. It's not good but I drink it anyway, and the jailer, same guy from yesterday, brings me more when I ask for it.

"So what time you think he'll be here Little Tim?"

I want to know when the judge will arrive.

"By nine for sure."

"Nah, sooner than that," says Blue Jeans. "He'll be here at eight. Bet you money."

I want Little Tim to be wrong, please let Blue Jeans be right, I just want to go home right fucking now.

Blue Jeans is right. There's a minor commotion outside when the judge arrives promptly at eight. There's a new catch handcuffed to a bench out front and he starts raising holy hell when the judge walks in. The jailers and patrolmen still processing the offender quickly restore order. Our three faces are pressed as close to the window as possible and I'm flooded with relief that the end is now literally in sight.

The judge is a neatly dressed Hispanic man, probably late fifties, with sharply trimmed facial hair and spectacles. He is short but fit. I feel ashamed just looking at him.

"What's next after the judge?" I ask.

"Then you can bail out," says Little Tim.

"Where you think my car is?" I've been having these nightmares that my car has been gone over with a black light by some crime tech and had the gas tank removed or something. Like I'm worth the trouble.

"Prolly in an impound yard," says Little Tim. "This ain't no CSI show around here," like he can read my mind.

"Shit show, maybe," says Blue Jeans.

They grin.

The door opens, and I'm first.

"Gray? C'mon. You're up."

The jailer closes the door behind me.

"First we gotta take your booking photo again," he says. "Something happened to yours."

I follow him around the counter and look in the mirror next to the bookshelf. My appearance shocks me. I've hardly slept in almost three days now, my hair is wildly uncombed and unwashed, and my beard is as unkempt as the judge's is neat.

After my photo is retaken, the judge beckons me.

"Mr. Gray come on up." He's serious, but kind.

He remains seated on the opposite side of the counter and I step forward. I look down and try to read what's on the paper in front of him. I can make out 'possession' and 'felony' but almost nothing else, and I can hardly focus on anything he says either. I hear "lawyer" and "court date" and "district attorney" and hear him ask if I have questions.

"Yes your honor did you say how much for bail?"

"No. But It's $8000. You can work that out with the clerk when we're done."

I almost whistle. I expected a grand. Instead I whisper a thanks that Little Tim had explained things better than the judge does.

"That it?" he gestures.

"Yes your honor. I'm sorry, how long does this sort of thing normally take?"

"Well, whatever it is that was found in your possession will need to be tested in the lab, the district attorney will review the case against you, determine what charges to file. It can take some time."

This isn't at all what I mean. I'm talking about making bail, getting the hell out of here. But I let it slide and don't point this out. We both know the lab testing is a waste of time anyway. The cannabis I had in "my possession" is clearly labeled right on the packaging, down to the milligram.

"What do you do for a living Mr. Gray?"

I look at the judge's tweed coat, his Windsor knot, I smell his cologne. I remember my face in the mirror and in my mugshot. The humiliation makes my ears hum as I stare at my orange slippers and tell him.

"I'm a physician."

II

A LIFETIME BEFORE…

"I still can't believe we live in Birmingham, *Alabama*."

It's my wife who can't believe it. We've been here a year now, and we are celebrating both our first anniversary and the completion of my medical internship. I've spent the last year on rotations at a private hospital in town, honing my skills on medical specialty services like cardiology, pulmonology, and nephrology. They're skills I'll need when I begin yet another three years of training in the field I chose back in medical school—anesthesiology. I've got a week off before that begins at the university hospital in town.

"I know you didn't want to come here," I say. "But you've done great." And she has. Her career in pharmacy is flourishing, and she's made more new friends during our year here than I have. It's just because I'm busy, I tell myself.

"Well hopefully it'll be worth it," Tami says.

"We'll find out next week." We toast. Her water, my wine.

She'd wanted to stay home, in Oklahoma City, after my medical school. But how did the department chair put it on the day I interviewed there? "We've just been placed on probation, and I'm leaving," I think he'd said. Well I guess that meant that we'd be leaving, too. Tami was my fiancé at the time, we'd marry right after graduation, and I told her that my training was just too important to take any chances with my residency program. She understood.

"Well maybe we could go somewhere close like Dallas. Or St. Louis. Someplace with direct flights so coming home is simple." Tami's family is very important to her, and she'd like to be able to visit easily.

"Yeah…Well what do you think about…Birmingham?"

"Alabama?" She didn't sound enthused. "Why Birmingham?"

"Because the program is supposed to be one of the best. Why don't I just see if I can get an interview. It's probably too late in the year, anyway. I doubt I'll get a spot. But it can't hurt to try."

I get a spot.

"I'm such a fucking fraud." This is the pep talk I give myself as I walk up the steps to the university hospital where I'll spend the next three years training to be an anesthesiologist. "They're all gonna find out I don't know anything." I feel like I'm wearing a Halloween costume.

I don't know how to be an anesthesiologist, I barely know how to be a doctor at all. But for some reason, I think I'm already supposed to. I hate saying "I don't know," have been known to lie just to avoid it, I hate not knowing what to do, and I *absolutely* hate asking for help. It might be why I picked this specialty. It's not the only reason, but it's definitely one of them.

Every applicant for anesthesia residency, and I mean every single one, professes a love for pharmacology and physiology on their personal essay. I did too. It's practically a requirement, an unwritten rule that we somehow absorb without being explicitly told. If you wanna get into anesthesia, say you love pharmacology and physiology. Because that's what we do. Administer drugs to make surgery possible, and monitor and manipulate the patients' physiologic responses to those drugs and that surgery so that they survive both.

Do I love pharmacology and physiology? Not particularly. But no one is honest always are they? Not me. But what I did love was the idea that maybe I could master them. Like I said, I hate to say I don't know. The predominant method of teaching during my four years of medical school and year of internship involves attending physicians asking students questions that they'll have a low probability of answering correctly. And even if you do answer correctly, ensuing questions will ensure that you eventually come to realize there is literally NO END to the list of "shit you should know but don't". There are twelve types of colon cancer, all with subsets, seventeen types of seizures. There's both obstructive and restrictive pulmonary diseases and you'd better know the difference. There's twenty different stages of the blood coagulation cascade and you gotta know how an abnormality of any of those enzymes might manifest itself. I'd wake myself up some nights concerned that I still didn't understand the Krebs Cycle.

Ok. I'm exaggerating. I'm also exaggerating to myself how much simpler it might be for me to master the skills of the anesthesiologist, but I don't know that yet, walking into University Hospital in my starched white coat, feeling like a fraud.

As expected, it'll be a few days before we're given any responsibilities in the operating room, the OR. First, we sit through various hospital and department orientations, get to know our fellow residents and a few of the attending physicians who will be responsible for our training. Then there are lectures about the handful of topics we absolutely must be familiar with before being entrusted with actual patients. And, as it turns out, actual drugs.

We are given crash courses on how to set up an anesthesia station without forgetting a crucial step, how to conduct a focused preoperative patient interview, how to operate an anesthesia machine. Caring for a patient in the OR during surgery is entirely different than being called to the emergency department to admit a patient for diarrhea or shortness of breath, the kind of patient care we are familiar with. These are the major areas that we were never exposed to in our medical education that could prevent us from making a fatal mistake with our first patients. We have to know it.

As I look at the agenda for the second day, I notice another topic that I'd never really considered necessary before, and though I don't appreciate it yet, it's also intended to prevent fatal mistakes. Not necessarily for our patients, but for ourselves. The topic is substance abuse.

"...so I guess I was just...curious. I saw how relaxed the patients seemed as they drifted off to sleep. Like they didn't have a care in the world. I guess I just wanted to know what that was like....I wish I'd never tried it."

We new residents are finishing up an educational video on "Physician Impairment", a catchall term for physicians whose judgment and ability to practice medicine safely has been compromised by a variety of conditions or behaviors—alcohol abuse, process addictions, anger issues. But it's obvious what the topic is focused on today—drug addiction.

The man in the video has been superficially describing what led him to first inject himself with Propofol, a potent IV anesthetic agent that would later be made notorious through the death of Michael Jackson. It is a cautionary tale. And one that makes almost no impact, on me at least. I simply can't relate. The thought of injecting myself with a substance where a cc or two could be the difference between delirium and a dirt nap is inconceivable to me. Wisdom is knowledge gained after it's too late to do you any good. What this man is saying may be wise, but it's also way too early to do me any good.

Our department chairman, whose qualifications to speak on substance abuse seem to be solely that he's The Chairman, follows the video. His words have more ultimate utility for me.

"Substance abuse is an occupational hazard in our profession. The only medical specialty with greater rates of drug addiction than ours is psychiatry. No one is exactly sure why this is. Studies have hypothesized that you'll be exposed to micro doses of aerosolized drugs that the patients breathe out during surgery, which could trigger certain cravings in susceptible individuals." He shrugs. "I don't know about that. The more obvious explanation is access. But the fact that other professions like pharmacy and nursing also handle controlled substances, but seemingly with lower risks for addiction, means there may be more to the story than just access. Maybe it has something to do with the types of personalities who choose to become physicians." The Chairman pauses to let that sink in, as if we're each supposed to take a moment to soul search. "What I do know is you're going to have access to powerful, potentially addictive drugs including versed, fentanyl, morphine, ketamine, propofol, you get the idea. And if you are foolish enough to experiment with any of these drugs on yourself, even once, your chances of becoming addicted are very high. And like the former resident in this video, your career will be severely impacted. If you even survive."

He seems to realize he's come on a little strong, forces a tight smile.

"But we want you to survive, and thrive, here in our program. Now, there are checks and balances with your narcotics in place to protect you. The pharmacy keeps strict counts on all controlled substances, and you'll be expected to account for everything administered to your patients, and to appropriately record and document your waste with a witness. Most if not all of you will do just fine. But we wouldn't be having this discussion if the risks weren't real. The prevalence of alcoholism and drug addiction in the general population is thought to be about ten percent, and as I've said, physicians are no exception. Now, when I was a young man and cigarette smoking was more common than it is now, almost forty percent of Americans smoked. I can remember when many of my colleagues took smoke breaks in the doctors lounge. We are not immune to self-destructive behavior."

I look down and wonder if the round shape of the Copenhagen snuff can in my coat pocket is perhaps visible.

The Chairman continues. "We want you to look out for your fellow residents as well as yourself. There are certain signs to look for in the impaired physician. One is general appearance. That often suffers. Wearing long sleeves is another, as they may be trying to conceal needle marks on their arms. A person's general disposition may seem more irritable, whereas before it was agreeable. You may find them around the hospital at odd hours, looking to pick up extra shifts or cases at night or on weekends so they can resupply themselves with drugs. And they will often chart that patients have received abnormally high doses of opioid medications, but since most of that was in fact diverted for the drug addict himself, the patients will wake up with more pain than would be expected. Be aware of this, and don't hesitate to notify a faculty member if you have concerns about a colleague. In fact, if you have reason to suspect a fellow physician may be impaired, you have an ethical obligation to report it. It's unfortunate we have to have these conversations, but this is the world we work in. Society has placed great trust in you as physicians, and especially as anesthesiologists, caring for them when they are most vulnerable. Do not betray that trust. Any questions?"

I have none. But I do have some answers that will come back to help or haunt me in my future. Maybe it's just the way my mind works, but it occurs to me that what The Chairman has perhaps inadvertently equipped us with is a "How To Manual of How To Not Get Caught".

Look sharp. Be nice. Wear short sleeves. Make sure your counts are correct. Do NOT offer to pick up other people's cases or shifts for no reason. And never, ever chart crazy high doses of pain meds.

Of course I never intend to need this information. It'll never happen to me. I'll never take any of those drugs he mentioned in the first place, never. But suppose I do. I surely will not become addicted. But *even if I do*... I will never, ever be that guy in the video. I ain't saying shit to nobody.

I picked the right specialty. I decide that pretty early on. One thing I quickly discover about myself is that I'm task oriented, not time. Put me on an ER shift from 7a-7p, and by 10:00am I'll swear it should be afternoon already. And if it's slow it's even worse. But tell me I have three gallbladders, a hernia, and a hip replacement, and I may not glance at the clock until quitting time. I don't know if that makes me impatient or the reverse. But I know it's a lot more satisfying to push a blood pressure medication and expect a result within two minutes than to prescribe one and say see me again in six weeks.

I also find that I'm at home in the OR. We spend a couple of months there during medical school, but I was always so preoccupied with not contaminating myself or simply screwing up that I never really knew if I liked it or not. Luckily, I do. As the anesthesiologist, I have just the right balance of authority and anonymity that seems to suit my temperament. I'm not the star, like the surgeon, but I don't really want to be either. The OR used to be referred to as a theater, people actually watched from a gallery, and while there are moments of tragedy for sure, the plot leans way more towards comedy. They're not that far apart. But what we do there is entirely unnatural, even grotesque. It's no wonder people sometimes pass out when they first glimpse it. So we armor ourselves with a brand of dark humor that helps keep us sane, in the face of the often inhumane-appearing acts being performed. I like it. Both the humor, and my role in the healing that ultimately takes place there. What happens is an honest to God miracle, and almost none of it would've been possible when my grandparents were born. A large part of that is because of development in my specialty.

I like it, but that doesn't mean it's easy. The list of "Shit You Should Know But Don't" isn't necessarily as broad, but it's much deeper. And the consequences for ignorance can be a lot more...abrupt. If you don't know something, there's often no time to look it up. We are vigilantly supervised early on, but that doesn't make it seem less stressful. Sometimes when a patient says "I'm a little nervous" before surgery, which is entirely natural, I want to admit "No shit, I am too", which is not. Or at least it's not exactly reassuring. Once, a patient asked me "How long have you been doing this," as I rolled her stretcher back to the OR. I did some quick math in my head, calculated that "This is my thirteenth day" would not engender confidence, and ad libbed "This is my second year of training out of medical school." Entirely true, but not exactly honest. A distinction I'll later sharpen like a knife...or a needle.

At the end of all this, sometimes I just want a drink. Not a drink as in "this red will go really nice with the prime rib," or "woo-hoo, we've finished our exams and let's party!" though I'm familiar with these types of drinking. No, the kind of drinking I discover in Birmingham is like this: it's like the waves of an ocean that lift you out of the sand, washing both over you coming in and beneath you going out at exactly the same time so that it makes no difference if you're coming or going either, rising or falling, and you can stay exactly, where you are. Or if you like, peace and ease. The kind you didn't even know was missing, you lost it so slowly, until you replace it, just like that, with a glass of cheap wine in a red solo cup, standing at your kitchen sink at 5:30 on a Tuesday evening. Or maybe it just makes me feel like I don't have a care in the world, just before the lights go out, and I never even knew I was curious what that was like.

———————————————

For as long as I can remember, I've had rules for alcohol. Some were given to me, and some I made up myself. The First Rule–Don't Drink. I learned this one early, like you do growing up in a Baptist church, with a grandmother old enough to actually remember when the 18th Amendment was passed, and why. "Is it a SIN to drink a BEER?"—This was what my teenage peers and I considered a profoundly philosophical question. There is deep wisdom in it we didn't recognize, but it can't be found by simply reciting that Proverbs states "Be ye not drunk on wine," or by boasting that when Jesus went to a wedding, by golly, He brought the wine! Har har har! It is in neither the black nor the white of the yin and yang, but in the thin gray line that separates them. I didn't know anyone who either had the experience to explain this wisdom or the openness to do so, we were Baptists after all, so though I held on to the First Rule much longer than most, eventually I'd break it.

And create for myself, Rule Number Two—When you drink, don't get caught. This one is juvenile, for sure, but there's an undeniable thrill from forbidden fruit. Before my medical career, I had spent two years in Japan teaching English and working with American Christian missionaries. The Japanese Christians are few, but they didn't have any of the same inhibitions with alcohol I'd grown up with. I embraced this on occasion, and once shared a beer with an older Japanese woman I worked with. "If Bobby-san come, we tell him no beer, is tea," and she giggled to herself covering her mouth with her fingertips. It made the beer all the more intoxicating.

By the time I left Japan I was more confused about who was going to heaven and who was going to hell than a missionary should ever be. But I was pretty certain that beer didn't have anything to do with it, and I felt no shame in breaking the "I drink/you don't tell" rule. This new-found freedom felt liberating, as honesty should. But it also felt powerful, in a 'yes I will have a beer with my lunch, so what?' kind of way. At first I respected the power. So I established for myself Rule Number Three—The two-drink limit. I'd read somewhere that two drinks was pretty much the daily limit to be considered moderate drinking, and as I'd probably also read somewhere that moderation was wise, I chose that for my limit. Never once did it occur to me that perhaps most people don't need to concern themselves with so many fucking rules about drinking. It's exhausting. Which is why eventually, inevitably, the two drink limit came to include the addendum "unless I'm out of town," or "it's the weekend." Or by the time I live in

Birmingham, "I'm standing at my kitchen sink on a Tuesday evening at 5:30 and I absolutely *deserve* this shit."

———————————

Once I break a rule, it's never any good again. It's as if it loses all of its authority. So in Birmingham I make a new rule, one I can believe in, and the only one I'll never have to break—there will *always* be wine in my kitchen.

III

40

Post-Pampa…

"Hey…boys. Whaddya say we drive back through Birmingham?"

The boys—my boys—the same ones I was supposed to pick up after school a month or so ago but didn't because I was stuck in a Texas jail cell, they say "cool." They don't remember that day I failed to show up. Their mom came through as always. As far as they know, Dad just had to work late. Which was a fact often enough that when it was needed as a lie to cover up an inconvenient truth, like say an arrest, it worked. They never thought twice about it.

Unfortunately, I'll be needing a new explanation. Because "Dad had to work late" sounds a bit suspicious when Dad don't work at all. I quit. I'd been off track for way too long, and it was time to make The Corrections. Evidently all I'd needed to read was the title.

Of course I told my partners at work about Pampa. It made it easier, in fact. "Look," I'd said, "I'm just burned out. I don't sleep well, I've lost the joy in this job, it doesn't feel meaningful anymore, and this foolishness in Colorado was just the wake up call I needed."

For most of them, that was enough. I'd been a good partner. Easy to get along with, took on my share of leadership responsibilities, never called in sick, ever, and would be happy to cover a shift for you in a pinch. But only if you *asked* me to. Only then. Every single reason I gave them for "retiring" was true. Maybe not honest, but true.

Besides, even though I may have kept myself awake fretting that they were analyzing what I was doing and why, the fact is, everybody else has enough in their own life to worry about without meddling in mine. You wanna quit? Then quit.

I might've heard an occasional "You really sure about this?"

But hell yes, I'm sure about this. I'm going to slow down, simplify my life, spend more time with the kids.

And spend a lot less money. That's actually the reason I'm pitching the idea of a side trip through Birmingham to my boys right now. When most people think of Alabama they think of college football. Or country music. Or the events of the civil rights movement. But they don't usually think about the part of Bama Tami and I came to love most while we lived there—the beaches. White sand and warm turquoise water, just a four hour drive south of Birmingham. As often as our busy schedules would allow, Tami and I would head down for a long weekend. It didn't seem possible that one day we might have our own place, right there on the Gulf, but just two years ago Tami convinced me that it was now or never, we'd been saving long enough, so let's just do it. And we did. The place is in a great new development, a very smart investment, and ours was completed just over a year ago. This is the second time I've had a chance to come down.

And I'm here to sell it. The rental income can be inconsistent but the mortgage payment's not, and we just don't need that kind of strain, not with my salary… gone. So as soon as school is out for the summer, I load up TJ, who is nine, and Tyson, who's seven, and we make the last trip down to the beach house because what else do I have to do anyway. And I've got to get this place sold.

TJ and Tyson, they don't actually say "cool" to my plan to detour through Birmingham on the way home, what they really say is "yeeeah, Dad!! Yeah!!" They'll be teenagers soon enough, but right now, they're still at that age where almost anything can seem like a great idea if you spin it just right, no matter how crazy. A couple of years from now it would've been a lot harder to convince them I knew what I was doing when I quit my job—"Look at all the time we'll get to spend together!" Or why we had to sell this beach house when we'd practically just bought it—"Real estate markets are complicated, kids. The timing just happens to be right."

Or this: "Watcha drinkin' Dad?"

"Juice."

"Can I have some?"

"No, Tyson. It's Dad's juice. But let's stop and I'll get you boys something."

This 'juice' I'm drinking, it's not juice at all, it's wine, poured from a box I'm keeping in the trunk. I stop to surreptitiously drain it into a red solo cup about every fifty miles or so as we make our way up through LA, Lower Alabama, towards Birmingham. I don't mind stopping for Tyson, I need a refill anyway. But I can't help wondering if he's going to remember this. I must have been about the same age when I asked my dad the same thing.

"Whatcha drinkin' Dad?"

"Coffee. With ice."

"Can I try it?"

"No."

He didn't offer to get me anything, just stopped at a new car lot, closed as usual on a Sunday afternoon, and set his cup on the floorboard of the backseat and went to roam around among the Chevys. Peace and quiet I guess. But the coffee with ice, I was curious what that tasted like, so I snuck back there and tried it while he wandered and it tasted like shit. Later I'd realize it tasted just like whiskey.

———————————

The rules, they don't work anymore once you've broken them all to pieces, but I haven't learned that yet. I'd been trying to quit a lot more than just my job ever since Pampa. It was part of the deal I'd made with Tami—that if she was going to continue to support the family with her pharmacy career, then I couldn't just be some bon vivant and be fucked up all the time, I'm gonna have to contribute. It's a reasonable request, and considering how my position in this family remains rather tenuous, one I'd best abide by. And I tried, tried like hell to reestablish the first commandment—Thou Shalt Not Drink.

I assumed it would be easy. I'd hardly drank at all in years, only when I was sick and I'd have to force it down. Like medicine. The cops, they took all the cannabis and the Kratom, and I'd burned every bridge to ensure I'd never go back for more, thought I'd never even have to. But that couldn't keep me out of the liquor store. I've been there every day, sometimes twice, and so while I've got to go to the beach anyhow to unload this condo, why not kill all the birds at once? I've been tapering off anyway, or trying to, so what better time to finally quit for good? This is my actual plan. And it's awful.

Tami doesn't know any of this, not really. Or she never would've allowed TJ and Tyson to go to Alabama with me. She thinks I'm doing as well as I tell her I am. It's not that hard, really, since I'm living on my own, and though she still loves me she hates me even more so she never gets close enough to smell. Later she'll think how could she be that fucking stupid, but it's not that at all, I'm just that sneaky. Until Don't Drink does work, I'm laser focused on Don't Get Caught, and doing a more than decent job. Well, maybe Tyson caught me, but I'm pretty sure a popsicle will make him forget, and even if not, he won't be able to tell anyone until he learns what whiskey tastes like for real and by then, it'll be too late. That's wisdom for you.

Both boys were born later, so they've never lived in Birmingham, but they've been here plenty. They know how to point out the house we'd lived in, the first one we ever bought, and where we liked to go for breakfast at this BBQ joint that for some reason also serves shrimp and grits. But they've never seen where I worked.

"You guys wanna drive by and see the hospitals where daddy learned to be a doctor?"

"No."

"Not really."

45

"Aw, c'mon, it'll be cool, I'll show you where the helicopters land when they bring in the super sick people. Maybe we can even see one come in."

"Ok!!"

It's all in how you spin it.

We drive up over the mountain from Homewood where our neighborhood was and down into Birmingham itself, the same drive I made morning after morning at 5am a lifetime ago. We pass the south end bars and there are residents and medical students on patios, sitting in their scrubs, sipping craft beers in the early evening after their shifts, laughing, drinking like normal people do. Not like I did, alone, standing in my kitchen, letting the imaginary waves wash over me as I waited on Tami to get home from another evening shift at the CVS. I look down at the red solo cup in the console, almost empty again and I'm so empty again that I don't even want to cry. I just shudder.

We pass the university hospital, still strong and just the same as when I left, and I point it out to the boys but hardly even look myself.

"What kind of doctor are you again Dad? An anesthethesographist?" TJ asks. He and Tyson both laugh. They never could say it, but I can't either now, both from the red wine and the regret so I just say "yep."

"When can we see the helicopters, Dad?"

"Hmmm…it doesn't look like we're in luck today boys. But that's good. It means nobody around here is super sick."

I swallow the bile and wish to God that was true.

———————

"Just one more place I want to show you boys and then we'll stop, ok?"

"C'mon dad, no, we're tired. We don't want to see any more of your hospital stuff. When are we gonna eat?"

"Just one more. This is the first hospital I ever worked at and I haven't seen it in forever. I just want to drive by and then we'll get a hotel. Ok?"

"With a pool?" Tyson is just learning to swim, and there's got to be a pool.

"Of course! And then we'll eat." Or at least they will.

"At Denny's?" TJ fucking loves Denny's.

"You know it! Where else?" I fucking hate Denny's.

We get on the highway and just a few miles north of downtown Birmingham I can see the huge blue cross of the medical center where I did my internship. From the front everything looks the same. It's getting dark, but it doesn't appear the neon lights on the cross have come on yet.

I pull around to the back where the parking decks are, expecting to try and find a spot on the upper level where the hospital staff park. Or maybe I can just park outside the emergency room if it's not busy.

It's not busy. It's deserted. The entire medical center is just as empty as my solo cup. I knew there were some rumblings of financial concerns during my year here, some administrative changes to hopefully keep this private hospital solvent and serving its community into the future like it had for what, a hundred years? How could it just be…gone?

The building is still here. But most of the windows are broken out, including on the second floor where the call rooms used to be, where I'd try to catch a few hours of sleep during busy nights. The parking deck still stands, I drive up on it and it holds us, but it's full of weeds and aluminum cans instead of cars. I wonder about all the people who used to work here. Not the interns and residents who would all move on to the bright futures they imagined for themselves, but the ones who thought they could stay. The nurses, the janitors, the cafeteria workers where the residents always ate for free. I try to recall the name of the woman on the 2nd floor who cleaned all the call rooms, who'd greet us every day with a "Mornin' ya'll. I'll be outta ya'll's way in just a minute, now." I can't remember her name but I can still see her face.

I park my car in a slot marked by weeds where yellow paint used to be and I get out and lean against the trunk as the sun goes down. This place is a corpse and it smells like one. It's fermented. What the fuck killed it? Was it *greed*? Did some people just want more money, more of everything? Or *envy*? Did they see the big hospitals to the south of them and think "we need a helicopter, too?"

Were they so full of *pride* that they could see the writing on the wall, but were too arrogant to admit it? Or just too *lazy* to do anything about it? What in the fuck has happened here??? Why couldn't they have just asked for help??? I only realize I'm crying, more like weeping, when Tyson says "Daddy what's the matter?", and TJ says "Dad you cussed." I never heard them get out but they're standing beside the car now, trying to ignore what's going on like kids do when their parents are fighting or something, but there's no one else out for me to fight with but myself.

I somehow manage to crumble my crying into a sort of laughter and let out a big sigh.

"I dunno boys. I dunno. It's fine." I can give a little more gusto to my chuckle now that almost passes for sentimentality instead of mourning. "Just some memories I guess. This was a great place once. I never thought it'd end up like this. Whew. Let's get out of here. We've got a motel with a pool to find!" I put a hop in my steps back to the car so they'll know I'm ok again.

"And Denny's dad. Don't forget we're going to Denny's!"

"That's right, TJ. We love Denny's don't we." I hate Denny's… but I fucking love these kids.

I steal a glance into the rear view mirror and the apocalypse behind me on the way out, and the broken glass stares back at me like eyes, and my reflection fills the empty spaces where the windows once were, and the effect is like one of those fun houses full of mirrors and you see yourself reflected into the past and a future that never happens and you can't figure out which way to go until you break

every piece of glass that you see like it was some stupid ceiling and
not some rule you should've followed, and you can't answer the
simplest question of *what in the hell has happened...*

50

IV

THIS IS WHAT HAPPENED…

"Where you going?" My college roommate wants to know why I'm putting on my running shoes at 10pm on a February night. A very cold one.

"For a run."

"Now?"

"Why not?"

"Didn't you go to the gym already today? Don't you need to study or something?" he asks.

"Yes. And no." I laugh, and he just shakes his head.

"How do you make yourself do it?"

I've never thought about it before, and I have no idea how to answer. What does he mean, how do I *make* myself. Is that what he thinks I'm doing? Forcing myself out into the cold to slog through seven miles or so like it's my job?

The only response I can think of that might make any sense is "How can you not?" But I can see by the look on his face that it doesn't. Maybe I should just tell him I want to stay fit, I don't want to gain any weight, that sort of thing. But c'mon, we're *nineteen*, it's not that hard to stay in decent shape. So I show him an ad for the kind of Nike shoes I've just laced up that I'd torn out of a magazine and saved. It says it better then I ever could. He reads it.

"Ten million decibels loud

And it doesn't care you're tired

Or it's your birthday

Or some holiday honoring a saint

So, though you'd rather not

You start down the road again

The road…

When it calls, it screams"

I'd understood it instantly, and he'll either get it or he won't.

He doesn't, just looks at me like whatever, man. Ah, well. Poetry's not for everyone. And neither is running.

"I'll be back in an hour, Dude." I slap him a high five with my gloved hand and head out of the dormitory into the dark. About a block away I silently add a line to the Nike ad—"Or that it's below freezing…" But within a mile or two I am warm, and by then I'm well outside of campus, headed east on a road I know well enough to run with my eyes closed, or at least with only the light of the stars and the moon. There is no sound other than that of my soles slapping the asphalt in a constant rhythm, my breath matching it—in for two steps, out for two steps. And on like that until I've gone further than I intended, almost four miles outside of town. I don't try to calm my mind, I just let it run too, and I revisit conversations I wish had turned out differently, and this time I'm always able to say just exactly what I'd meant to say all along and everyone is always very impressed.

I get to a turn in the road that I know from mapping it with my car's odometer means I'm almost exactly four and a half miles from my dorm. And though I didn't time myself, I know from my breathing that it's taken me thirty-three minutes to get here, give or take thirty seconds. I stop, not because I'm tired, but because the trees off to my right seem to have something to say. But it's a whisper, not a scream. I stand still and listen, my breath coming out like crystals, it's so cold, and the sweat comes off my shoulders like steam. I stare at the four trees, naked and dormant for the winter, nothing out there but bare branches and barbed wire and I just feel so…grateful. The perfect winter scene has manifested itself for me, here in the moonlight and the middle of nowhere in a pasture I've passed a hundred times. It feels almost like Christmas, and there is joy in my world.

———————————

Although I don't know it, something specific has happened in my brain, has been happening even before I ever made a conscious decision to put on my shoes and run. Don't tell the poets, but the road, it really wasn't screaming at all. But my brain was. It wasn't screaming for the road or a run, but it knew that was a way to get what it wanted, even if I didn't—it wanted dopamine. It never seems to have enough. When I was a kid my brain would suggest to me subconsciously that eating all the icing off a birthday cake until I was physically ill would do it. And it did. Dopamine is a chemical messenger, a neurotransmitter, in the brain and nervous system. The reason I want more icing, or anything else, is dopamine. Because dopamine is pleasurable. It's also the only reason I'm in college at all. It allows us to strive for achievement, and makes us want to do things again and again. Without dopamine, life seems meaningless, and things that should seem obviously enjoyable, aren't.

So as I'm standing in the middle of the road beneath the moon and the stars, staring into the branches and beyond, it seems to my conscious mind that something mystical has happened. I'm no longer beating myself up over what I should've done or said yesterday, and I'm not worried about what might happen tomorrow. I am simply present. I feel connected to all that is around me, to my friends even though they're not here, and to God, who so obviously is. It is the very definition of euphoria, a feeling of well-being.

On a subconscious level, nothing mystical has happened at all. My brain has simply gotten the dopamine it craved through my exertion. And a scene which would have otherwise seemed ordinary and mundane, seems magical and full of meaning.

———————

This cuts both ways, and I'm acutely aware of it now, two decades later, standing in my suburban backyard outside of Oklahoma City. I'm not thinking about Nike ads or neurotransmitters, although I've used the motivation from both to get me exactly where I am. I've achieved a lot, done all the things I thought I was supposed to do so that there'd always be joy in my world, and in my family's world. I finished college, spent time teaching both in Japan and in Oklahoma, and then went on to medical school, fueled by dreams and dopamine, though I only knew about the dreams. Tami and I were married and were both convinced we'd found a love that would last the rest of our lives. By the time I finished my residency in Birmingham, my fears of feeling like a fraud and a failure had largely faded. I passed my board certification exams, and soon after landed a job at what I considered to be the most outstanding anesthesia practice in Oklahoma City.

Life is good. Or it should be. Our house sits in a gated neighborhood, the right cars are in the garage, we've been to all the coolest places like Costa Rica, it's all just so obviously enjoyable. Our family has grown, TJ is a toddler and Tyson, he's just a baby, and Tami takes great care of them both. A year ago I made partner in my practice. No more exams to cram for, I'm capable and confident in my career, and now it's time to simply relax and enjoy.

Except I can't. Seems I'm used to going up. And standing in my backyard on a warm summer evening, that's exactly where I look—up, up into the sky. My mind is imaginarily transported above and I can see myself, standing in the grass, next to a new gas grill, surrounded by a privacy fence from the yard next door. Which is exactly like mine. And the one next to it. And on and on around the block, and over into the neighborhood beyond, just as far as my mind's eye can see. If I could read my own lips from way, way up here I would see myself asking—"What now?"

This isn't a mystical moment at all, it's more like misery, and instead of feeling gratitude, what I feel is much more like guilt. I feel guilty. *All this and you're still not happy? What exactly is it gonna take?* This life, which should seem so obviously enjoyable…isn't.

55

And neither is this red wine. It's not living up to its end of the bargain. We made a deal all those years ago in Birmingham—you provide the peace and ease, and I'll keep you around forever. I've kept up my end of the deal, but the wine, unfortunately, has not. It seems we've gotten used to each other. Those ocean waves, they used to be both effortless and economical. Two glasses, that's all it took. But little by little, the glasses got bigger and bigger. The price for peace and ease kept going up. By now, I don't even bother with bottles, it's too easy to see how much I've drank, or how many. With boxes, nobody can see, including me.

Although I should know it, something specific has happened in my brain, has been happening since I first began to rely on alcohol to ease the tension of the day. My dopamine system is drained. Every time I take a drink, my brain enjoys an unnatural spike that's simply not achievable without cheating. It's a crutch. And even though I wasn't hobbled to begin with, by now I am. I need it. My brain got so confused with all the ups and downs and what I expected of it, eventually my natural neurotransmitters just said fuck it, and now they're gone. And without their cooperation, the wine has revealed itself as the depressant it really is.

Not that I'm giving it up. The thought is inconceivable. Without it, and without any dopamine of my own, there's no beauty in all this bounty whatsoever. Every ounce of color is gone, and all I'm left with is...plain old Gray. And I can hardly bear to be myself without changing the way I feel with a drink.

It's entirely possible that my life could've proceeded on this path for another twenty-five years, a parade of monotony, punctuated occasionally by periods of self-pity. For me, alcohol strikes just a precise enough balance of creating low-level misery but countering it with just enough relief to keep me perpetuating this cycle ad infinitum, never knowing exactly what the problem is, or having a clue how to fix it. And I have way too much pride to consider asking anyone else.

The thought of such a future isn't exactly a comfort, but I needn't have spent any time pondering it. Because I'm about to make a decision that will ensure such a future is impossible. There will never be enough relief to balance the misery it causes, never, and the gray will fade away with the rest of the color 'til all that's left, is black.

V

"TJ, run inside and say hi to Granny. She's excited to see you."

TJ does, runs up the wood steps that lead to my mom's back porch and bursts through her unlocked door and yells "Hi Granny! Gran-ny I'm here!"

He finds her in the living room, semi-confined to her couch where she almost always is, her arthritis so bad that getting around has become a chore. She'd had me at thirty-five, uncommon for those days, and I'd waited even longer, so she's more like a great granny to TJ, and she's the only grandparent he has. He loves these visits.

"Where's your brother?" She asks TJ, but she's looking at me.

"He didn't come," I tell her. "He's with Tami."

"Ah well, it gets to be just you and me, then," she tells TJ, and he giggles.

This has become normal for us. Tami takes care of Tyson, and TJ, he's with me. He's always with me. When Tyson was six weeks old, we kept waiting for him to start sleeping through the night, like TJ had. But that was eight months ago, and he still wakes up every ninety minutes. And all he wants is mom. I'm useless. So I do what I can, which is mostly make sure TJ is taken care of and Tami, she's got Tyson. And postpartum depression. But she won't admit that any more than I'll admit I've got a drinking problem, so here we are, pretending

58

everything is normal, because how is anybody supposed to know otherwise? We've never done this before.

My mom, she's just spry enough to keep TJ entertained while I go for a quick run around the block. If you can call me dragging my bloated belly down the street running. But this is my hometown, and these are the roads I first fell in love with and I want to at least pretend. When I was twelve I wanted to run, needed to get in shape before my first football practice, so my dad watched the odometer on his car as he drove me down the street from our house until he said "see that sign? That's where you turn around." It was a sign letting us know who'd built the chain link fence it hung on. It's just my mom's house now, but the rusted sign is still there, a half mile down the road. Back when I was twelve a mile seemed like it went on forever, and now at almost forty it seems even farther, so when I reach the sign I wheel my fat ass around and head back the way I came. I know what I'm missing, though. I'm missing my friend Jeff's old house which is another half mile farther and the turnaround point for the two miles I'd run sometimes in high school. There are more markers the farther you go and the older I got. Some of them as far as thirteen miles away, where my dad would meet me with Gatorade and Gu Gels so I'd be able to get back home again. But I can't get to any of those places anymore, so this run is good for the memories but not much else, and I come home almost as empty as when I left.

My mom is seated in a chair in the hallway, outside a closet where TJ is exploring his favorite spot in her house. The closet's been converted into a fort, and it's full of all the toys he keeps here, mixed in with a few his older cousin left behind when he outgrew them. There's even an Evel Knieval action figure that once was mine but the motorcycle that goes with it is long gone.

My mom wants to know "How was your run?"

"It was fine. I just wish I could do more than a mile. I barely worked up a sweat."

"You can always just go across the street to the track and walk, you know. I bet you'd enjoy it. TJ and I'll sit on the porch and watch you, won't we TJ."

TJ says yeah.

I shake my head. "I'm not walking, mom."

"Daddy can we read these before bed?" TJ pulls from the closet two Curious George books, and one with Uncle Remus stories that lost its cover about a hundred reads ago.

"Sure, Buddy. But first I'm thinking we get a Mr. Pizza, rent one of the Toy Story DVDs, and…" I wait for him to finish my sentence.

"Take a bubble bath!"

He knows he always gets a bubble bath at Granny's. No wonder he loves it.

———————

"'Where have you been George? I was worried about you,' said the man with the…"

I leave TJ an opening just like my dad did when he read this book to me, and TJ says "Yellow Hat!" and we both smile. His head is still wet from the bubble bath and he smells like Prell shampoo and Ivory soap.

We finish both Curious George books and I tell him it's time for bed.

"I wanna wead Uncle Wemus! Wead the one where Bwer Wabbit eats all of the…the hucklebewwey jam!" He's trying to pout with his lower lip out, but he cracks himself up and laughs like only a kid can. He only mispronounces his R's when he really wants something he thinks he's not going to get.

"No buddy, it's time for you to go to bed." He might not be tired, but I'm exhausted, and I can't do the voices for Brer Rabbit and Brer Fox right anyway, not like my dad did.

"O-K", he pouts but he yawns, too. "Tomorrow can we make cinnamon toast?"

"You bet, buddy." Another tradition at Granny's.

"Night buddy."

"Night Daddy"

"You sleep tight."

"But lay down here daddy. Until I fall asleep." TJ points at the bed, where he already knows I'll join him.

———————

"He asleep?"

"Finally, yeah," I tell my mom as I slip out of the bedroom that used to be mine.

"You do so good with him, Tommy, you really do."

"Thanks, Mom." But there's no gratitude in it.

"You loved it when your dad read those books to you, I'm so glad I kept them. TJ really seems to love them, too, doesn't he."

"He does."

"Well, your dad loved it, too."

If he were here I'd ask him how he made himself do it. Maybe he has a poem that can explain it for me.

I can tell she wants me to say more, but she can tell I don't want to, that I'm done for the day, so she just says "G'night, son. I'm glad you boys came out to spend the weekend with me."

"G'night mom. I'll see you in the morning."

I give her a little peck on the top of her head as she hobbles into her bedroom.

I'm exhausted. But that doesn't mean I'm sleepy. I wonder if I'll be able to sleep at all. Because I don't have my medicine. I don't think of it that way, but that's what it is, the wine. It's medicine. Something I take without thinking about it, every day, just to maintain homeostasis. To stay balanced.

I didn't bring it for two reasons. One, I'm trying to cut back, have been pretty much ever since I'd made partner. I'd tried to hide things, turned the bottles into boxes, but I wasn't blind, I knew I drank too much. And I feel guilty. But I always had an excuse, a goal that was always just a little ways off, and I could tell myself "I'll do it then." After residency. After boards. After the kids are born. Just so long as tomorrow never turns into today. I don't want to quit today.

The second reason is my mom. I don't want to deal with disappointing her. I don't want her to see me struggle through the door with my arms full of matchbox cars for TJ and Merlot for me. Oh, she knows I drink, I've had to listen to her lectures on more than one occasion, just like she'd done to my dad when I was little and they thought I wasn't listening. And she'll tell me that all my dad had to do was ask Jesus for help, and mean it, and he just…quit. She can think it was Jesus if she wants to, but I'm pretty sure it was the stroke that stopped him, and I'm not sure I can pray it and mean it anyway so what's the use of worrying her. I can cut back and keep my mom off my back at the same time. Kill all the birds at once. Surely I can do without it for one night.

————

In med school we learned mnemonics for everything, and there's one for identifying problem drinking, too. It's called CAGE.

——Have you ever tried to Cut back?

—Have you ever felt Annoyed by anyone asking about your drinking?

—Have you ever felt Guilty about how much you drink?

—Have you ever had an Eyeopener?

Whenever this crops up in my mind, I go straight to the end. The eyeopener. I've never had one, never even thought about it. The idea of drinking in the morning disgusts me. I've only had a hangover once, after my first ever six-pack, and I've never had so much as a shiver or a shake. I never had to get straight in the morning. Hair of the dog, and all that. No, I wake up right as rain, every single time, and escaping these consequences has convinced me I'm special. I can do things other people can't. An eyeopener? I'll never get that bad. And that's what it means to be alcoholic. Right? Never mind that if I had unexplained weight loss, a change in bowel habits, and a family history of colon cancer, I wouldn't wait until I was shitting blood to schedule a colonoscopy. But that's different, I tell myself. That's a disease. There's no shame in shitting yourself when you can't help it. Besides, I'm gonna cut back.

It's almost like I'm reminding myself every thirty seconds, "See? Not drinking over here, you're not drinking Tommy, you're doing it!" Like I'm Peter walking on the water or something, and not just some schmo doing something as simple as not drinking. It takes a lot of…effort, this not doing. It seems like my mom and TJ went to sleep hours ago but it's only been twenty minutes. I'm certain because I keep checking. And the next thing I know I'm standing in my mom's kitchen going through the cabinets where she keeps her medicines, the real ones like for her hypertension and diabetes. Because my brain, it's reminded me that something might be in here, that a decade or so ago, don't you remember, you found a Xanax in here. And though the Xanax was a disappointment, maybe there's something else now, anything that will just make me stop feeling like I have to fucking walk on water just to stay afloat. And I'm almost to the back,

I'm about to give up, when I find one more vial that looks like it doesn't get opened often and I pull it out to check the label and before I could've even had time to read it out loud, I feel better. My brain, it's salivating dopamine it probably didn't know existed, because now I know I don't have to try to walk on water anymore, I've been saved, and at this point it really would take an act of God to stop me from what I'm about to do, standing here all alone. Because that label doesn't say Xanax. It says Hydrocodone.

VI

Hydrocodone. I'm familiar with it, of course. It's the generic name for one of the more commonly prescribed opioid pain medications. Potency-wise, it's somewhere in the middle, used typically for mild to moderate pain. Although like with all opioids, what matters isn't so much the potency. It's the dose. And what my mom is holding here, is smack dab in the middle—7.5 milligrams. I assume someone must have prescribed it for her arthritis.

I've even had a script for it once myself, back when I was in my twenties. Had a little mishap with a greasy cement floor at a restaurant where I waited tables, and ended up in the ER with a lacerated chin and a broken jaw. The doctor prescribed me a steroid and told me "you HAVE to take it", and some hydrocodone that I could take "if I needed it." When I got home I couldn't remember which was which, and since the doctor seemed emphatic about one of them, I just kept taking them both to make sure. And how was it? Meh, I suppose it was ok. Didn't really seem to leave much of an impression one way or another. I even took a couple right before a trigonometry test the next day and did just fine, made a 98. A couple of days later, I got my jaw wired shut, and never even bothered to finish off the bottle.

So, while I'm profoundly relieved to stumble across my mom's pills, I don't expect them to do much more than put a soft edge on my jagged senses, and perhaps help me get a little sleep. Tomorrow I can always get more wine. The *last* thing I expect is to alter my life forever.

Not that I need any justification for what I'm about to do. I'm way beyond that. Like I said, it'd take something akin to an earthquake to stop me. Or maybe just my mom walking in, but I know that neither is gonna happen.

Somewhere in the back of my mind I know there's a technical term for all this—it's called diversion. Taking controlled medications that were prescribed for someone else, for symptoms I don't even have. Non-technical people call it stealing. But I'm just calling it my lucky day, because who am I hurting, really. My mom's got plenty in here, she'll never even know these two are gone. So just like that, I pop them into my mouth, and I go to bed.

Except sleep doesn't come. What does come is a state of being that is something like being asleep and awake at exactly the same time. My mind and body rest as if in the midst of a pleasant dream, but I'm also completely alert and aware that it is happening. It's as if my brain had been a desert and a spring rain has come and washed away everything worrisome. Or it's a sponge, once dry and brittle, but now soaked. When I was a kid I'd go to the lake with my best friend Daniel, and after a long weekend of boating and eating burgers at his parents' cabin, we'd all load up into their pickup truck for the long drive home. Daniel and I got to ride in the back like they don't let you do anymore, I suppose because it's dangerous, but we either didn't know or didn't care, and neither did his folks. We'd both have a sleeping bag even though it was summer, and the wind would inflate the sleeping bag to make the warmest cocoon. The asphalt would hum a constant tune beneath our backs as we laughed at the old inside jokes or made new ones like you do when you're young and you're best friends. The closer we got to home, the further away it seemed. Or at least we hoped so, and we didn't know that this kind of happiness isn't supposed to be permanent. Our minds were sated with memories of water skiing and marshmallow roasting, our bodies were sunburned, and my spirit, to the extent I knew I had one, was in heaven.

Well, the hydrocodone…it's better. And it doesn't require going anywhere at all, or even a best friend to go there with. Maybe it's like the womb, if anybody who knew could tell us. But I don't come out screaming the next morning, quite the contrary. After several hours I suppose I must've fallen asleep even though I don't recall it, because I do know when I woke up. And the first thing I thought was, I'm going to do this again. Talk about an eyeopener.

VII

The cinnamon toast smells good. TJ helps me make it, insists on sprinkling the cinnamon on his own toast and I don't fight him even though I know he'll fuck it up. He does, puts way too much cinnamon on it, but I just tell him it's fine, and I compensate by adding way too much sugar. For balance. Might as well triple the butter, too, while we're at it, and the toast not only smells good, it's delicious. TJ tells me so, that's it's the best cinnamon toast, ever.

I'm in an uncommonly good mood this morning, and my mom notices, says I must have slept real good.

"I sure did, Ma. Best sleep I've had since…well I don't know. Maybe it was the best sleep, ever!"

I'm talking to my mom, but I'm looking at TJ, and he laughs, with crusted sugar and cinnamon caked on his cheeks. It's beautiful. Life, feels beautiful.

"I think I'll go for a run if you guys will be ok."

"Of course," my mom tells me. She and TJ will be just fine. They've got cartoons to watch. So I tie up my shoes and trot on down the road towards the rusted sign on the chain link fence. I search myself for traces of guilt, any second thoughts that maybe last night should've never happened, or should stay just a one time thing. I mean, I've got to keep this shit secret. In all the casual conversations I'm ever a part of, it's perfectly acceptable to mention "Hey, I tried this really nice whiskey last weekend. I think you'd love it." Or even "Man, I way overdid it on the brewskis Saturday night. I really gave my smooth endoplasmic reticulum a workout!" And we'll laugh as if we party like rock stars, knowing we're just nerds at the same time. That sort of thing, well that's typical. But try saying "Oh wow, I 'borrowed' a couple of my mom's hydros last night, and it was amazing! I can't wait to do it again!" Well that would be highly frowned upon, by anybody. So it's gotta be a secret.

My favorite sports radio guy, he often says "you wanna know if something's a good idea or not? Say it out loud. You'll know." So I do. All to myself, alone on this road, I say, "Last night I took two of my mom's Hydrocodone." And that's where I stop. It's all that comes out, like if I can avoid saying anything more, then it won't become…insane. Because the sports guy, he was right, what I've said sounds awful. So I swear I'm never gonna say it out loud again, to anyone, ever.

But I still feel so good I keep on running, right on past the rusty sign and all the way out to Jeff's old house where I turn around and head back for what will be a respectable two miler. I'm actually looking forward to today. I'll take TJ to the new splash park, at one of my hometown's city renovation projects. When I was a kid it wasn't a park, it was a sewer, but it's really well done and TJ will love it. We'll eat lunch at the old cafe that's still in the Main Street strip that's otherwise empty. This town…what used to be a literal shithole is now a place to swim, sort of, and the old downtown is dead. Things change. But it's gonna be a good day, I can feel it. Or maybe, it's just because I'm looking forward to tonight. Either way, at least I know I won't have to bother going to the liquor store. This cutting back is way easier than I'd thought.

_____

"You having fun, baby?" TJ is talking to Tami on the phone, and he tells her all about the splash park, and how we got the best booth by the window for lunch. He says "uh-huh" a lot and nods, and I can tell he's tired of answering questions, he's anxious to get to his bubble bath, so I take the phone from him and tell him to go take his clothes off. I know Tami and I won't be talking long. She mostly says things like "good day, huh?", and I say things like "yep." She and Tyson are fine, will probably go out to her brother's in the morning and might still be there when we get back. My mom, she doesn't do things exactly like Tami's mom does, or like she would've if that car wreck hadn't killed her, along with Tami's older sister a couple of years before TJ was born. Tami still feels the loss, probably will forever. So coming to my mom's is painful for her. No matter what other excuses she might make, it's just a reminder that her own mother isn't here, and how much different it'd be if she were.

We don't have to talk about any of this, we know it by heart, so I just tell her I'll see her tomorrow and I run in to pour Mr. Bubble in the bathtub and let the suds fill up until I won't be able to find TJ when he gets in. I'm not in any hurry, I'm enjoying this. I let him soak until his fingers and toes wrinkle and he says, "Look, I'm Granny!" and his giggles echo off the bathroom tile. When the water gets too cool I wash him up with the Prell and the bar of soap until he squeaks. He makes me sing the little ditty I made up when he was a baby, "gonna wash your neck, yeah, I got your neck," and on down until his toes get tickled. And just like that, he's putting on his PJs and hopping into bed, and he's opening up Uncle Remus like it's a jar of huckleberry jam, only sweeter.

"Ok buddy, let's see what happens to old Brer Rabbit and Brer Fox," and we read it until he's almost asleep, and then I just lay there until he is for real. I've got patience to burn.

I'm so patient I talk to my mom for almost a whole half an hour after TJ's asleep. I tell her how Tyson's doing and I promise to bring him out here next time, even if Tami doesn't come, which she won't. My mom tells me about how her friends are doing, which ones can't drive anymore, and which ones are dead. She tells me my friend Steve's mom died too, which is a surprise to me because Steve and I are close, or we used to be, and he hasn't said a thing. When I call him the next day with condolences he'll say "No, she's sitting right here." So my mom's not right about everything. But she's right about this—she tells me to treasure these times with the boys, because someday I'll miss them. I tell her "I already do, mom. I already do." She says "Huh?" which she does about every other sentence anyway, and I tell her "Never mind, let's go on to bed. I'm tired." She goes on to bed with the same kiss on the top of her head. But I don't.

I've been patient, yeah, but I can't hold on forever. I wait for the sound of her door closing, but not for the light to go out in the crack beneath it, and I tiptoe into the kitchen, which is unnecessary since she wouldn't hear it if a buffalo barged in. But I do it anyway, tiptoe right up to the cabinet where her medications are. I look where I swear I left the pill bottle, but it's gone. I put it right there, I know I did, and a jolt of electricity surges through my gut because it is simply not there.

And I simultaneously feel the disappointment that I won't get to take anymore mixed with the shame of being convinced that my mother has caught me, and instead of confronting me she just hid it, until I look down and I see, oh....there it is. It's sitting on the counter. The lid, it's just sort of sitting there, half on and half off, like she sometimes leaves them so she doesn't have to mess with child-proof features, because it's hard for her with the arthritis. And I think to myself, "Fuck! Was that lid off last night or not? Because I know I put it on tight, like I always would, and did she think to herself today when she struggled to open it, "somebody's been sleeping in my bed," like she's mama bear or something, and I'm as guilty as Goldilocks? But no. It was on tight. I fuckin' shook the thing before I ever opened it. I remember being happy at how full it felt.

Which reminds me, I should count them. I don't want her to think any have gone missing. So I pour them out on the counter, and I do my best to count them like a pharmacist would, like I saw Tami do back in Birmingham when I'd actually visit her sometimes at her work. I don't have the fancy tray and stuff, but counting them is simple, and I'm pretty sure there are forty-two here. Forty-two. I look at the date on the bottle, do a little quick math in my head and I figure she must be taking what, a pill and a half a day? Counting the two I took last night? Yeah, that's it exactly. So she is, in fact, taking them. Well...I just can't get greedy, that's all. What's a couple of pills here and there when she started out with sixty. And without another thought, I pop two more into my mouth.

I don't go straight to bed this time, though, and I won't for several hours. I go to the living room, turn the TV on low so I don't wake TJ, and try to relax. I'm about twenty minutes into the second half of a movie about werewolves fighting vampires with a British actress I like, and I don't like vampires and shit but I like her, so I keep watching. And I'm pretty into it, have sort of forgotten that I'd taken the pills at all, at least for the past five minutes, and I begin to notice that every so often, it just feels like…honey. There's the warmth of honey inside. It kind of comes and it kind of goes, it's nothing overwhelming, certainly not like heaven, or anything you'd die (and go to hell) for. But it's nice. Really, really nice. I don't feel sleepy at all, and unlike the night before, I don't have the sensation of slumber, either. I'm alert. Like I could almost do trigonometry if I could remember how. I finish the movie, and I watch another one with the same British actress, must be a marathon or something going on, and afterwards it feels kind of like I just got home from a really nice date. Nothing that blows the mind. Just a nice first date, and you'll be more than content to wait a week or whatever, until maybe, you can see them again.

As I lay down for another night's sleep at my mom's, I don't know it yet, but I have in fact had a date. But it wasn't with Kate Beckinsale. It was with a dragon. And I'll either be chasing this dragon, or he'll be chasing me, until one of us is dead.

VIII

I'm a chipper. I don't know it yet, and I won't even learn the term for months, but that's what I've become. I don't really know any drug users, at least not ones who are open about it, so I'm not familiar with any of this terminology they—or should I say *we*—use to romanticize our plight. It'll be months before I'm not just surfing, but scuba diving the internet in a secret search for anything that might magically turn me back into what I once was. And I'll find a lot of good advice that I won't have any use for and a bunch of inside lingo that I will, if only in conversations with myself.

But all I know at this point is that as often as I can since I first discovered my mom's pills, I load up TJ, and sometimes Tyson, and say "Guess where we're going this weekend?" And TJ says "Granny's!"

That's right. We just love these visits.

And I'm being a good son, really. I'm spending time with my mom, and making sure my boys have memories of their grandmother from their childhood. Everything is true about that. But why I come so often, why I start planning it before the week is even half over, is the chipping. I'm not a drug addict, not at all. I'm an occasional user, couple times a month, three or four tops. I take a couple of the pills Friday night, a couple more on Saturday, and I have no trouble at all waiting til the sun goes down. I don't need an eyeopener with the pills any more than I do the vino. And this, as I'll learn much later, is called chipping. But by the time I learn where it leads, there won't be a thing left worth romanticizing at all.

I have the occasional warning sign, what I should assume is an omen, a wake up call. Once, when I'm headed home from my mom's, still digesting the pills I'd popped for the road, I catch part of a news story on the radio. Seems a notable basketball coach in the state had done something stupid. Got himself caught with the same exact pills I've just taken, only he ordered them through the mail. But I don't think "that could be me," I think "that guy's a dumbass," and how could he have been so desperate. He should've known he would get caught that way. And he had so much to lose.

Then there's Barry, one of my old classmates. We'd been pretty decent friends back in med school. Not best of friends by any means, but decent. We had a lot in common. Some people compare the first year or two of medical school to trying to drink water from a fire hydrant. It's not so much how complex the information is, just that there is so much of it. It seems that Barry and I had each figured out our own ways of staying on top of our studies without having to give up everything else we loved. I once ran into him at a Wilco concert on a Wednesday night during exam week. Nobody does anything for fun during exams. We might've had to stay up the rest of the night studying, but it was Wilco in 1997 and it was worth it. Although Barry probably went home and slept because he was brilliant. He could get away with it. We also both liked to play guitar and would jam a bit together now and then.

Another thing we had in common is we were both pretty quiet. Neither of us was the one to do all the talking, and that might be the reason we weren't better friends. We were too much alike. After graduation we lost touch, but I knew he was planning a career in anesthesiology just like me, and quite a few of our other classmates. He headed up to the northeast to one of those Ivy League institutions. Small town Oklahoma boy makes it in the big leagues, it'll be a story like that, and that was the last I heard from him.

Until another friend, Cade, calls and says "Did you hear Barry's dead?"

"Say what?…He's dead? Whaddya mean he's dead? I just saw a picture of him on Facebook. He was at a Sox game."

"Well he died. I think he might've…he might've had a drug problem." He doesn't want to disparage Barry's memory by saying any more. Just wanted to let me know. I tell him thanks, and also how sorry I am. He was closer to Barry than I was, and he can't believe it.

But I think back to those videos we watched in Birmingham, and everything the chairman said about "occupational hazards," and it suddenly makes perfect sense. I wonder if Barry'd seen the same videos I did, listened to the same sort of speech. I'm sure he thought "no, it'll never be me," just like I did. But it was. It is. Barry is the guy in the video. But he didn't live to tell anybody about it.

In the weeks to come I'll see the sad messages that pop up on his Facebook feed. They're like telegraphs sent to a doomed ship, after it's already been lost at sea and isn't ever coming back. There will be a newspaper article or two from the northeast as well, and I'll be able to fill in all the blanks I haven't already figured out for myself about what happened to him. And I'll think about all those things we had in common.

If this isn't an omen, I don't know what else could be. It's like an SOS that I get to read in advance, before I have to send it out myself. "Dangerous waters ahead". But I still cling to the thought that I'm special, like that's some sort of life raft. No one will need to come save me, I'll be just fine. *I can do things other people can't*. Even if Barry couldn't.

And besides. Barry was a drug addict. And all I am is a chipper.

IX

Sometimes things just get out of hand. Especially when nobody is paying any attention. And right now, nobody is paying any attention to Daniel and me. Why would they, we're maybe six, seven years old at the most. Our dads and all the other men around, they have more important things to do, like build a baseball field, a whole giant complex where kids like Daniel and me will live out our Little League dreams. They'll pay attention then, but now they've got work to do laying the bricks on the concession stands and building backstops.

While the men work, Daniel and I play our imaginary games, swing imaginary bats, and watch balls soar over fences that don't exist yet, and jog around where the bases might be just like Reggie Jackson. Mr. October. It's October here, too, and it's cold. So they can warm up during their smoke breaks, the men have built a fire, out away from where they're working so it won't be in the way. Like Daniel and me.

We get cold too, eventually, my best friend and I, and we use this fire that burns in a barrel to warm up between imaginary innings. I'm not sure if it's during the long 7th inning stretch or not, but Daniel and I stay at the barrel a few minutes longer until we find a new game to play, and it's not an imaginary game at all. It's playing with fire.

Daniel finds a paper cup from the ground, says "watch this," and lets the flames lick it until it burns. Tosses it into the dead grass where those flames spread. The fire spreads fast but we're faster and we stomp it until it's only smoke. We grin. We don't stop to wonder whether this is a good idea or not, it's my turn now no matter what, and I find another piece of trash to feed to the flames. This time we let the grass burn just a second or two longer, the fire gets a little bit bigger, and then we stomp the life out of it again and only it's black breath lingers. Our grins grow into laughter. This is fun. I'm not sure how many innings we play to in this particular game, or who is up to bat, but eventually the wind whips up and though we stomp and stomp like we're trying to bring the rain, the wind wins. And everything burns.

Eventually the fire department comes, but the future ball fields are toast. The men blame themselves, wonder whose bright idea it was to build the fire in the first place, on such a windy day like this. Or point to packs of cigarettes and say, "You sure you didn't get careless with one of your Camels over there, Bob?" But what they don't do is suspect Daniel and me. We just stand in stunned silence and stare. We might be just six or seven, but we know when to keep our mouths shut.

Playing with fire, it'll later be one of those inside jokes we share like best friends do. "Remember when we burned down the baseball fields?" In the retelling, the sizes of the fires we were able to stomp out will seem bigger and bigger, like we had more and more control, and as far as when we lost it, only the wind knows.

———————————

"Are you sure your mom will be able to drive out here?" Tami asks me. "You don't want to go get her?"

"No, I think she'll be fine. It's only a forty-five minute drive. It won't be close to getting dark yet. She said she can do it."

It's a Sunday afternoon, and my mom is coming to spend the week with us. I'm happy about this for two reasons. First, it means Tami is going back to work. Tyson is well past a year old now, he's *this* close to sleeping through the nights, and we figure it's time to put him into one of those educational daycare programs like we did with TJ when he turned one. We don't want to screw this parenting thing up, accidentally find out when our kid is four that he doesn't know his ABC's or something. And this makes me happy because I'm hoping it makes Tami happy. Or happier. She never was big on the staying at home thing, and I don't blame her, her career is important to her just like mine is to me. But she felt it was best to stay home with our boys when they were babies, and I agreed. I'm not sure how she could have functioned at work anyways, waking up five or six times a night whenever Tyson cried. But those days are pretty much over, and she's excited about her new job that starts tomorrow.

My mom is coming to bridge the gap. The daycare school where TJ goes won't have a spot for Tyson until next week, but Tami's new job wants her right away. So we've been sort of scrambling to arrange babysitters for Tyson in the meantime. My mom has offered to help. And that's the second reason I'm happy. Because I figure if my mom will be spending the week with us, then so will her hydrocodones.

It's been a busy few weeks, and it's probably been a month since I've been to my mom's. A month since I've borrowed her pills. A month since I've chipped. But it's not like I've stopped thinking about it. Sometimes when I drift off to sleep with who knows how much red wine in my belly, I even have dreams about it. Murky, incoherent illusions about how satisfying it is to have a whole bottle of pills, ones that are mine, or a whole bowlful like it's cereal. They're the kind of dreams that are so disappointing to wake up from.

But when I have a moment in secret to unzip my mom's bag, what I find is more like my worst nightmare. My mom got here safe and sound a half hour ago, we all met her in the driveway, and like a dutiful son I said, "Here, let me grab those bags. Boys, come say hi to granny and give her a hug." TJ does, Tyson just drools, and me, I'm kind of drooling too, just being more discreet. I rushed inside to stash her bags somewhere so I could have a moment with them in secret, and now that I do, I can't believe what I find. Or don't find.

"Dammit. Shit. What the..." There's no bottle of pills. And I don't even have to look hard, because I immediately find one of those plastic weekly pill organizers, the kind seniors use to keep all their meds straight. I had no idea she had one, but here it is. A Lipitor, glipizide, and metoprolol for Monday. And one and a half hydros. Same for Tuesday, Wednesday, and forever. There's no way I can take any, not even one. She'll notice. And I can't help but wonder, "shit, does she know? Is that why she's doing this?" It's been months since that first weekend when I went back to her pills for the second time and found the lid half on. "Has she known since then? Is that why she insisted on driving herself?" I've tried to be so careful, always counting her pills, checking the refill dates, doing the math. But maybe I got careless, I can't say. The paranoia is gripping. But I'm also getting mad. I'm not gonna get what I want, and dammit I've been expecting this. I've been working my ass off and I deserve it. My depth of disappointment is disturbing, but I'm too pissed to consider it. And I'm irrationally upset with her, my mom. Why's she doing this to me?

I try to talk myself down. It's not the end of the world, have another glass of wine, you'll be just fine. But I don't *want* wine, I'm sick of it, and my synapses are screaming for me to fix this. Just fix it, there's gotta be a way. And I don't know if it's my mind or it's me and what's the difference anyway, but I come up with a plan. I know where the rest of her pills are, right there in her cabinet. I just need to get to them.

––––––––––––––

"Hey, I'm going to Home Depot. I need to get some of that sealant stuff. You know, the kind you can spray on a screen door and make a boat out of it? Like in the commercial?"

My mom and Tami are catching up. It's been awhile for them, and they've got lots to talk about.

"What do you need that for?" Tami asks.

"I think there's a leak around one of the vents in the roof. It's supposed to rain this week. I wanna get it sealed up."

"Does that stuff work?" She wonders.

"Yeah it works, it works great. Didn't you see the guy's boat float? Doesn't leak a bit."

I've no idea if it works or not, and I don't care. I don't have any leak to use it on. But I couldn't exactly tell them I need to go make a copy of my mom's house key, could I? Because without that, my plan won't work.

My plan, it's stupid simple. My mom doesn't live that far away, just forty-five minutes. I'm pretty sure if I speed I can make it in thirty. So in the morning, I'll leave an hour early for work, slip inside my mom's with the key I'm about to copy, grab what I need, and be to work right on time. Nobody'll be the wiser. It can't fail.

"Mom, I'm gonna take your car. Make sure it's running ok. Check your oil and all that. Where are your keys?"

This is the kind of thing my dad always did for her, and it makes her think I'm being a dear. There's a joke I haven't heard yet, but I'm already proving it true—that an alcoholic will steal your wallet. But a drug addict will steal your wallet and then help you look for it. Or maybe he'll just buy you a tank of gas.

I know it won't be for today, I'll have the pills tomorrow, but my disappointment is vastly relieved. Now that I've got a plan, I can be patient. My mom's tank is still three quarters full but I stop to top it off on the way to the Home Depot. There's plenty of air in the tires, too. But her oil, it's just a little low and I want to add some. I'm just not sure what kind. I'm thinking of my dad already, of him doing all the things for my mom like I'm doing right now. He was no mechanic but I remember him saying once, "Oil is oil. In a pinch just put in 5W30. It's the standard. It'll be fine." And I don't even remember forming the thought, it seemingly just appears, but I think to myself…"opioids are opioids." By the time I reach the depot parking lot, I've already done some more math, purely for hypothetical purposes.

"If two 7.5mg hydrocodones is 15mg…and intramuscular morphine is triple the potency of oral hydrocodone…then all I'd have to do is…"

It's just a thought, nothing I'd ever say out loud, certainly nothing I'd ever actually *do*, for crying out loud, I'm not crazy. But now that I know…I can't unknow. Five milligrams is all it would take. And five milligrams, is nothing.

And I run into the Home Depot, head straight for the sealants and grab a can of that Flex-i-whatever it's called. Who knows, someday I might need it, and I can show it off when I get back home—"Here it is! I got what I went for!" And I head back out, straight to my mom's Toyota and I realize, I never even bothered to copy her key. Which is fine, because I know I won't be needing it. That idea was so stupid, anyway…

———————

Sometimes when nobody's paying attention, and things get a little out of hand, you learn from it. I never set anything on fire again, on purpose or otherwise, and so far as I know, neither did Daniel. But sometimes, you don't learn. Sometimes you don't even know how completely out of hand they've become, and the rains you'll pray for never come, not even if you stomp and stomp doing the same damned thing over and over like you're insane. And it'll be pointless to wonder when out of hand became out of control because by the time you consider it, the wind has already won, and everything, is burning.

X

"…And if you are foolish enough to experiment with any of these drugs on yourself, even once, your chances of becoming addicted are very high…"

That's what The Chairman had said to us years ago during my residency, and I remember it. In fact, he gave a number—fifty percent chance. He gave a drug—fentanyl. And he gave a method—intravenous. If two of us residents, were to inject IV fentanyl, then one of us would become addicted. It's quite a vivid image, two of us sitting there about to inject, wondering which one is doomed. He must've meant to make an impact, and he succeeded. None of us can imagine using IV drugs. On ourselves? I couldn't fathom it. And fentanyl? Most of us are just becoming familiar with it, you don't hear much about it as a med student, and what we hear makes you go whoa. A hundred times the potency of morphine? That's some strong shit.

So for some stupid reason, this is what sticks in my mind. *That's* how you become addicted. That's how the whole thing starts. As if two otherwise healthy, well-adjusted physicians just one day decide to inject the most powerful pain killer available straight into the vein, because what did else did they have to do today anyway. And one *still* walks away unscathed. It seems ridiculous…because it is.

Of course, The Chairman wasn't trying to sound absurd, he was being sincere. He was doing the best he could with what he knew to try and save us from ourselves. But most of the time, we hear what we want to hear, and we see what we want to see. And right now, I see a way to make those fifty-fifty odds of becoming addicted tilt way in my favor, even if I don't see that it was all bullshit to begin with.

Well, what if it wasn't fentanyl? Fentanyl is potent, but it's also fast. It's rapid onset and short duration are what make it so effective in the operating room, but those are also the exact same qualities that increase a drug's potential for abuse. Like freebasing cocaine. And what if it wasn't intravenous? It's that immediate rush of an IV bolus that's addicting, too, right? I've got a fix that will avoid all that unnecessary risk. And also...what if it wasn't me. Because it's already been Barry. It can't be both of us. I mean, just look at the odds.

I've grown adept at managing the hydrocodone usage. I've learned how to take it and when, so that it gives me exactly what I need, when I need it. Need a couple hours in the Land of Nodding off before sleep? It's got me. Need a little boost to play with the kids in the evening? It's got me there, too. It can actually be energizing. I don't see myself as a drug abuser at all, this isn't harming my life, it's an enhancement. It seems so obvious. I've kept it confined to the weekends, I don't suffer any sort of withdrawals, and I'm pretty sure that if I really wanted to, I could quit. Hell, if I am a drug abuser, I'm a very successful one.

So, what if I could find a way to mimic the pills? A way that mitigates the risks of an IV bolus, fentanyl, all that. What if I just used...morphine? It's sort of the standard that most other opioids are compared to anyway. How potent is something, compared to morphine. And injecting into the muscle isn't ideal, but I can't just drink it. The dose is tiny, just a half a cc or so. Besides, it's not like I'm going to make a habit of this. The only reason I'd ever considered it is because my mom left all her extra pills at home. This will be just for today. Although if all goes well, and how could it not, this could be a great regular weekend substitute for my mom's pills. I can finally stop stealing. At work, I'd only take what I was already going to waste, that's it. It'd be like stealing trash.

———————————

This seems like an awful lot of thinking, a lot of careful consideration. But the fact is, I knew it all in an instant when "opioids are opioids" flashed in my brain. It's like a movie where the plot unfolds in reverse. You know how everything ends up from the very beginning and the whole exercise of how to get there is nothing but a continuous suspension of disbelief, willing or not, it doesn't really matter.

The morphine…it's easy to get. It's nobody's fault but mine, but it's no problem. Like I said, five milligrams is nothing. The security mechanisms, with the wastes, the witnesses, and the worry about mass spectrometers and such, they're about as sensitive as any safety protocols could be. But the fact is, they might be decent at detecting advanced disease, and I'll have to deal with that later, but when things have first metastasized from your mouth to your muscle, flying under the radar is as simple as dropping it in your pocket. And although I should, I don't feel any worse about it than if I'd squirted it out in the sink.

Much later I'll remember how easy it was and I'll wish I'd stolen more. Maybe a lot more. Maybe things would've turned out differently. Maybe if it would've been spectacular. Or nearly killed me. Or made me immediately want more like they say crack cocaine does. Maybe something like that would've shocked some sense into me. But nothing like that happens, and what does happen doesn't surprise me at all. Because it's almost exactly what I expected. The needle in my deltoid, it stings a little, like I knew it would, but nothing bad. Hardly a drop of blood at all. It's all very clinical, with alcohol swabs and sterile syringes. Nothing gritty. Nothing dark. I even apply one of those little round bandages like you get after a flu shot, I've got my shit together. And it only takes about ten minutes instead of half an hour, but when that warmth starts to click, and lubricate everything that's been irritating me, all I think is "Huh. I'll be damned. My dad was right. Oil is oil."

It's perhaps the worst thing I could've thought.

"What was I thinking?" Usually when we ask ourselves this, there's only one answer—I wasn't. We assume using logic keeps us sane. We think a cautionary tale will prevent calamity. Knowledge is power for sure, but fruit from its tree isn't always sweet. We can do everything the conscious mind can conceive of to protect ourselves and others, but the truth is, the subconscious mind has knowledge too. It remembers everything, and it can't tell the good from the bad. It doesn't care of you're running a marathon or mainlining morphine, it's all the same. It doesn't judge. It can't.

There's an actual term for this, when the subconscious mind alters rational thinking in such a way as to get you to do it's bidding, even if you ordinarily wouldn't. Reality actually seems different. It's called brainshift. Fear can trigger it, even something silly like the fear of looking stupid in front of your friends. But so can reward. And the rewards my primitive self is used to are just out of this world, they're not natural, at least not in the way I've been using them. It doesn't matter how smart you are, how rich, or how poor, black or white. It doesn't even care where you've chosen to align your moral compass. Because when the brain shifts, it's more like it blows up, and all the barriers to badness that you thought would stand forever between you and the thing you'd never do, well they're gone. And what you see instead, it seems to make perfect sense. What's even worse, what once felt impossible can never quite seem so again. How could it. You're already doing it.

None of this is an excuse, it's just an explanation, and it's not even one that will do me any good. It's just more…knowledge. But I'll seek it just the same. I'll read everything from evolutionary biology to the Bible, both to tell me why and also what to do now, but none of it will help. What would help is something so simple even a child could comprehend. But even though I may already know what it is, I've got a hell of a long way to go before I'll be willing to do it.

XI

"You not drinking any wine tonight? Again?"

It's Thursday, and Tami wants to make sure she's seeing straight. It's one of those questions that's full of hope and doubt at the same time. It seems too good to be true. I don't know if she's gotten past the point of paying attention to how many times I topped off my wine glass every night, but she's definitely given up on hassling me about it. We've had an unspoken truce for years. So my fourth night of not drinking is noticeable.

"Why?" she wonders

Because there's gotta be a reason, right?

"I dunno, I guess I just don't really want it."

Which is half true, the only half of it she could handle. The other unspoken half is "because I've got morphine coursing through my veins this very minute." That half, I'm quite sure, she could not.

Still, she doesn't believe me. "It's because your mom is still here, isn't it. You can not drink for her, but not for me, is that it?"

"No, Tami, that's not it. But you know, I need to cut back, I've been saying that for a long time. And maybe the time is now." I shrug and pat my belly. "I mean, look at me. I'm thirty-five pounds heavier than when we got married. You're not, and you've had two kids." I pat her butt, and the flattery seems to satisfy her. She leans more into the hope.

"Well whatever the reason, I'm glad. The boys will be, too. They like you playing with them more"

———————————

So obviously, the idea that the five milligrams of morphine from Monday was a one time thing, that really didn't work out like I'd planned. But everything else…everything else couldn't be better. My new disregard for alcohol is only one of a half dozen reasons I'm convinced this new morphine experiment is gold. It's a discovery.

In every way I can measure, I'm a better man. The alcohol never made me angry, like it does some people, I wasn't a belligerent drunk, ever. And I was never looking for oblivion, it's not like I'd get blitzed. The sweet spot was it for me. Just pure peace and ease. But the booze, it made me lazy, and getting me to do much more than change the channel was a big ask. I just wanted to sit there, sipping, and not say shit.

The morphine is an improvement. A noticeable one. It's only been four days, but I've got a routine down. A habit. Not everybody needs morphine during a surgery, fentanyl is far more common, but during the longer procedures it's easy to justify. And by late afternoon, I can escape the OR with enough of the standard for my two hydrocodone equivalents, and I head home happy. I'm out of my CAGE. I don't need to Cut back, nobody is Annoyed, and I don't feel Guilty. At all. Why would I? The morphine has cured my alcoholism. In

1910, this would've been normal, why not now? As far as I'm concerned, this physician has healed himself with an ancient remedy.

Even in these last few years, I've continued to either run or go to my home gym and do as many pull ups and push ups as I can every day after work. Some primitive part of myself has continued to crave it, but I'd found a more practical reason as well. I make sure it's the first thing I do when I get home. Sweat out as much water as I can in the summer heat especially, and having a glass of wine is like having three. It's a great recovery drink. And I had to get started before dinner, because drinking on a full stomach is a drag.

I've been saving the morphine for a post-workout reward, too. But instead of anchoring me to my armchair, it's more like a second wind. It's like my natural neurotransmitters, my endogenous dopamine, struggle to the finish line, depleted. But the morphine is there to give them a high five, pick up the baton, and I can keep going, and going, right up through bedtime stories for the boys.

It's not like living with a blossoming opiate addict isn't noticeable. It is. But when the notable changes are positive, and can easily be attributed to a precipitous decline in ethanol consumption, who's gonna complain? We see what we want to see. Much later, I'll read story after story about addicts and their experience, in both a conscious effort to uncover their secret to surviving and an unconscious desire for connection. In one of the books, a famous rock star claims that if you were to give an opioid to five people, four of them would either go to sleep or get sick. The fifth one will start cleaning the house, and there's your drug addict. I guess I'm guilty.

Not that there aren't telltale signs, but they'll expose themselves gradually. And I'll disclose them even more slowly to those who might notice, like Tami, as if they were bargaining chips that will buy me just one more day of freedom to supposedly make my own choices.

But all that's a long way off and I needn't worry about it now anyways. It's Thursday already, and I need to worry about what to do this weekend.

———————

TGIF. Everybody knows what that means. It's supposed to be a celebration, a small, weekly reminder of what it felt like on the last day of school and an endless summer awaited. This weekend will just be for two days, but if I don't figure out a way to make the morphine last until Monday, it's gonna feel like forever. I should've started thinking about this back on Monday, but then again, I wasn't thinking at all, was I. My planning has been piss poor. The party wasn't supposed to even get started until today.

Fortunately for me, my Friday is busy. I won't be finishing work until well after six. There was a time when that would've bothered me, when the first thing I'd look at when the next day's schedule came out was "what time do I go home." Time was my currency. But then I made partner, and the pay scale changed, and the more I worked, the more I made. Money is a pretty good incentive, for most of us, and I began to pay more attention to how much I could earn in a day rather than how many hours I'd have left at the end of it.

But today, I'm not paying attention to either of these things. My money is morphine, and the currency I'm concerned about, is drugs.

It's not like manna from heaven, I won't get any daily bread, so I'm gonna have to store some up. And I can't just break into the automated drug dispenser and check out whatever I want, it has to be skimmed, little by little, case by case. Luckily, today's schedule should allow me to do just that. I should be able to give each patient just what they need to wake up in reasonable comfort (I can't ignore one of those cardinal rules for not getting caught already, now, can I?) while still being able to take home five milligrams for today, five milligrams for Saturday, and if I'm lucky, a whole ten milligrams for Sunday. To celebrate my success. TGIF indeed.

————————

It feels good to be holding. This is more drug slang, but this one I know already, from movies and television shows about people whose lives seem a world away from my own. It means I'm in possession of drugs, more than I've ever had at once. I'm sure appropriating the term, even if only to myself, is some sort of defense mechanism, a form of denial that my darker nature uses to bully its better angel. As in, "what the fuck are you worrying about, man? Everything is gonna be great! We're holdin' over here. Just chill." And it works. The whole drive home is a high all its own, and every once in a while I'll give my pocket a pat and remind myself, you're set 'til Monday.

Except by Sunday…I'm not. It's not my fault really, shit happened, and I've never been holdin' before, how was I to know how to handle it. On Friday night, Tami was complaining that her back hurt, like bad, and she never complains so I knew something must be really wrong. And I thought maybe I could tell her, "Here, I've got some morphine, maybe that would help," but I thought, no, no, I can't do that, and the sheer absurdity of it made me want to laugh, but there was nothing at all funny about her back pain. So rather than saying something stupid, I just went and took an extra five milligram shot for myself, and I took her to the ER instead. Fortunately, those doctors knew what they were doing, and it turns out she had pyelonephritis. A full blown kidney infection. Of course I hadn't been serious, but morphine would've done nothing but mask what was really wrong with her, and the irony of *that* I wouldn't have found funny even if I hadn't missed it.

So I fucked up Friday, but I've still got a full ten milligrams to last me through the weekend. I can still stay on somewhat of a schedule. Saturday morning comes, and Tami is feeling a bit better. She'd gotten an antibiotic shot in the Emergency Department, and a prescription for more pills that she'll start this morning, but she's nowhere near back to normal. She needs to rest. Which means breakfast is on me.

"You boys want cinnamon toast?"

"Cinnamon toast?" TJ's eyes get big. He usually only gets it at Granny's house. It's not the only thing I know how to make, but it's by far the easiest, and I figure my mom is still here, so why not.

"Or I could bake everyone some muffins?" My mom says it as she walks into the kitchen, and TJ looks at me and says "Granny waked up!"

"Yeah, buddy, Granny's awake, you want her to bake us some muffins?"

He does, and somewhere between me showing my mom where Tami keeps the muffin mix and TJ asking for a glass of milk, I think to myself…"Wake and bake."

———————————

"You know what we should do in the morning?"

"What, Billy."

Billy is my roommate, and he's drunk, which means I'm irritated with him. Because Billy is an asshole when he's drunk, and he pees in places he shouldn't like the dishwasher. But he's also my best friend, and pretty much has been since I'd seen him walk into the restaurant where we both wait tables with a big pinch of Copenhagen in his lip. Which I thought was pretty cool for a guy who said he was gonna be a dentist. We're also in the same science classes at college, and both a little older than most of the other students. I need the classes to get into medical school because all I've got is an English degree. Billy needs them because all he's got is two ex-wives.

"We should wake and bake."

"What's 'wake and bake', Billy."

"It's this." He shows me a little plastic bag full of the marijuana I know he sometimes smokes. I've tried it twice, once to no effect at all, and once to merely mediocre results, and I don't really get the appeal, especially considering its illegality.

"You want to wake up and smoke pot in the morning? What time will that be, noon?"

"Oh, don't be such a puss." He's so drunk he can't pronounce an S to save himself. "You jus' gonna finish your…your two little Miller Lites and go…go study or something?" I haven't yet adjusted the two drink limit rule with endless amendments. He'd call me self-righteous but he can't pronounce it.

"Well I do like you better when you smoke than when you drink, that's for sure. Just go to bed, Billy. I'll see you in the morning, and yeah, let's 'wake and bake'. That's a great idea. And make sure you piss in the toilet." He weaves down the hallway towards his bedroom and gives me the finger over his shoulder.

I don't expect him to remember any of this, he never does. I also don't expect to see him at 7am, but there he is, grinning like an idiot, telling me to "wakey, wakey."

"What the fuck, Billy. Let me sleep."

"C'mon, man. Get up. We're gonna wake and bake. You'll love it. We'll smoke some of this kind green, we'll walk down to the Coyote Coffee Shop, we'll read the paper, eat banana muffins. We'll come back, catch college football game day, and then about eleven, when the OU game starts, we'll take a nap."

"You're serious."

"Get up, Tommy Boy. You're gonna love it."

Billy was right. I loved it. The richness of the coffee, the freshness of the muffins, and the way time seemed to pass by so slowly. You could savor everything. Fortunately for me, they didn't sell

98

weed at the 7-11, and I didn't make it a habit. But that first time, it was an eyeopener. And right about the time my mom says "The muffins are ready!", I remember the morphine, and instead of wondering why, I say "why not."

Saturday night I'll succumb to some similarly flimsy excuse, so instead of celebrating my success on Sunday with a double dose, I'm back down to drinking.

"I haven't had any in a week," I say to Tami, as she looks at me sideways when I start my first pour from the box that's been sitting untouched on the kitchen counter.

"Uh-huh…your mom's gone now, so what, you're back to normal?"

"Hey, I never said I was quitting. Maybe I'll just save it for the weekends now, or something. It's not a big deal, I can have a couple of glasses on a Sunday, right?"

"Yeah, you can," she says. "I was just kind of hoping maybe you wouldn't. But it's fine, it's fine."

Which it might be. For her. But the wine's not fine for me, I barely even enjoy it at all. It's like sipping saccharine when I've gotten used to the sweetness of syrup. It seems like there's no point. But I tell myself maybe that's a good thing. This week I know I have to get back on the schedule with the morphine, just saving it for the weekends. I've gotta get back to just chipping. And if the wine is going to be this sorry of a substitute, well…forget cutting back. I could probably just quit entirely. I mean really…I think I'm right on the verge of just being able to say…fuck it.

XII

"Got anything to waste?"

A nurse in the recovery room asks me after I've handed off my patient, still a little sleepy from the anesthetic.

"Yep. Got one cc of morphine." I show it to her, clear in the syringe. It's morphine, says so right on the blue label I've stuck to the side of it. MORPHINE. I point to the pharmacy sheet I've filled out with how much I've given and how much we're wasting, and she attests to its accuracy with her initials. And I squirt the MORPHINE into the sink.

"That might as well be saline for all I know." She gives me a look with one eyebrow raised.

This is an old joke, one I've heard before from various nurses going all the way back to Birmingham. Sometimes I just go with a shrug, like "what can you do? System ain't perfect." Today I go with a "Ha. Ha. You got me." My delivery is dead pan. She gets it of course, and we both laugh.

But I'm dead serious. Saline is exactly what it was. Salt water from an IV bag. The morphine, it's in my pocket, where it belongs. Where it can do some good. What's the use of it swirling around in a sewer? Wasting it seems like such a...well, waste. Better to save it instead.

And after I did it once, I never didn't do it again.

It's been a month since that first time. The month of August. And normally in Oklahoma, August absolutely sucks. It's hell. The temperatures are in the 100s, the humidity isn't much lower, and you can't remember the last time it rained. September seems to come slower than Christmas. But for me, it's been more like spring. I've been reborn. Nothing bothers me, not even the heat.

Well, almost nothing. I've got my own little opioid accountability system in a notebook I'm keeping. Kind of like the pharmacy uses, only instead of tracking patients, it's keeping track of me. I started using it two weeks ago, when it became evident that I wasn't going to be reserving the shots for a reward just on the weekend like I had with the pills. Oh no. Why would I do that when life has become just so much sweeter with morphine? I've quit drinking entirely. I'm not even sure if there's any alcohol left in the house other than an old bottle of grappa someone once left as a gift. About a week ago Tami finally threw out the half empty wine box that had been sitting there like a piece of obsolete electronics, just useless, incompatible. Didn't say a word, like she was afraid she might jinx me. One day it was just gone.

And my gut, it's not gone yet, but it's definitely going. I've eliminated so many empty calories just by not drinking that I'm losing almost a pound every other day. And even though food tastes just fine, I'm not really all that hungry, and I certainly have no need to comfort myself with cake and ice cream. I've lost ten pounds in August alone, Tami tells me I look great, and I'm pretty sure if I can keep it up I'll lose twenty-five more by our anniversary. I'll be back to the man she married.

But it's not the things on the outside that are beginning to bother me. It's what's on the inside. On the inside of my little newly kept notebook, to be specific. Not that anyone else could see it even if they looked. It's just some numbers—a one, two, or three. Sometimes there's a four. And the letter M, which cleverly stands for morphine. But in the last week, there's been a few D's, and also F's. They're not grades, although they do reflect my failure, they're more drugs. The D is for Dilaudid, and the F, the F is for fentanyl. There's nothing any more special about them, morphine is still my favorite, but just depending on what hospital I happen to be working at, or what kind of cases I've got, I've had to adapt. Be flexible. Especially with the fentanyl. The morphine and dilaudid can be administered to hospital patients intravenously, but intramuscular injections are also common. IM. And that's my preferred route on myself for a number of reasons. It's like sipping on whiskey slowly instead of doing shots. And I like to make it last. Also no blood, or almost none, and no track marks left behind. Only tiny bruises. So even though fentanyl is always given IV in the hospital, I figured what the hell, what's the worst that can happen, and I tried injecting it into my muscle like it was morphine. And other than burning like shit, it's a fine enough substitute for the standard.

But it's not so much the letters in my notebook that are concerning me. It's the numbers. Each one represents the number of times I used in a particular day, or sometimes just the total dose. And just a week ago today, last Friday, I'd written a giant 40. Traced over it multiple times and added an exclamation point, like I could hardly believe it. I don't even have to write the M beside it because I just know, it stands for forty milligrams of morphine. In an evening. I guess

103

I was all TGIF or some shit, and things just got a little out of hand, but I had to head on out to my mom's for the rest of the weekend. Lucky for me, she'd just refilled her prescription, but I'm afraid I took enough in two days that I pretty much cleared my quota if I don't want to get my hand caught in her cookie jar.

The date in my notebook, it also concerns me. It's August 29th, a Friday. Which means Monday will be the first of September, and that means it's Labor Day. And unless you're on call, and I'm not, it means there's no work. I guess a lot of the surgeons got an early start to the holiday, and there's not much work for me today, either. Not that it matters, considering my attempts to ration on previous weekends have been a disaster. But I've got to look at the bright side. Maybe this is just what I need. A little three day holiday, not on drugs, but from them. It'll be intentional. I can tell my tolerance has been building up, it's right there in my notebook, and hitting the reset button will be refreshing. And nothing gives you confidence like shooting up all your stash, which, of course, I do, this very evening.

————————————

"You have to work Monday? Really?"

"Yes, I told you that two weeks ago. I'm the newbie. I get Labor Day and I'll probably get Christmas, too."

If Tami had told me, I'd forgotten. Her new pharmacy gig is going well. She's glad to be back to work. But having to occasionally work weekends and a holiday like this is one of the drawbacks.

"You said you'd be off, that you'd watch the boys," she reminds me.

104

"Oh yeah, yeah. I know. I remember." I don't, but this is not entirely unwelcome news. A plan is forming. "I think I'll uh, I think the boys and I'll go somewhere. A little guys holiday weekend."

"Really? I figured you'd just go to your moms. She can at least help you watch the boys."

It's tempting. But that's just it. It's *too* tempting. Besides, I can do this. I need to do this.

"Nah, we were just there last weekend. I'm thinking maybe I'll take them to Tulsa. Go to their zoo and stuff. Or Dallas! We'll go to Dallas! Maybe the Rangers are in town."

"You're going to take Tyson to a baseball game? He's just a baby."

"He's not a baby anymore, he'll love it. It'll be a night game, not too hot. TJ too. He loves baseball. He'll be playing T-ball himself soon. It'll be great!" I've convinced myself.

"Well...ok. I guess. You won't be able to just come home if Tyson won't sleep you know."

"I know, I know, it'll be fine. Our first all boys trip. Hey TJ, guess what! We're going to Dallas, buddy! To a baseball game!"

TJ, he thinks that's a home run.

_____

"You see that big yellow sign with the red letters buddy?" I ask TJ.

105

"Yeah...I see a D!"

"That's right! And Denny's starts with a D."

"What's a Denny's?"

"A Denny's is quite simply the finest food a family can eat. If you're on a road trip, anyways."

"What do they have?"

"They have...everything!"

"Do they have mac & cheese?"

"Of course they do."

"And chocolate milk?"

"Chocolate milk too. You wanna go to Denny's buddy?"

"I want mac & cheese and chocolate milk!"

When I was a kid, any car trip longer than two hours demanded a pit stop, but my dad never took us to Denny's. It was always a Howard Johnson's, or if we were lucky, a Tastee Freeze. I loved the feeling of going somewhere else, especially with my dad, and Tastee Freeze tasted like freedom. All of them are long gone now, the restaurants and my dad, so Denny's will have to do. Maybe when TJ and Tyson are older, freedom will taste like a Grand Slam Special.

I've got another reason for picking Denny's though. I've got a soft spot for it from my time in Japan. Kobe, where I lived, had numerous western franchises like McDonald's and KFC, and there was a Denny's not far from my apartment. I ignored all of them for the first year, and lived on ramen noodles and yakisoba, but by the second year I began to crave more familiar flavors. I'd occasionally take a two hour train ride to the far side of Osaka just to get a real pizza at Pizza Hut, and I started stopping in at the Denny's by my apartment from time to time. From then on, Denny's has pretty much tasted like home.

———————————

The sound of "Save Your Life" by the Australian Christian pop band The Newsboys is unfamiliar to most people. But not to this crowd of Rangers fans. It's the walk up song for their star player, Josh Hamilton, and when they hear it, they go nuts. It means Hamilton is up to bat. He's having a helluva season, he'll go on to win the league MVP, but where he's come from makes it even more impressive. He'd been the first player drafted a decade or so before, but his career had been derailed by cocaine addiction. It's been a long road back, but people love a comeback story almost as much as they love a winner. And right now, Josh Hamilton is both. He's lived out the lyrics to his walk up song.

The Rangers are having a great season, but most people are evidently saving their money for the playoffs, and tickets are easy to get. Maybe because they're playing the Twins. I overpaid for three seats in the boxes down close to the backstop, on the third base side, and I'm pretty sure former president George Bush is sitting off to our right close to the Rangers dugout. I tell TJ to go say hi to him, but he won't. He doesn't know what a president even is, or care.

But he does care about cotton candy.

"I'll take two," I tell the vendor.

"That it?" he asks.

"And peanuts. One pack of peanuts."

"Anything to drink?"

"We'll take a Coke." We can share it.

"Ok, it's fourteen." He passes us our snacks and I start to pass him the cash.

"Wait. What kind of beer do you have?"

"I got Bud, Bud Light, and Shiner."

"Gimme two Shiners."

"Ok it'll be thirty."

I hand him two twenties and tell him to keep the change. And to come back in a couple of innings.

TJ wraps his little hands around the giant Coke cup and sips through his straw. He doesn't have a clue who Josh Hamilton or any of the other players are, or why they're chasing after that little ball like life depends on it, but the sights and smells of the ballpark alone are enough to captivate him, at least for a couple of hours. I pull off strands of the cotton candy and feed it to Tyson between huge swallows of the shiner, and I'm not sure which one Tami would disapprove of more. But hey, it's a ballgame. Not drinking's gotta have some exceptions.

————————

108

During the seventh inning stretch my favorite vendor stops by again.

"Last call for alcohol. U want another Shiner?"

I show him two fingers. He looks at the scattered peanut shells at my feet surrounding the stack of beer cups. There's gotta be eight.

"Alright man, last round."

He hands me two lukewarm cups. TJ is ready to go, and Tyson is getting cranky. I'm pretty sure he's crapped his diaper but I'm going to try to wait until we're leaving to change it.

"Let's go, daddy. Daddy, let's gooooo."

"Hang on buddy. Josh Hamilton is third up this inning. After he bats we'll go. Promise."

The first batter singles, and quickly steals second base on the next pitch. The Rangers bunt to move him up to third, and the go ahead run is ninety feet away from home with only one out. Everyone in the stands is on their feet when "Save Your Life" announces the arrival of Hamilton for the third time. He's 0 for 2, and he's due. We're so close we can see the flames tattooed on his forearms flicker when he adjusts his grip on the bat. He takes a big swing at the first pitch, but misses, and we can almost feel a breeze from his bat. TJs eyes are big. The pitcher doesn't want to make a mistake with Hamilton at the plate, but Vlad Guerrero is up next so he has to pitch to him. The next two pitches are close but they're both balls, and Hamilton takes them.

"Home run, buddy, he's gonna hit a home run, I can feel it!"

The next pitch is a little low but Hamilton goes down to get it and sends it soaring as high as I've ever seen a baseball go. Andrus runs back to third to tag up and everyone in the stands screams at the ball to get out of the park. But it doesn't listen. The right fielder is camped out near the warning track by the fence, and when Hamilton's ball comes down, he catches it easily. Josh is out. But Elvis Andrus takes off from third as soon as the ball is caught and he's across the plate with the go ahead run before the ball even reaches the infield. The crowd goes wild.

"Was it a home run Daddy?"

"No buddy, he got out."

"How?"

"He sacrificed."

_____

I wake up in the king sized hotel bed next to Tyson and TJ, and two things immediately come to mind. The first is that I feel like shit. And strangely enough, the second is "if you surrender, you will live." The feeling like shit I can attribute to how much I drank last night. After the boys fell asleep, I followed up the Shiner Bocks by raiding the mini-bar, and since there are seven empty airplane-sized vodka bottles next to the TV, I guess that's how many I had. I'm pretty sure it's a hangover, but since I never get them, I can't be certain.

The suggestion that "if you surrender, you will live" seems to have surfaced from somewhere subliminal, and it takes me a minute to recognize where it's from. And then I remember. Fuckin' Josh

Hamilton. It's a line from his walk up song. I'd downloaded "Save Your Life" to my phone last night and listened to it a few times while I drank the vodka. I had a couple of Newsboys albums in the 90s, and this newer song, well it's not very good. But that one line… "if you surrender, you will live," it sticks with me. I guess I can see why Hamilton likes it. And I'm rooting for him, I really am. But I don't want to have to go through all that devastation myself, and surrendering's not gonna save my life, it would fucking destroy it. Holy shit, I can't even imagine. After what I've been doing? Thankfully, I still have a choice. I know this can't go on forever, but it's not too late for me yet. And I've got a walk up song of my own, courtesy of Keith Richards and the Rolling Stones, and those are the lyrics I'm gonna live out. I'm gonna walk…before they make me run.

I can still just walk away, right now. And nobody will ever know a thing.

XIII

"Mommy!"

"Hi baby! I'm so happy you're home! Mama missed you!"

"Missed you, too mama!"

"Tell me what you did this weekend with dad and brother!"

"We went to a baseball game, and we went swimming, we stayed in a ho-tel, and we went to a Denny's, and we got room service, and, and that's it!" He holds up his hands like everything's disappeared.

"What else did you guys do?" She's asking me.

"Not much, I also took them to the book depository museum at Dealey Plaza."

"Yeah, where a man shot the, shot the prezudent in the head." TJ remembers now.

"Why'd you take them there? Did you take them to mass yesterday?"

"No, we didn't go to mass. We kind of slept in. I always wanted to go to that museum. And we saw George Bush at the ball game. Figured TJ could learn what a president is. Or was."

"Well, sounds like you guys had fun. Is it good to be home?"

"Yeah. Yeah, it's good to be back."

———————————

She has no idea how good. The truth is, after I woke up yesterday morning with the strange hangover, I was pretty useless. I figured it was a "beer before liquor, never sicker" kind of thing, or is it the other way around. Either way, it seemed to last most of the day. We probably only spent an hour at the book depository, but it seemed more like six. We just went back to the hotel, and I made TJ take a nap with Tyson, but only so I could take one, too. It didn't help. I took them downstairs and beached myself by the kiddie pool and made sure they didn't drown, but I didn't so much as get my feet wet. Fortunately room service was a novelty for the boys and we just stayed in the rest of the evening and watched movies on the hotel television. I ordered a bottle of wine with the room service but I didn't even finish it. I thought hair of the dog was supposed to help, but it didn't do shit.

Thankfully, today I woke up feeling much better. Not normal, but almost. Music helps, and we listened to it the whole way home. It's funny how music can trigger everything from the blues to bliss, it's way better than the bottle last night, and today's playlist was like the soundtrack to my own comeback story. It's pure audio optimism, most of it straight out of the 80's. "Don't Stop Believin'". "Eye of the Tiger". A little Bon Jovi. And even some new stuff. There's this singer I've just heard of, I think her name is Katy Perry, and I really like her. Maybe I'm not supposed to be the target audience but I never cared about that shit anyway. She's good. She just put an album out, and somehow she seems to know exactly how I feel. I do feel "paper thin". I do want to "start again". And baby, I *am* a motherfucking firework.

Then there's Keith Richards. I've always kind of been a Rolling Stones fan, I know most of the hits, and since I lean more towards Keith than Mick, I know all the songs Keef sings, too. Like "Before They Make Me Run." My new walk up song. I never particularly cared for the melody, but I've taken a new interest in the lyrics, for obvious reasons. It's hard to be a heroin addict, even for a world famous rock star, and in 1977 Keith got busted with enough smack to be charged with trafficking in Toronto. Even though it was all for himself. Ultimately he paid his penalty by putting on a benefit concert for a girl who couldn't see, but before that he'd been looking at real prison time. The Canadians were looking to make an example out of him. He knew how lucky he'd gotten. The heroin, it had become just too much trouble. He'd had his fun with it, and now it was time to walk away…before they made him run. Not bad. From then on, he'd choose other medicines.

I don't know any of this backstory yet. It'll be another month or two before Keith's autobiography comes out, and I'll be so hungry for it by then I'll devour it in one sitting. All I know at this point is that it's been almost seventy-two hours since I've committed a criminal act of my own, I didn't even drive home from the ballpark, and as far as I'm concerned, all the statute of limitations have expired. All I've got to do now, is walk away.

———————————

I drive to work on Tuesday with Johnny Nash, or at least his voice. "I can see clearly now, the rain is gone." It's gonna be a bright sunshiny day indeed. It's September. It'll be a couple more weeks before the weather gets comfortable, but I'm totally cool when I walk towards the hospital. A little bit of butterflies, but that's not anxiety, it's anticipation. It's that feeling you get before you leave the locker room at a football game. I'm about to prove to myself I can do this. It might take a little will power these first few days, but I've got as much of that as anyone. I've run marathons, nine of them in all. That's twenty six point two miles worth of will power. I also willed myself to lose twenty pounds when I was twelve because I figured Melanie Murdoch would notice me more if there was a lot less of me. It didn't work, but that's beside the point. The point is, I can fucking do this.

And I do. All the way up until my third case. Almost four whole hours. About the length of time it would've taken me to run one of those marathons I'm so proud of. But I've got a really good reason, it's not even an excuse. It's a plan. It's intentional.

The half life of the high from the Johnny Nash harmonies must've been about seven seconds, because by the time I get inside the hospital, I don't feel nearly as good as I thought. My pulse is uncomfortably quick, and my mouth is dry. It feels fucking unsafe, not just for me, for my patients, too. I'm on edge. But I still say no, and my answer is firm, every single time my sinister self says "Oh Tom, you know what would just fix *all* of this…" And it's not really a demand at all, it's just a suggestion that seems to say "if you've got a better idea, then I'm all ears… so long as you just stop saying no. Because *I'm* not going anywhere." Eventually, inevitably, my no becomes negotiable, and it almost feels like a decision, when I conclude that this cold turkey stuff, well it never works, what was I thinking. Every ounce of confidence that I could quit, it's all still there, only I don't need to start today. I need to start with a taper. That's it! And so, I do. Right away.

All I need are a few supplies, a syringe, a needle, and a swab of alcohol, and I make my way to a restroom in a rear corridor of the surgical area. Slide the silver latch to lock the door in place, and in less time than it takes to take a piss, I stick myself in the shoulder and sink the morphine into my system. It's a relief, really. Not so much the drugs, just that the fucking fight is finally over.

———————————

"Hey Tom, this is Kate, she's gonna be running the marathon with us tomorrow. We used to run cross country together at UC Santa Barbara. Kate, this is Tom Gray. We're med school classmates back in Oklahoma." My buddy Ray is introducing me to one of his college friends. Ray's from here in LA, and we've come for spring break to run the Los Angeles marathon.

"Oh cool, you're from Oklahoma then?"

"Yep."

"Nice!" Kate is beautiful in that sun-kissed California kind of way. She and Ray both look like they could still compete.

"Is this your first marathon?" Kate asks me.

"No, it'll be my sixth. First one in LA though. I ran San Fran last summer."

"Very cool. This'll be my first. I'm kinda nervous." Kate smiles like she couldn't possibly be more relaxed. "What kind of time you thinking?"

"Well, my best has been about 3:45. But I'm shooting for 3:30 tomorrow. If I do as well as my training runs, I should be able to do it."

She's stoked to hear this. "Right on! 3:30 is my goal, too! We should totally try to pace each other. Ray here is gonna kick both our asses, though, right Ray? What are you shooting for, 2:30?"

"Naaah, dude. I'd be good with sub-three. This is gonna be so cool, bro, I can't fuckin' wait!" Ray gives me a high five, and his enthusiasm, it's contagious. It's his first marathon, too, and he will indeed kick our asses, but I don't really care. I'm gonna be running with Kate.

We all meet up early and join the thousands of other runners crowded at the starting line. We share whoops, hollers, and high fives, as if we aren't going to be begging for all this energy back a couple of hours from now. When the gun goes off, we walk several steps as the massive crowd lurches forward, and then break into a slow jog.

"I'm so stoked to be doing this with you bro, this is so cool!" Ray gives me a high five, and he looks like he could run all the way back to OKC. We've put in hundreds of miles together there while we work our way through medical school, and he's right. This is pretty fuckin' cool.

As the crowd thins out some, Ray says "catch you guys at the finish line," and he's gone, leaving Kate and me to settle in at what I hope is a steady 3:30 pace. Eight minute miles.

"How you feeling?" she asks.

"Good, you?"

She nods. "Good."

But I'm not really sure. It feels kind of fast. The adrenaline dump has dissipated, but now I'm fueled by a desire to not look like a dumbass in front of this girl I'd just love to impress. She's a college runner, and if she says this is the pace, then dammit, it's the pace.

The so-called distance markers don't help. The first few are missing, and someone has clearly confused kilometers with miles, so who knows how fast we're actually going. If I had breath to speak I might say something.

It appears that the distance markers are finally accurate when we approach 10K, only when I look down at my watch to check our time, I can't really believe it. It says thirty-eight minutes. That's less than 6:30 per mile. I've never run a 10K in thirty-eight minutes in my life, my best is more like forty-two, and this would be fantastic if I were finished but I've still got twenty more miles to run. Shit.

"Kate…hey…this is way too…fast for me. I've gotta…back off." I struggle to tell her.

"Yeah I thought it…was kinda…fast." She can't breathe any better than I can. Maybe she was waiting for me to slow us down, I'm the one who's supposed to have done this before, but who knows if nobody speaks up.

"I'm gonna use the porta potty, try to drink a little, too. Go on if you feel like it. Maybe I'll catch up with you later." She says ok, and her blonde ponytail disappears into the crowd.

I tell myself it'll be alright, I'll slow way down, I'll recover, and I got such a head start, maybe I can still hit 3:30. Only in a few more miles, I know I'm screwed. At mile ten, I start to walk some. At mile thirteen, it's the only thing I can do, and by mile seventeen, I'm flat on my back. I'm done. My race is over.

And what landed me there on a dirty LA sidewalk, sticking my tongue out, was not altogether different from what would later lead me to that locked hospital bathroom, sticking a needle into my arm…but probably not for the reasons you think.

———————————

My brain, it's just one of my organs. It's not "me" any more than my liver is. But its function has an awful lot to do with the choices I make, and with my actions that have a lot to do with determining the type of person I am. I've known since well before I arrived to work on this particular Tuesday after Labor Day that I faced one of these huge choices. It was Nike versus Nancy Reagan. Just Do It…or Just Say No. When I woke up, a tiny part of my conscious mind wanted to Just Do It. It's a frightening thing to face a future that doesn't involve mood altering substances, once you've relied on them like I have. But overwhelmingly, I'm with Nancy. Just Say No isn't the better choice, it's the only choice. My mind is made up. Or at least the part of it I'm aware of. I've steeled myself with fight songs, and I swear I won't stop believin', no matter what.

But there's an unconscious aspect of my brain that feels differently. And it's all "Just Do It", baby. It makes no difference if I'm aware of it or not, it's been paying attention, and it's aware of everything. When my alarm clock went off at the typical time, it noticed. When I put on scrubs to go to work, it noticed that too. It noted the familiar route I took, the exit sign on the highway, and the hospital parking lot. It's got expectations, and they take conscious form in the thought that the morphine would make me feel better. It's what I need. Don't think, Just Do It.

At first, saying no to this impulse is simple. I Just Say it—"No." But if I think that's it, I've got another thing coming. It may not be for another five minutes, but inevitably I hear it again—Just Do It. Saying no a second time is almost as easy, I might even put a little pepper in it—"I said, No!" When I walk by the drug dispenser, it happens again—Do It. Hell no. And it goes on like this, and on like this, until one of these sides finally says fuck it.

Mediating all this drama are other little parts of my brain, like the anterior cingulate cortex. Part of its job is to help me make a choice, to exercise self control. To exert my will, or to even decide what my will is. And in this conflict between do it or don't, one side has got an enormous advantage...and it's not Nancy Reagan. I'm sure she didn't know it, but it turns out, Just Saying No is costly.

So is starting out a marathon by running the fastest 10k of your life. Glucose is a simple sugar and it's basically the building block that fuels most of what the body does. The fuel for running a marathon is a glucose combination called glycogen, and the body stores up as much as it can in the liver and the muscles. If I pace myself right, it'll last me the entire twenty-six miles. But if I don't, I bonk, and I wind up flat on my back, unable to will myself to walk another step.

And not only can more will power not get me out of this mess, it's part of why I'm there in the first place. I can thank my ego. For wanting to impress a girl. For not listening to the rest of my body. For telling me I can just do it…when I can't. Will power and wisdom are not the same thing.

So sprinting a marathon is costly. Just Saying No might be less obviously so, but it costs just the same. The brain needs glucose, too, the cortex requires energy to put up with all this bullshit, and every time I have to say No, it uses more up. It's not glycogen this time, it's glutamate and other neurotransmitters my brain uses to communicate with itself. And little by little, with no after no after no, it gets exhausted, literally. My cortex bonks.

But shouldn't it be equally as costly to say Just Do It? To ask again and again and again, are we there yet? Turns out, not at all. Because one side is fighting for morality. It's playing by certain rules. But for the other side, it's about survival. And instinct. If I were dying of thirst, I'd never stop wishing for water. I know I'm not gonna die if I don't get morphine, at this early stage it doesn't even hardly feel like it. But to my brain, it really doesn't matter. Fighting for survival or trying to play by the rules, it's just the flesh versus spirit, and the enormous advantage the flesh has is it never gives up. It doesn't have to, because it never gets tired. Not unless you die.

When you bonk in a marathon, it's easy to learn from it. It should be obvious what happened. And even if it's not, someone will tell you. It's not like you'd have to hide it.

—"I dunno what happened man, I was running great for the first 10k."

—"Well, dumbass, you might try pacing yourself next time."

But when you get tired of Saying No and start saying fuck it, it's not at all obvious why. If the more and more you try, the more likely you are to fail, and if in order to succeed you have to do almost nothing, how in the hell is anyone supposed to figure *that* out. It's like a sea you cannot swim in, you just have to sink…and hope you find a whole new way to breathe.

XIV

"Dr. Gray, you can't go see your patient like that."

One of the pre-op nurses tells me, and for a split second, I freeze. What does he mean, "like that"? How could he tell?

"You got blood on you."

I look down at the front of my scrub top like I'm looking for mustard.

"No, not there. Here. On your sleeve." He points.

Near my left shoulder are several scattered dots, like I've been squirted with a red ink pen. I neglected to put a little bandage on my injection site, thinking it wouldn't bleed, but evidently it did.

"Ah, shit. Thanks man. Must've gotten on me during the last case."

"No problem, Dr. G. Lemme grab you some peroxide, it'll dissolve it right out."

I rub the peroxide on the blood stains, and they turn white and fizzle. After everything dries, my scrub sleeve is all baby blue again. Nobody can see a thing.

And so long as I'm not careless like that again, I'm quite confident that my secret is safe. This isn't like the movies, I didn't just slam my whole score and nod out before I've even had time to untie the tourniquet, there's no drama here at all. I walk, talk, and work, exactly as I did before. Hell, I could even do trigonometry, if I had to. This is a childish satisfaction, but I allow myself a moment to enjoy it anyway. "I've just injected morphine, not twenty minutes ago, and nobody knows." It doesn't make me feel isolated, it makes me feel special, as if having secrets is a superpower and not a sickness.

This isn't the first time I've used drugs as a crutch on the job. Back in medical school when I wrote my personal statement for my residency application, I included all that obligatory stuff about my "keen interest" in pharmacology and physiology, even if it wasn't especially honest. But I also related a little personal story that was. My first experience in the OR wasn't as a doctor, it was as a patient, back when I'd slipped on the restaurant floor and broken my jaw. I had to have surgery to wire it shut. And the surgeon, he was nice enough I suppose, but he'd done this so many thousands of times before, he seemed to forget that what was routine to him wasn't familiar to me at all. It was scary. My anesthesiologist, he seemed to remember that. And in my personal statement I said that no matter how many thousands of patients I get to see myself, that I'd remember it, too.

Except I didn't. Eventually I just relied on the drugs. Versed is an intravenous anti-anxiety medication. A "don't care shot", some people like to say. And it's commonly given to patients just before they roll back to the OR.

It's supposed to work like this…

"I'm going to give you a little medication that will help you relax before we head back, Ms. Jones." Ms. Jones is about sixty, and she's cranky. She's been waiting all day without anything to eat or drink, and she's got a kidney stone that needs to be removed. Her surgery was supposed to be at two, but since the earlier procedures took longer than expected, it's almost five before we can get started.

"You'll know that medicine is working because I'll start to look young and beautiful again." Karen says it. She's about sixty as well, and she's the circulating nurse. We'll be pushing Ms. Jones back to the OR on the stretcher. Versed works fast, like in less than thirty seconds, and by the time we roll into the room it should be in full effect.

"That versed workin' yet Ms. Jones?" Karen wants to know.

"Well…I guess not. 'Cos you're still ugly."

It's the first time Ms. Jones has smiled. I guess the versed is working fine.

So versed is a substitute for giving a shit, but not just for the patients. At some point it became one for me, too. I could rush through my spiel, do my little routine, then boom—push the versed, and all is forgotten. Just like my intention to remember what it's like to be a patient myself.

———————

Once I get the blood out of my sleeve, I'm in good shape to see my next patient. And with the morphine in my system, it's like I'm doing this for the very first time. All my idealism is back. We might already be forty-five minutes behind, but so what? I've got patience. We've got plenty of time. I can say "tell me more" instead of "moving right along" when the patient wants to address a particular concern or fear. Instead of treating them with versed, I can treat them like a person. A person like I was, who'd never done this before, and might be scared.

During the surgery, I'm vigilant. It's the motto of my specialty, and I live up to it in every way, paying attention to each little detail. I calculate the drugs, correct the fluid imbalances, anticipate the swings in surgical stimulation to keep the patient's vital signs stable. Everything is interesting, even the stories the surgeons tell to entertain themselves. I even tell a few of my own.

This day, it's turned out even better than I could've imagined. So good in fact, that I've abandoned all thoughts of a taper. I've even got a couple cc's of fentanyl in my pocket to take after dinner for dessert. Their saline substitute is circling a sewer pipe. But I'm not impaired, I'm engaged. I know nobody could ever understand that, but I remind myself that nobody knows. Nobody can even tell.

I still run when I get home, and I do five miles instead of 5K. It feels fabulous. Losing the pounds has helped, but so do the pain meds. Shit is performance enhancing. After dinner, a quick shower, and a quicker shot, I open up my notebook. After three blank days I add a one and two, both with a big M, and a three followed by an F. It's what I used today. Two shots of morphine, three or four hours apart, and the fentanyl I just took. If by chance I do ever want to taper, this seems like a reasonable plateau. I can't imagine I'd ever need to use more. Today, it was the sweet spot. It can't get any better.

———————————

It can't. And it won't. But it can get a lot worse. It won't be long before "nobody knows" won't be just a secret, it'll be a secret weapon, too, and my survival instincts will know just how to wield it. People still won't be able to tell if I'm on drugs, only when I'm not, and I'll need a few more letters to add to my notebook. WD's. It'll stand for withdrawals. What I've done today, it isn't chipping. From now on, I'm not just a chipper. I'm just a junkie…

XV

Of course I never intended to become a junkie. When I was a kid, I didn't really want to be anything at all when I grew up. Well, maybe a pro football player, but that wasn't particularly realistic considering I was hardly any good even in middle school. People sometimes ask me if I'd wanted to be a doctor since I was little, was there a doctor in my family, that kind of thing. And the answer is no, my dad was an engineer and my mom stayed at home, and all the doctors I knew, I was scared of. My older brother and I went to work with my dad a couple of times on a weekend when he had to finish a project, but we just wandered around in some industrial warehouse while he stayed in his cluttered office. I had no clue what he did in there other than smoke cigarettes and drink coffee. With ice. What most other adults did during the hours I was in school was equally mysterious, and the only grown ups I saw whose lives made any sense to me were the ones teaching me, either in the classroom, or at church. I knew exactly what they did. So I sort of figured maybe I'd do that, too.

My first choice was church. A lot of the kids I knew started to experiment with alcohol by the time we were teenagers. Somebody would somehow score a six pack, and they'd go down some dirt road and drink it all and howl at the moon or something. At least that's what I imagined, I never went. But I got *my* first high at church camp. I was old enough to know what a lot of people thought about church—that people were fake, that it's full of hypocrites, that they spoil all the fun, and all God is there for is to judge you. But that's not what I experienced at all. To me it wasn't full of people who thought they were better than you, they were people who knew that they weren't. It was the first place I saw people being real. Maybe I just saw what I wanted to see, but I saw people being vulnerable, and admitting that they sometimes felt like I did. Inadequate. Lonely. Not good enough. I thought that's exactly what church was supposed to be like, I couldn't get enough of it. And when you find a place where you fit in, then that's a place that makes you feel like everything is going to be ok. I assumed I'd be able to feel that way for the rest of my life. I thought our youth minister was the coolest adult I knew, and I wanted to be just like him.

When I went to Japan to work with missionaries, I'd just graduated from college, and I was hoping to find my vocation, my calling. I didn't exactly find out what it was, but I guess I found what it wasn't, and I knew that being a professional Christian wasn't going to be a possibility for me. God was either a whole lot bigger or a whole lot smaller than I'd ever imagined, and until I figured that out, I'd have to find another way to earn a paycheck. Teaching school was the only other thing I'd ever really considered doing, and so that's what I did. I taught high schoolers English.

I say I taught. Because it would be disrespectful to the profession to say I was a teacher. Being a teacher, a sensei, takes years of practice, and I only did it for a year. To this day it was harder than anything I ever tried to do in medicine. That's not really the reason I moved on though. I'd figured out that the world was a whole lot bigger than I'd ever imagined, and what other adults did all day didn't seem quite so mysterious anymore. Before I left for Japan, my mom had read me this quote from a book my campus minister had given me—"We lead limited lives until we step over into the concrete world of another culture, another tradition of worship." I still didn't fully understand what it meant, but I did realize that I'd been limiting myself, that there was a whole world of possibilities that I'd never considered before. My students who were graduating from high school believed they could do anything they wanted. I decided that I could, too.

After a great deal of thought, I narrowed my choices down to two. I'd either become a physician, or a long-haul truck driver. Like John Steinbeck, I had the ancient shudder. "Four hoarse blasts of a ship's whistle…the sound of a jet, an engine warming up, even the clopping of shod hooves on pavement brings it on…once a bum always a bum." I just wanted to go somewhere. In the end I decided that medicine was a safer bet, and the only place I went was medical school. I even tried to romanticize that a bit, telling myself I'd tried to find a place of service in the realm of the mind and spirit, and maybe helping heal people's bodies would be my final calling. But I was equally motivated by the thought that I had to start looking out for myself. I wasn't sure I could trust God to do it anymore, and somebody had to.

So that's when I went back to college. Took all the prerequisite science courses I needed, waited tables to pay my tuition and rent, met wake & bake Billy, all that. At first I had some concern about whether or not I could get accepted, medical school admission is competitive. But then a guidance counselor told me the science department had a fifty percent acceptance rate into medical and dental schools. I looked at myself, and I looked at Billy, and I thought if one of us is fucked, it's that guy. But turns out, we both got in, and Billy is a fine dentist today. I guess what that means is that when it comes to betting on your future, the statistics don't mean shit. Between Billy, Barry, and me…we're batting a thousand.

———————————

It seems like just yesterday was that long Labor Day weekend, but September is already almost over. All this thinking about what life used to be like when I was young, it's just because time seems to pass so differently now, there's no rhythm to it, and summer is just another season, only hotter. I do notice things I didn't used to though, and one of my favorite days of the year is that one when the heat finally subsides, and the temperature tops out at about seventy. It's always towards the end of September where I live, and today is one of those days, and it's a Sunday. Some people like to pretend that it's cooler than it really is, break out the sweaters and the chai tea, and imagine they live in Colorado, but not me. I like to go to the lake.

It feels different when nobody else is on it, except for a few fishermen here and there. The sun is warm and the water is cool, it makes me think of what it might be like to go to the lake in Minnesota or someplace. But I think the real thrill comes from the fact that summer is already over. We really aren't supposed to be out here. We're running out of time. I don't know why that makes it sweeter, it just does. Like you're riding a motorcycle out in front of a storm, trying to outrun it.

But I don't feel any of that today. I don't even really want to be out here. The only reason I am is Billy's in town. He's a dentist in Tulsa, he's got a son who is a year older than Tyson, and if the boy's mom is lucky, she'll be wife number four. We've stayed in touch since the college days, and it's my first chance to meet his new family. I promised everyone we'd take the boat out when he came down. The girls didn't really want to go out, Tami gets motion sick so bad she really doesn't enjoy it anyway, so it's all boys out on the water today. And Billy's got some beers.

"Here man, want one?" He offers me one from his ice chest.

I do. I'm supposed to be enjoying this, it's exactly the kind of day I love, with no wind, and the water is calm. But all I feel is melancholy. What I feel isn't the opposite of joy, it feels worse, it feels like joy's absence. Like it doesn't exist. I want the beer because maybe it could bring it back. That was always alcohol's specialty, making a good time even better, but even as I take the bottle from Billy's hand, I know it won't work. I know because I've tried it.

Each weekend in September since Labor Day, each one has been a little bit worse. I'd blamed the ballpark and all the booze the first time I started feeling bad, so the next weekend I didn't drink at all. And while it wasn't the worst, it still wasn't good and I was afraid that maybe this is just how people are supposed to feel without a drink or a drug. Maybe it's just been so long I forgot. Then after another week I thought that can't be true, this has got to be something more and I convinced myself that underneath it all, I'm just depressed. Maybe I'll get on something like prozac, but in the meantime, maybe the grappa that's in the back of the pantry will help. But it doesn't. It makes me want to throw up. And just holding this ice cold beer that Billy has given me makes me want to do the same thing.

"Nah, I don't want it. You can have it back."

"You sure?" Billy puts it back in the cooler slowly. Looks at me longer. "You good man? You seem a little off. A little checked out."

I think about just telling him what I've been doing. But I can't do it. Telling him about the morphine means telling him about my mom's pills, and I'm not sure which one I'm ashamed of more, so even though I know if anyone would understand, it's Billy...I just can't. Besides, he cares about me. He might try to help me. And help is the last thing I need.

"I dunno man...you ever just think to yourself, is this all there is?" I decide to go with something broad. Existential. Who can't relate to that?

"All the fuckin' time, Dude." Billy tries to give me a toast with his bottle, only I don't have one. Billy's dad is a Baptist preacher, and I guess he's been running from that since the time he could walk. I knew a little philosophical misdirection would take the focus off of me. And besides, it's the truth.

"But right there, man. That's what life's about for me now." This time he points his beer towards his son and nods his head. "I'm gonna do it right this time." Billy had a daughter with his first wife, she must be fifteen or sixteen by now, but he almost never sees her.

"Don't fuck it up," I say it and smile the best I can, but it's almost painful. My face, it just wants to sag.

"No shit. Hey, gimme a pinch of that Copenhagen, will ya?"

I toss him my can. "Thought you quit."

He flicks his wrist, slaps the lid of the can with his index finger. Shrugs. "Does anybody ever really quit? Or have they just not started back again."

"Good point."

I somehow fake it through the rest of the afternoon on the boat. I wish time could drag like this when I'm having fun. I hate being an ungracious host, but by the time we get the boat stored and are back at my house, I'm ready for Billy to leave.

"You sure you guys can't stay for dinner?" Tami says. But her heart isn't in it, like my reluctance has rubbed off.

"Nah, we gotta roll. Got an early clinic in the morning," Billy says. While his future wife gets their son settled in the SUV, Billy pulls me aside, says "Whatever's up, you know I'm around. I've been there. Talk to somebody, see a shrink, I dunno. I'm not used to seeing you like this."

Billy has been diagnosed with bipolar disorder since before it was fashionable, and he thinks he knows how I feel. And maybe he does. But I'm pretty sure by now that it's not for the same reason.

"I know, I appreciate it man. I'm glad you guys came down. Sorry to be such a downer, I'll bounce back. Just some mid-life shit, you know."

We give each other pats on the back, I tell him I'll be up to Tulsa next time, and I'm relieved when he's off.

———————————

"Want me to fix something for dinner, or you want to just get take out?" Tami, she's not blind, she knows something is wrong. She just doesn't know what it is and has a hard time asking about it. She and I have made a habit of this, just ignoring things until hopefully they get better. And almost always they do. Well not better, that implies growth, and it's hard for a marriage to grow when half of the people in it have been drinking two bottles of wine or so a night. But at least they don't get worse.

"You know I just…I don't really feel so great. Maybe going to the lake when the weather is cool isn't the best idea. Maybe I'm catching a cold." Tami likes this idea, it's a reason, one she won't have to worry about.

"Ok, well I'll fix something for the boys and me. You can eat later if you feel like it."

"I think I'm just going to go to bed."

We're separate sleepers, Tami and me, have been since Tyson was born. It didn't happen because we'd drifted apart, but that might be what it's starting to cause. Because I like sleeping upstairs. I don't mind if it stays that way. Especially since I've been sleeping with sister morphine.

Tonight, of course, I'm not. And even though I've been trying to deny it since Dallas, and I desperately clung to any other possible explanation, it's time I admitted the truth. I'm not depressed, I'm dopesick. What's wrong with me is that I'm in withdrawal.

XVI

Today was a one. It wasn't that bad. I haven't made up a scoring system yet, but I will soon, and I'll use it to grade the severity of my withdrawal symptoms. To document how dopesick I am. A one is no fun, but it's mostly tolerable. A two is worse, but if I really, really put my mind to it, I can fake it. I can convince people around me, which will mostly mean Tami, that I'm straight. But a three? That'll be as bad as I care to qualify, and when it's a three, hiding it ain't happening.

I did not expect this to happen to me. That seems ridiculous, even to myself, but I just didn't. But then again, I suppose everyone who ends up strung out on opioids starts with some form of magical thinking, that either they'll quit before it gets this bad, or they just won't be affected like everyone else. Me, I thought I had some kind of immunity, like I just got to experience all the upsides with none of the drawbacks of drugs. Like with alcohol. It's a drug too, of course, the only difference is you drink it, and I know all about the consequences of alcohol withdrawal. Most doctors do. It's not like being just dopesick, you can actually die. DT's can be deadly. Opioid withdrawal just makes you wish you were dead. I'm sure I'd drank heavily enough and long enough that if I were going to develop some physiologic dependence, it would've happened already. But it didn't. It's probably why I've never had an eyeopener, never needed to drink first thing in the morning. It's definitely why I don't think I'm an alcoholic. Alcoholics get DTs.

And drug addicts get dopesick. I've suspected this might be happening for almost a month, but I'd diagnosed myself with everything from dehydration to depression in order to deny what was really happening. But now I have to accept it. Everything is different. I have fundamentally changed. When I don't use, time will inevitably transform me, like a werewolf. And a full moon is coming, there'll be nothing I can do to stop it. Or I'm a vampire, who must feed to feel normal. My basic bodily needs are now altered. These comparisons are accurate, because the realization…it's horrifying.

I went to bed early tonight, but I can't sleep. It's like a stranger is in the house, but the stranger is me. I don't really know much about opioid withdrawals, and I've mostly been informed by movies, ones where people beg and scream, heave their souls into toilets, and stare into the abyss. It seems possible that all this is awaiting me in the hours to come. But today, it's just a one, even if I don't know that yet.

Some days when I get to work, there will be a struggle. I will fight this. I'll swear solemn oaths, vow to vanquish this dragon, and only go lock myself in the bathroom once I have battered my will against the stone surface of my own tombstone until my cortex is completely depleted. Today isn't one of those days, but it wouldn't have mattered anyway, because whether I go in like a lion or a lamb, I always wind up in the same place—in the motherfucking bathroom, with the silver latch slid into place, and a 25 gauge needle stuck in my ass. Which is exactly where I wind up today. And even if it bleeds, it won't show. My scrubs are dark blue, almost as if I'd planned it that way.

The morphine revives me. It shouldn't, I know. After a night of no sleep, you'd think I would fade into a fog, but that's just not what happens. The fatigue I felt is gone. It's like I've just come back from vacation, rested. Relaxed. Refreshed. I've injected myself with life. I feel normal, although it's becoming harder and harder to remember exactly what that means. But I need some of this clarity. To work, yeah, but also to work on what to do. I need to become an expert on opioid withdrawal, and fast. I need to know what to expect, and what, if anything, I can do about it. I spend some time on my phone scouring the internet for more information. Some of what I find seems sound, some is clearly quackery, but I'm fairly certain that even though I failed, I had the right idea a month ago. I need to taper.

If I were a doctor who prescribed opioids, and I guess I sort of am, and I had a patient who needed to stop them, and I guess I sort of do, the best strategy would be to taper. It's really quite simple. You start with the average daily dose that the patient is accustomed to, and then little by little, day by day, the doses decrease in increments, until at last the dose is zero. If the time frame is long enough, and the dose decreases are small enough, a taper can be accomplished with little to no withdrawal symptoms at all. And that's exactly what I hope to achieve. By now I recognize that I've had a fairly mild case of dopesickness, and a two-week taper should be all it takes to restore my independence. It's just what the doctor ordered.

With that settled, the rest of the day passes uneventfully. It's a day with a kind of two dimensionality I'll come to recognize. It's not that I won't be able to remember anything about it, it's more that nothing about it will seem at all memorable. Nothing sucks, but

139

nothing seems special either. That's just the way it is when you're numb. Nothing makes an impact. Since today is the start of the taper, I figure I might as well take as much as I like, or as much as I can get my hands on, and I do, so that by the time I finally lie down to bed at night, I settle into that familiar state of sleepless slumber.

But it's not entirely peaceful. In fact, I'm wracked with regret. I should not be feeling this way. I should not be this at ease. I've fucked up, and I see it now. Two weeks? I'll taper myself off in two weeks and be back to normal? I shouldn't have to. I should've already done it by now, could've done it a month ago, if I'd really wanted to. I wasn't even getting sick then, not really. Why didn't I just do it then and I wouldn't be in this mess. I didn't fail, I didn't even fucking *try*. Even this past weekend, on the boat with Billy. Was it really all that bad? Could I not do it again, if I had to? Could I not have gotten through today without starting all over? Because that's what I'm doing, starting over. And I was this close. Fuck. If I hadn't used today, I'd probably feel normal right now, wouldn't I? I guess I'll never know.

But what I do know, is that nothing is either as good or as bad as I remember it. The highs, were they ever even all that good? I remember thinking it…"For this? People throw their lives away for *this*? No possible way. This, I'll be able to quit." And the withdrawals, they weren't all that bad. It was for what, a day? Maybe two?

But I have to stop beating myself up. It's not doing me any good. I don't have to fix this now, and I don't even have to fix it tomorrow. Will I use tomorrow? Yes. Yes I will. Will I be using two weeks from now? Not if I can follow a very simple schedule. It's right in front of me.

And I'll be damned….in just two short weeks, I've done it.

XVII

Tapering wasn't easy, not with the tools I had to work with. Ideally, you want a smooth, steady descent. Like an airplane landing. You want to let that dopamine down easy, not pull the rug out from under it all at once. The ideal delivery system would be a patch, which is why they use it for nicotine. The drug slowly seeps into your system through the skin, and as you switch to smaller and smaller patches, your body has time to adjust. You could accomplish the same thing by smoking successively smaller cigarettes. You could still land the plane, but it'd be like doing it in a shit storm. The drug may be the same, but smoking—whether it's a Camel or crack—is the fastest way to get a drug to your brain. That's a great way to create an addiction, but a terrible way to taper. But I guess it beats jumping out of the plane without a parachute.

I didn't have any fentanyl patches, all I had were needles. But I did it, I actually fucking did it. I flip back through the last two weeks in my little notebook, and each day the doses dropped. I wasn't able to avoid withdrawals entirely, not when I was injecting into my muscles, because the sudden surges this creates do not exactly make for a smooth descent. It's not a walk in the park, it's more like trying to walk a rabid Rottweiler, but it got the job done. When I started feeling the first hints of withdrawal symptoms, I'd wait as long as I could and then make myself wait one hour longer before I used. At first it happens by noon, then not til two or three o'clock, and now exactly two weeks later

142

it's almost five, and holy shit, I don't feel a thing, except for freedom. I can't believe it. It's Independence Day.

But then…I get to thinking. What's the problem with opioids, really. Especially pharmaceutical grade, like I'm getting. I'm not gonna get a hot shot, and OD. It's not really damaging to my organs, a professor told us so in med school. I guess he forgot the brain's an organ too, but that's beside the point. My liver, kidneys, and heart will be fine. It's easily less harmful than alcohol in that regard. Right? The real problem with opioids, as I see it, is the dependence. You develop tolerance, need more and more to achieve an effect, and if you don't get it, you get sick. That's the reason I've had to quit. And if I could avoid that, or at least escape it every so often, then perhaps I've been a little hasty. I've overreacted. I know I can escape, because I just did it, didn't I. I tapered myself right off. And if I can do it once, I can do it again any time I want. Which means, I can also use morphine again, *any time I want.*

I guess when I prescribed this taper, I forgot one important thing—my patient is a drug addict. Drug addiction and drug dependence, they're not the same thing. They're connected, but not contingent. You can be one, the other, or both. In this case I'm both, or at least I was until I tapered myself off. But I was only treating half of my problem. Now I'm no longer physiologically dependent, and my body can do without it. My treatment plan, it worked. But that doesn't mean I'm not still addicted.

An addiction is by definition, harmful. If something's not really doing damage, or if it's helping at least as much as it hurts, then I'm probably not going to try very hard to change. If I have that second donut that I just can't resist, but the worst thing I've got going for me is an extra ten pounds around the waist, then no, those donuts are not "Soooo addicting." I just don't give a shit. I just like the donuts more than my skinny jeans. But if my diabetes is so bad that I can't feel my feet, and my heart surgeon is suggesting a quintuple bypass, but I *still* sneak into the kitchen so my wife won't catch me chowing down on my third slice of cheesecake, well…welcome to the club. I might be an addict.

Once you start to see that harm, whether it's weighing four hundred pounds or waking up in withdrawals, you have to want to do something about it. In my case, "I have really got to do something about this nasty little opioid habit. I don't want to be a slave to something like this, I want my freedom back." And then you have to act. You have to smoke your last cigarette and start chewing the gum, sign up for weight watchers, taper yourself off the morphine. And then…you have to fail. Because that's the thing. Even when you want to change, you can't.

That's what it means to be an addict. What was once a solution has now become the problem. And you just never know when the line is crossed, when what was once a luxury becomes a necessity. When the power to choose, is lost. But even more maddening is that you refuse to believe it's even happened, even when choice is just an illusion you cling to. The only way to know for certain is after it's already happened. The knowledge then is no more useful than an autopsy.

As soon as I was free from physical dependence, I used that freedom as an excuse to go right back to the habits that had created the dependence in the first place. And tapering will become the white whale I pursue again and again and again. And again—it works, I know it does, I've seen it work with my very own eyes. Even if it never will again.

———————————

"If you are a doctor or a doctor's representative, please press 4..."

"Yes, this is Thomas Gray, MD, my office number is 867-5309. The patient's name is Randall Wayne, date of birth 2/25/69. The prescription is for Clonidine, zero point two milligrams, take one po, q eight hours, dispense ninety with two refills. Thank you very much."

Randall Wayne, he's my best friend from high school. He doesn't need any Clonidine, though. That's for me. It's part of my next escape plan. I'm not worried about getting caught calling it in for myself. It's not controlled, it's just a blood pressure medication, and if I pay cash, nobody'll even notice. They won't even ask for my ID. I don't know why I didn't just make a name up. Randall's just came to mind as I was calling it in.

After two weeks, I tried to restart my taper, but it hasn't gone so well. The withdrawals started getting worse on the weekends, and by Sunday evenings I've barely been able to function. I'm easily at level

2, it's taking everything I've got just to fake it. There's no way I can keep doing this. And that's where the Clonidine comes in.

A large part of the nervous system is subconscious. It's a complex network of reflexes that regulate bodily functions that are not under conscious control. The nervous system automatically regulates things like heart rate, blood pressure, and digestion. It's called the autonomic nervous system, and there are two major parts to it—sympathetic and parasympathetic. The sympathetic system basically revs you up, and the parasympathetic chills you out. The sympathetic helps you chase down and kill your prey, and its counterpart lets you chill out after you've eaten it. And opioids fuck all this up. They basically put the brakes on the sympathetic branch, and the parasympathetic dominates. This is partly why chronic constipation is a common affliction for opiate users. Or why it's hard to pee.

When you take opioids long enough, your body decides, "well, I guess this is just going to be the way it is from now on," and it stops doing the things it normally does to keep the nervous system balanced. And since you're injecting yourself with joy directly, it assumes it doesn't have to carry out the work in that department either. The natural well of endorphins runs dry. Dopesickness is just the symptoms of all this deterioration when the drugs wear off.

With the opioids out of the way, the sympathetic system comes screaming back to life. The heart races, you get the runs, and you can't stay still to save your life. Clonidine lowers blood pressure by inhibiting the sympathetic system in the brainstem. For an opiate addict in withdrawal, it should also mitigate the effects of the runaway sympathetic train. Or at least that's what I'm hoping. I haven't tried it out yet.

A lot of people I know have a lake house. Some of them are opulent million dollar affairs on Grand Lake north of Tulsa. Most are more modest, and others are nothing more than a mobile home a mile or two from the water. It doesn't matter, you just call it a lake house. Tami and I wanted something we could use year round, or maybe just I did, but we bought a lot in a small development outside of a tiny town called Medicine Park just after Tyson was born. It's right outside the Wichita Mountain Wildlife Refuge, and I've been going down there since I was a kid. I love it. Billy taught me how to rock climb there back when we were roommates. There's also a lake nearby, and I imagine it as a vacation spot close to home that my sons will grow up loving like I do. The house isn't much but it'll be perfect for weekend getaways. We finally got moved in just before my experiment with the morphine began, and I haven't been back since. It's been two and a half months.

"I think I'll head down to Medicine Park this weekend. Take some more stuff down, clean up around the property. TJ can come with me."

I don't want Tami to go, and she doesn't offer, but I also don't want to leave her with both boys to look after. I'm not sure how helpful this Clonidine is going to be, and I'm planning to detox. I'm hoping for a magic bullet that will let me breeze right through it, but in case it's not, I'd rather not have Tami around. But TJ and I should be fine. He's pretty self-sufficient, and he isn't likely to notice if I'm not a hundred percent.

"Ok, well TJ's been asking when you guys are going to go back. Will you be gone all weekend?"

"We'll head down after I get off work Friday, be back sometime Sunday. I'll see if I can get an appointment for the guy to come set up the cable TV on Saturday."

TGIF doesn't exist for me anymore. It's become OGIF—Oh God, It's Friday, and I end up just praying I can make it through the weekends. Until Monday brings the Manna from heaven. It's become a dreaded monotony in the short span of a month, but I'm expecting the Clonidine to cure it.

"You ready to go buddy?"

"Yep!" TJ races over to Tami, tells her "see ya, mama," and he and I are off. We've loaded up the Honda Odyssey with stuff for the weekend, and other things we've bought to make the place feel like home, and the mini van is full. It's coming in handy, like I'd told Tami it would. I love mini vans, it's like driving around in your living room, but Tami hates it. She wanted something sporty.

It's an easy drive to Medicine Park, just an hour and a half or so to the southwest, and we make it just as it's getting dark. There's not really a grocery store in town, but there's a Dollar General at the highway exit and we stop there to get some essentials before we go on to the house. We pass by the town, and then turn up into our development across the street from an old market that advertises having "Live Rattlesnakes", for what I'm not sure. Our neighborhood is basically one long street that ends in a cul-de-sac, and ours is one of only a few houses that's already been completed.

We unload the groceries and clothes, but leave the rest for tomorrow. Eventually I hope this place has everything we need to enjoy, we won't need to pack a thing. Just get in the car and go. We had an outdoor shower installed off the back porch, to wash off after sweaty summertime hikes, and TJ wants to use it before we get ready for bed. It's too chilly, really, but it has hot water so what the hell, and I let him take his shower there.

There's not a whole lot else to do here yet, so we sit on the couch and I pull up classic cartoons on YouTube and we watch them on my phone until TJ gets tired. He likes Fat Albert, and Hong Kong Phooey, but the one he loves best is Tom & Jerry. There's one where Tom lands on a board full of nails, and when he takes a drink, the water squirts out of the holes in his butt like he's peeing. Or at least that's what it looks like to TJ and he wants to watch it over and over.

His laughter makes the empty room echo, and I imagine what it'll be like when we're done, when the whole family is here, enjoying hot summer days at the lake, or cold winter evenings by the fire. Maybe this is where we'll come for Christmas time from now on. TJ's so happy and I'm so content, even if it's manufactured with morphine, it doesn't matter now, tomorrow seems a long way off, and that's just how it always is.

––––––––––––––––––

149

When I wake up, I have an eyeopener. As soon as my eyes pop open I think "drugs". But it's not really a thought or the word itself, it's just an awareness, I'm immediately aware that I don't have any. It's dreadful. I'm full of dread at the thought of facing the day, not because of how I feel now, but of how I'm afraid I'm going to later. But oh yeah, the Clonidine, and it's comfort enough that I can put my feet on the floor and get up.

TJ's still sleeping. It's a gift he has, he always sleeps great, and I always felt bad for those parents whose kids wake them up at 5:30 on Saturday mornings. TJ sleeps like a rock. I slept ok too, of course, drifted off to sleep just fine, but it feels like I woke up someplace different. I can't imagine any of the warmth that existed last night. Everything just feels empty.

I dig a few things out of the minivan that I've brought for the kitchen, a coffee pot and a Bluetooth speaker for some music. I get both up and running and I sit on the back porch in a folding lawn chair, listen to the Rolling Stones, and sip the coffee. "Before They Make Me Run" isn't an inspiration any more, it's too late for that, but I hated that song anyway. Today it's "Torn and Frayed". Fuckin' A.

I figure I've got about five hours left. By one o'clock I'll start to feel the fatigue. I don't know how it will end, but that's how it'll start. In the meantime, I fix TJ some cereal for breakfast, and I just have another cup of coffee for mine. I'm not hungry. I've got an appointment for the guy to come install the cable TV between twelve and four, and I'm praying it's closer to twelve.

150

I get the rest of the Odyssey unloaded while I still have strength, and TJ and I have the rest of the morning to play. This place is awesome for a kid. It's hilly here, especially for Oklahoma. Not mountainous, but kind of close. The lake is on the backside of a hill to the north and we can see it when we hike up. There's also an old abandoned water slide nearby, and it's concrete skeleton sticks out of the hillside. TJ runs up and down it like a race car. But the coolest thing for him by far, is the construction equipment. The builders have various bull dozers and loaders on the vacant lots, just sitting there empty on a Saturday, and TJ climbs on everyone of them and shifts all the gears. It looks like fun. I can see that it is with my eyes, I just can't feel it, and I wonder how he's able to do it. Enjoy himself like that. It's like I've forgotten how to breathe.

The cable guy comes not at twelve, but 11:30, and by 12:15, we're watching television, if we want to. I tell him thanks, and he's gone almost before he was supposed to get here. Thank God. I make a Hot Pocket for TJ, but he doesn't finish it, and the leftover is lunch enough for me. I top it off with the Clonidine, I figure I've waited long enough, and let's see what this sucker has got.

The first thing I feel when the withdrawals start is sheer exhaustion. It's overwhelming, with an unstoppable urge to sleep. I put on the cartoon channel for TJ and tell him dad needs a nap. We'll play again later. If the Clonidine is any sort of shelter, that is.

I sleep like a dead man for two hours, dreamless, and I wake in exactly the same position I started in. I immediately know I'm no better, it's worse, and if the Clonidine has done anything at all it's just further sedated me. Like that's what I needed. It's fucking awful. I feel hollow, with a shell that weighs a thousand pounds. Things smell funny, too, and this house, with its new strange scents, is not welcoming anymore.

"Hey buddy. Whatcha watching?" I allow myself to drop on the couch beside him and I can feel my soul sag.

"Blues Clues!"

It's an episode he's seen before, I can tell because he knows what's going to happen before it does, but that just makes him enjoy it more. The people who make the show, they know this about kids, and they run the same episode five times in a row before airing a new one. And it doesn't make it boring, children watching are much more engaged on the fifth viewing than on the first. It seems it's human nature to like knowing what's about to happen next.

I have no idea what's about to happen to me. And it's terrifying. I feel like I'm inching out onto a frozen lake, step by step. It's dark and it's foggy and I can't see how far it is to the other side or even if it's there at all. Every bodily sensation feels like the ice is groaning, and at some point it's going to give way and swallow me.

Fuck you, Clonidine. All that talk about sympathetic this and parasympathetic that, but it all just boils down to bullshit. Apparently nothing helps…except…

"TJ, how'd you like to go to spend the night at Granny's?"

XVIII

"Granny doesn't know we're coming buddy. Let's be quiet and surprise her."

We make it to my mom's house by six or seven. She's home, of course, which means her door will be unlocked, like it always was when I was a kid. I'm not trying to be sneaky. I mean, we're staying. I just need a minute, is all. Or more like twenty seconds. We slip in quietly, surprises are fun when you're a kid like TJ, and the TV is blaring from the living room around the corner from the kitchen. She couldn't have heard us if we shouted, but I wave TJ on to tiptoe in to see my mom, and before he's even around the corner, I've swallowed three of the hydrocodones. It'll take them a half hour to kick in, but I already feel a hundred times better.

"Weeeellll....Lookie who's here!"

"Surprise Granny! It's me!"

"Well who's with you?"

"Hey mom." I come around the corner. Wave. Smiling isn't easy, but almost.

"Isn't this a nice surprise. You boys gonna spend the evening with me?"

"Yeah I thought we would. We went down to the Medicine Park place last night, got a few things moved in and spent the day there. I wanted to watch the OU game tonight though, so thought we might just come watch it with you, probably spend the night. Has it started yet?"

"I think it started at six. Here, see if you can find it." She hands me the remote. The Sooners are playing Iowa State tonight. I normally wouldn't watch, but having some sort of an alibi makes me feel like less of a liar, like the more lies you tell, the less they all mean.

"Did you all eat yet?"

Eat. I totally forgot. TJ's had a bowl of cereal and half a hot pocket today.

"Buddy you hungry?"

He's playing in his closet, hollers back "Huh-uh," but I know he will be soon.

"Maybe I'll go get us a pizza. Would you eat some?"

My mom says she would, and I figure by the time one is ready, I'll be able to eat, too, and I call Mr. Pizza and order a large pepperoni.

———————————

I guess I just couldn't go through with it. I got about as far out onto that frozen lake as I've ever been, but I chickened out. The voices that call you back to the shore, they're soothing. And you know it's not a place you can stay forever, but at least it's solid and it feels familiar. Besides, there's always tomorrow, it's not like I'm giving up. I can try again.

And I do try again, but for weeks and weeks it's not like I try anything new. Each one is pretty much the same. I go to work on Monday thinking lemme just get my shit straight for just this one day, and then Tuesday I can start to taper. But the next couple of days find excuses of their own, and by Thursday it's too late anyways to do any good, so by Friday I'm just like, fuck it. On one of the vials, it could've been fentanyl or maybe it was morphine, it says in bold letters, "This product may be habit forming." Well no shit. But when it's Friday and you've got the fuck its, reading that is kind of funny. But the weekends aren't. I survive them by experimenting with the Clonidine, taking it sooner, then later, then doubling the dose, trying to find some damn combination that will work like the websites say, but it just doesn't. At least not for me. I borrow from my mom just as often as I feel like I can without getting caught, but otherwise I just suffer through it.

It's like all week long I'm in a vegetative state. Not that anybody'd know, I still do all the things I'm supposed to do. TJ, he seems too young, but everybody else's kids have started fall T-ball, so he does, too. And I take him to practice, stand on the field with him like the other dad's do, encourage him to "run, run, no not that way!" when he hits the ball off the tee. I have superficial conversations with the other parents, but it's not like I'm really getting to know them, and they're sure as hell not getting to know me, are you kidding? My soul is asleep. I'm a potato.

The only time I seem to come alive, when my body is animated with a spirit, is when I'm dopesick. It's the only time life blows up into three dimensions, but everything feels alien. On those weekends I look at the people around me, and I just can't figure out how they do it.

It's only been three months or so, but I've completely forgotten what it was like to be able to get through a day without drugs. When I watch the NFL pregame shows on Sunday mornings, the ones where the hosts are always chuckling a lot for no apparent reason except to make it look like they're having a great time, I wonder if they must be on something, too. They've got to be taking pills or something. Or else how could they do it, just make themselves laugh like that when nothing is fucking funny about football.

I've kept browsing the websites, everything from wikipedia to webMD, trying to learn all I can about opioid withdrawal. But the advice hasn't really helped. I can't seem to taper, and I've run out of patience with the Clonidine, don't even bother with the refills I wrote for. I've surfed internet message boards trying to find any alternatives, and it seems people try everything from eating M&M's to masturbating, but mostly just stay miserable. One guy says the first few days were rough, but he's ten days clean now and he's never felt better. The message is four years old, though, and I have this image of him reading it himself from time to time and wishing. Wondering how he can ever get back to ten days clean. It feels impossible.

I know I can't keep this up forever, though. So far I've only had to go at most forty-eight hours, and the withdrawals sometimes don't start until the second day. I seem to be living life in two-week windows, never imagining a tomorrow when I won't be using drugs, but never imagining a future beyond two weeks when I will. But I know that if I ever hope to fulfill that future, eventually I'm going to have to get through a full blown detox, go all the way across that frozen lake, no matter what. Showing up to work on Monday's with the job half done, it's hopeless.

The holidays are coming soon, and those two-week windows are about to have some major holes in them. I just need to decide which one is right for the trek. Thanksgiving is out. I'm on call for all of it but Thanksgiving Day. Christmas and New Years will both be on a Friday, which makes for a four-day desert. But will that be enough time?

———————————

My brother is great at buying Christmas gifts. I guess I don't actually know if it's him or his wife, but the presents I get from them are the best. They're never that expensive, but they always mean a lot. They're personal. Maybe I don't pay attention like I should, but I just never seemed to have that ability. The first Christmas after we were married, I spent as much as I thought we could afford, and I bought Tami something like eight gifts. And she returned eight of them. I'm sure that says something about the both of us, but the next year I just went with gift cards.

My gift from my brother and his wife this Christmas, it's a book. I can tell that before I've even torn into the wrapping paper. I just hold onto it while everyone else opens their gifts. Christmas is for children and old people, my mom likes to say, so they all get to go first. Besides, all of I've got is a book. How good could it be.

Mark and Ellen, that's my brother and his wife, they watch me when I finally tear the paper off. They want to know if they got it right, but it's hard to tell with me. I'm staring into the mug of Keith Richards, who's covering half his face with one hand and lighting a cigarette with the other, like he needs it to steady himself after getting off a roller coaster that was perhaps as frightening as it was fun.

"Don't you like him?" Ellen asks me. "Didn't you see them in concert when they came to Norman? I remember you talking about it."

Yeah, they got it right. And that show was almost fifteen years ago, but I guess that's the sort of thing they pay attention to.

"We thought you might like that," Mark tells me. "Maybe get you back to playing some guitar." He knows I haven't played in years.

"Thanks guys. This is awesome." And I mean it. Keith Richards' autobiography is simply called *Life*, and I don't know it yet, but it's about to change mine.

Keith Richards heroin use is the stuff of legend. He used a lot of other drugs as well, but the one he's most closely associated with, is heroin. And for good reason. Heroin use can define your life. It can tell you where you can go, when you can go, and who you can go with. The same goes for morphine and all the other bastard brothers of the poppy.

Humans have been cultivating and using the poppy seed and its offspring for probably around five thousand years, all the way from plain old opium to OxyContin. And Keith Richards is just another junkie who happened to join that parade of poppy users which will probably stretch another five thousand years into the future. Because like they say—if God made anything better, he kept it for himself. And if my brother had given me a book about the Rolling Stones and their famous guitar player on any other Christmas, I'm sure I would've still enjoyed it. But now that I've joined him in that pathetic parade, it seems as if we're links in the same chain. I realize I'm just being sentimental and stupid, but I feel connection. And it makes his story resonate with me like it's one of his famous open G chords.

Of course this is all just coincidence. Mark and Ellen just knew I kind of dug the Stones, and would undoubtedly enjoy the book. Were they trying to speak to my secret opioid addiction, other choices might have been more apt. Perhaps a book on William Halsted, the American physician who had as much to do with inventing modern surgery as anyone else. He also inadvertently invented the one hundred twenty hour work week for surgical residents because he'd leave the hospital early every day to go shoot up morphine and somebody had to stay in charge. Or maybe one about Florence Nightingale, who treated both her patients as well as herself with morphine—"I could not have got through the day without this wonderful little pick-me-up." Yeah…I think I would've known what she meant.

But instead, for Christmas I got Keith Richards. And since there's no way you could digest him on an empty stomach, I gift myself a handful of my mom's hydros, and settle in to read *Life*. There's a lot I'm going to learn from this book. Interesting stuff about the band's history, how they got started, and how they managed to keep it together so long. I'll read about some of the secrets to his sound, like tuning to an open G and removing the low E string, and I'll do it to a guitar of my own. But I'll also read about Keith's relationship with his son Marlon, how he struggled to be a dad and use dope at the same time. And I'll think of TJ and our trips to Medicine Park when I didn't have the strength to fake it. Had I just read about Halsted, perhaps my addiction would've remained rather clinical. But because I'm being informed by the "world's most elegantly wasted human being," I can't help myself from romanticizing it a bit. I don't just have 3cc syringes and a 25 gauge needle anymore, these aren't medical supplies, I've got *gear*. And I won't be striving to detoxify myself from drugs, I'll be kicking.

I'll be astounded at the effort it takes just to maintain a heroin addiction, even when you're a world famous rock star. It's not an act you can just take on the road. With very few exceptions, being a drug addict also makes you a criminal, or at least a potential one. It's not like being an alcoholic. And because of this, Keith was an expert on kicking. And with all due respect to WebMD, that's exactly what I need.

XIX

"I think I'm coming down with the flu"

It's New Year's Eve, and some of her family and a few of our friends are just arriving to celebrate the coming year, but this is the time I pick to tell Tami. It's not like I can help it, it's been more than twenty-four hours since I've used, and I'll be turning into a pumpkin well before midnight.

"You are? Didn't you get a flu shot?" Tami asks me.

"Well yeah, but you know how well those things work. I don't know if it's the flu or not, but I feel like crap. I'm achy and I have the chills."

"Well go upstairs I guess. Don't need you making everyone else sick. I'll tell everyone you don't feel well." I feel like a kid faking an illness so I can skip school. But it's not like I have to pretend. I feel like shit and Tami can see it in my eyes, they're sinking.

"Just text me if you need me to bring anything up, some juice or some soup."

"I'll be ok, prolly just going to go to sleep. Maybe I'll feel better tomorrow."

But I already know I won't. In fact, I'm planning to be up there until Sunday. Seventy-two hours. That's how long Keith said it takes. He also said it's kind of like having a really bad flu, which is where I got the idea. If he's right, and how could he not be, by Sunday morning I'll be resurrected. I'll be reborn into a brand new year. I can't change the past, but come Monday, I will rewrite my own future.

I've got everything I think I'll need. I've got medications—Imodium for the inevitable diarrhea, Benadryl for when I can't sleep, and a bottle of whiskey for when the Benadryl won't work. I've got books—two more about the Stones, and one by Lance Armstrong that he wrote way back before everyone knew he was as good at lying as he is riding a bike. I've got snuff, six cans of it, and I've got sugar. A sackful of Halloween candy that TJ never finished. By now I know enough about dopamine depletion, and I'm hoping the sugar rush will at least dampen the despair that I know is coming. And with that, I fall into the last fit of sleep I will get until sometime early on Sunday.

———————————

Sometimes when you've lost a loved one, you forget. Just for a brief moment, like when the phone rings and you think it might be them, or in the morning when you first wake up. You forget that they're gone, and when you rebound back to reality, it's almost like getting the news all over again. When I wake up Friday morning to a brand new year, it's sort of like that. For the briefest of moments I think once I wake up just a bit more, I'll run downstairs and see what the boys want for breakfast. But before I can blink, my senses snap back, and I remember I can't. I'm broken. I'll be celebrating New Year's Day in bed.

162

Tami texts me—"Happy New Year. Everybody missed you last night. Party was good. You feeling any better?"

—"No. I don't feel good at all. Def have the flu."

—"Sorry. Need anything? Boys and I going over to my brother's in a bit. Want me to pick anything up? Meds?"

—"No, I'll be fine. I got ibuprofen if I need it. Ya'll have fun. Happy new year and sorry. Tell the boys I love them. I'm just gonna try to sleep."

This isn't like the fucking flu. With the flu, you might feel miserable, but there's no despair. In a couple of days your strength will return, the aches will pass, and you'll feel better. There's hope. You know what's going to happen. But I don't feel any of that. I feel like death. Not that I'm going to die, but that everything else already did and it's never coming back. I'm having these weird smells, and everything seems toxic, like the house is a rotting carcass. And out of nowhere I sneeze three times in rapid succession, it's always three, like my body is trying to purge something from inside my skull. But when I desperately want to yawn, nothing comes out, it's stuck inside of me. I'm getting out there on the frozen lake now, so far I can't see where I'm going, but I can't see back to where I came from either. There's nowhere to go. I'm lost and I just want to sit down and cry, so I do. I just...I just want to be *clean*. It's a sob and it's a prayer.

For now, most of the suffering remains in my mind. Other than having almost no energy, my body is relatively intact. I try to distract myself with reading, and I start with Lance Armstrong. His story is interesting, even if I don't entirely believe it. He's still several years away from admitting the whole truth about his use of performance enhancing drugs, and the defiance in his denials is palpable. 'You think I'd risk my health to take those drugs? I had fucking cancer!' The drugs I'm using have very different effects, but I can't help recognizing that we both have a dark secret, a double life. Or at least I do. Maybe Lance is telling the truth. His belief is almost contagious.

I delve into the Rolling Stones books, and they're like a road map to a deeper discovery of their music. "Gimme Shelter" has a whole new meaning for me now for obvious reasons, and I listen for the part when backup singer Merry Clayton's voice cracks under the strain of singing. "Rape…Murder", and Mick Jagger responds with a whoop, all left deep in the track, but it's there if you listen. I play "Coming Down Again" over and over, Keith sings on that one, and it's like the soundtrack for the starved.

None of this is an inspiration. It's like air with no oxygen. I try some of the tunes I would've listened to as a teenager, Christian rock. Jesus Music. If there's a central theme to Christianity, it's that there is hope for the lost. That even after we've fallen from Eden, or wandered off like the Prodigal Son, that in the end, all will be overcome. There will be an Exodus from Egypt, a resurrection from the grave, and we will reach the promised land. But it all just feels like Jesus got sent to the wrong planet. It's a world away.

It's hard to tell when day fades into night. This room has blackout curtains and soundproof windows, for those times when I might have to work all night and need to sleep during the day. I tell myself not to look at the clock, just sleep when you get tired, but I can't. I take the

164

Imodium even though I don't have any diarrhea, because it works by stimulating opioid receptors in the gut. It's basically an opioid itself, but it doesn't cross the blood-brain barrier, but I figure it can't hurt, and I wonder if I could've found a way to alter its chemistry so that it would cross into my brain, as if no one's ever considered that before. Benadryl doesn't help either, even after I take so much of it that my fingers won't work and I have to turn the pages of a book with my knuckles, and I can barely hold on to the bottle of whiskey to pour it into my mouth. But even the whiskey won't work. It's a long and most miserable night, spent entirely awake.

———————

—"Any better?"

I only know it's morning because Tami texts me, and I wish I had good news but I don't.

—"Not really. Not any worse tho. Basically been sleeping. Surely I'll be better by tomorrow."

Lies. All lies. I don't even believe the part about tomorrow.

—"Well just stay up there then. Don't want the boys catching the flu."

That's my only solace, knowing the boys are safe. They're lucky to have their mom, she's strong enough to handle this without me, but I know they're going to need their dad, too. It might be the only reason I'm not considering blowing my brains out. I'm not, but I've got no judgment for anyone else, and I especially don't have any for Barry. At least I have my kids to cling to.

It's Saturday, or at least I think it is, and Tami takes the boys out for most of the afternoon. I take the opportunity to go downstairs and see if there's anything I can eat or drink. There's some soda, and it almost tastes good, but it's the only thing I can put into my stomach. I watch a little TV but seeing any other humans at all, even on the television only worsens my self-pity and I'm certain I'll never feel normal again.

All this bullshit? It's mostly been in my mind. Not to minimize it, it's hellish, and it might be the worst part of withdrawals, but it's still just about at level two. If I had to—*really, really* had to—I could've forced myself to function. I was fortunate I didn't have to. But I'm about to go beyond where I've ever been, to level three, kicking and screaming, it doesn't matter.

Starving, Hysterical, Naked

I have a T-shirt with these three words printed on the back, bought it at the City Lights bookstore in San Francisco, back when Billy and I ran a marathon there. I knew where it came from, it's from the opening line of Allen Ginsberg's poem "Howl". I wasn't sure what it meant, though, the whole poem or even just these three words. I just thought it was a cool T-shirt.

But I'm not wondering anymore. I'm soaked in sweat, somehow hot and cold at the exact same time. I try lying on my back, focusing on relaxing each part of my body in some sort of self-guided meditation, but my body rebels. I have an uncontrollable urge to flip on to my belly, hoping I can find any comfort in this position, but I can't, and I curl into a ball on my left side and hold that position for all of fifteen seconds before everything involuntarily unfolds like a spring. I sit up, pace the room, do five pushups, try holding my breath until I almost pass out and then start the whole cycle all over again. Hour, upon hour, after hour.

This…is kicking. Anytime I try lying still, a spasm erupts from somewhere deep and it ripples towards the surface of my skin and finds an outlet in one of my extremities. Which one is anyone's guess, but either an arm or a leg will shoot towards the ceiling and it'll shake and spasm until the evil spirit is exorcized. You literally kick. It's where the phrase "kicking the habit" comes from.

I'd do almost anything to escape my flesh, but it's almost like an out of body experience witnessing what is happening to me. "Well you're the real deal now, Tommy boy. You're a real live drug addict." Although I'd settle for a dead one. I take deep chugs of the whiskey, but it has almost no effect.

I pray to Jesus, please let it stop, I'll never take a drug again ever, even if I break my leg, or crash in my car, just please…let this pass.

And as all things do…it does. It passes. The next thing I know I'm in the kitchen. Tami has hollered up the stairs to me that she and the boys are going to church, it's Sunday, but she's got what I need, it's on the kitchen counter. I walk down the stairs, and there's a paper sack sitting there with the logo of some minute clinic on it. And inside the sack are three huge pill bottles—one full of Soma, one with Xanax, and the largest one with oxycodone. It's the pill mill trifecta. What the fuck? How does she know when I never told her? And why would she do this to me? I want to take them, and I know that I will…but I don't, not yet. Just having them is making me feel better, and I simply sit with them in the kitchen, until my eyes open. And I'm still in my bed.

I guess at some point I finally fell asleep. But I feel better, I honestly feel better. The dream, it came from some place of sleep I've never experienced before, and I have to go downstairs to convince myself that the pills aren't there. It was so real I'd swear it had to have happened. And of course they're not, but I'm still relieved. Nobody else is here either, I guess Tami really did take the boys to church, and maybe even hollered up at me before she left.

I've spent all night hysterical. Naked. And now… I'm fucking starving. I'm so ready to eat. It's been three days, and I'll be damned…but Keith Richards was right.

———————————

"Look who's up."

Tami finds me in the kitchen when she gets home with the boys after church.

"You better?" she asks.

"Yeah. I feel fine. Must've been like a three day flu or something. I feel great, actually." I'm surprised, myself. "You guys want to get something to eat? I'm starving."

Finally, as a family, we celebrate the new year. It's the perfect time for it. If New Year's Day were in July, who would even notice? Right in the middle of summer when it seems like time will go on forever. But here, in the dead of winter, it's right where it belongs, when we need it most. Just to remind us that anytime we want, we can start anew. That even when the days are short and the nights are long, that spring will come again, and life will go on.

I feel as if I shed my skin last night. My entire nervous system went through some sort of regeneration, and all the overactivity was just growing pains. And it was worth it. I've spent the last five months dormant, in darkness. And today, I feel light. I have crossed that frozen lake, and reached the other side. Finally, I am free.

Later in the day, I hoist myself up over the pull up bar one last time, and I'm finished. The workout feels better than it has since I can remember, and it's a reward unto itself. The sweat is honest. My home gym, it has a big mirror, which I've mostly avoided for months, but I inspect myself, and I'm pleased with what I see. I can look myself in the eye. I've lost almost thirty pounds these last five months, without even trying, but it's not only that. I see relief. I see gratitude. I'm relieved and grateful that it's over, but also that I got away with it. It's a relief that's almost as wide as my despair was deep, like the suffering carved out a space for it. I almost smile. I can't be a chipper anymore, I know that now, I'm past the point of no return. But I can still do things other people can't. I am proud of myself.

Out loud I tell myself—now…just don't fuck it up.

And a grin blossoms.

XX

Las Vegas, Nevada

Four Years Later…

"I think we should do it, Tom. We should at least go to a couple of the presentations and listen to them. I've been saying this for three years."

"Steven, I dunno. I dunno, man. It just makes me nervous. And I think that's what they want—to scare us, so we'll sell."

Steven, he's one of my partners, and a super guy. We're in Vegas for a practice management conference sponsored by our national society of anesthesiologists. It's a trade show of sorts, where private practice outfits like ours can come and learn about important trends and regulations that will impact our profession. Steven is referring to one them.

"I just see it as the future. It's happening all around us whether we want it to or not, and if it's inevitable, we should do it early while we still have a choice."

Steven doesn't say it, but I'm pretty sure what he means is 'while I can still make some money off it'. I don't hold it against him though, I really am torn myself, and if I were in his position, it'd be a no-brainer.

He's getting close to retirement, and for him "the future" means less than five years.

"Well, here's how I see it, Steven. These guys are a bunch of very wealthy venture capitalists, with money that we can't imagine. And I'm sure they take advantage of opportunities in tech, energy, and other places, but now one of those other sectors is in healthcare. They wanna know where they can invest and make some money in healthcare. And they've figured out that a large part of a hospital's bottom line is in the OR. There's a lot of money in surgery. And then of course it doesn't take a rocket surgeon to figure out there's some money in anesthesia, too, and 'are you kidding me, it's just in the hands of these private practice doctors? Working for themselves? Well how in the hell can we get some of it?' So now they're trying to buy our practices for a fraction of what they're worth, so we can spend the rest of our careers as their employees, at 75% of our previous income, and they keep all the rest as profit. Helluva deal…for them."

"But it's a good deal for us, too, Tom. We don't have any guarantees of the future. It's better than the hospitals coming along and trying to turn us into *their* employees. They wouldn't pay us a dime for our practice."

"No…they wouldn't. But if being a hospital employee is inevitable, selling to one of these corporate outfits won't stop it. Look, I can see why it's appealing to you. You get a nice little payout a couple of years away from retirement, and then you don't have to stick around and watch them siphon off your future income. I get it. That's why they want you at the presentation and not me. These guys are like the fuckin' mafia. Making us an offer we can't refuse. Like 'Hey, this is a really nice pizza joint you got here. But you really need somebody lookin' out for you in the neighborhood, see?' Really all they want is their hand in our pocket off the work that we do."

We laugh. This isn't confrontational, there's no clear answer on what to do. These venture capitalists, they've already convinced a lot of younger and middle-aged physicians like me who are years away from retirement, that we need them. How else could we wade our way through the labyrinth of governmental regulations? And they throw out acronyms like P4P and MIPS that seem murky and hard to grasp, most likely because they haven't been fully developed, let alone implemented. And they assure us that without them, we could never effectively negotiate with the big bad insurance companies, but since we'd have the corporate muscle on our side, we'll be paid more for doing less, and almost certainly will end up increasing our pay in the end. Even after our new bosses get their taste. We'd be fools to turn them down. And, who knows, maybe they're right.

"Just come to the presentation with me," Steven says. "Listen with an open mind, and when we get home and report to the group, I'm sure we'll reach a decision that's best for everyone. You'd get the same buyout I would, don't forget. But keep that mafia shit to yourself."

We grin. "Deal."

I suppose this is why the executive committee of our practice chose Steven and me to come to this conference. Different ages, different perspectives, and we work well together. Steven is actually the managing partner of our group, and as his newly elected replacement, I'll be taking over in a couple of months to serve my own two year term. Things are going well for me, better than I could've ever dreamed of just four years ago. Professionally, at least. Steven's wife joined him on the trip, and they plan on catching a show later. I didn't bother inviting Tami, and I know she wouldn't have wanted to come even if I had. Things at home, they're not so good. But we're making it.

"Afterwards, Diane is going to meet us for drinks at the bar. You sure you won't go to Cirque Du Soleil with us tonight? I know a guy. He can still get you a ticket."

"Nah man. I'm good," I tell him. "But I'll meet you guys for drinks. I'm gonna play blackjack or something later."

———————

It's amazing I'm able to do this. We left OKC Thursday afternoon, and it's already after three on Saturday. And I feel fine. I won't ever forget "Oh God, It's Friday", what it's like to be told where I can go, when I can go, and who I can go with. But here I am. I'm not walking across that frozen lake, I'm walking on water, it feels like a miracle, still. You detox like that, kick cold turkey like I did, and it'll put the fear of God in you. It's not a memory that fades.

I've got a couple of hours to kill before I'm supposed to meet Steven for the first presentation. I think it's some firm like Continental Anesthesia Partners or something, I don't really care. They all sound the same. I'm worn out from sitting in conference rooms all day, and I figure I'll just take a nap.

173

But first, a wee bit of tea. Back in my room, I look through the complimentary selections. There's green, and black, and jasmine infused, but I don't need any of them. I've brought my own. Mine is something called Red Indo, it comes in a powder, and I mix it with some warm water straight out of the tap. It's gritty and tastes awful, so I don't sip it, I just force it down and try not to choke. But I'm used to it, I've done this before. A lot. This is my third time today, and I'll do it again before bed. I fold the package into itself four times before stuffing it inside an old sock, one which I'll throw away before we leave, but in the meantime, I don't want to risk anyone reading the wrapper and getting curious. I won't make that mistake again. Because the red wrapper…it says Kratom.

XXI

Kratom. Most people have never heard of it, or at least I hadn't until I discovered it on a message board, found it among the shipwrecked souls as I scuba dived the internet trying to salvage my own life. See, I never really stopped. I just found a way to survive.

The seventy-two hour detox wasn't entirely a waste of time, though. I did feel good, genuinely good when it was over. So I know it's possible. I just haven't been able to get back there ever again. Seems the longer I use drugs, the longer it takes to detox from them. Seventy-two hours just doesn't seem to be enough anymore. It's been four years, I know, but I can't give up. Or maybe I'm just addicted to quitting.

Some people say you quit one day at a time, but for me, that's how I use—one day at a time, as if every single day will be the last. That's how it was supposed to be after that long New Year's holiday. Just this once, who's gonna know, I almost felt like I deserved it after what I'd just been through. And so I did. And the day after that, and the day after that, and by Friday it was like "Oh fuck…Here we go again…"

I've become a big believer in MAT—medication assisted treatment. It's an approach to treating addiction that combines counseling and other behavioral therapies, with medications. It's supposed to maximize the chances of success. I don't participate in any formalized way of course, that would require a degree of transparency for which I'm nowhere near prepared, so I just skip the counseling part. Besides, I'm doing pretty well on my own.

The Clonidine, it didn't help much, but that was just my first attempt. Since then I've gotten a lot better. I started out by just asking myself basic questions, like what exactly is wrong with you when you're in withdrawals? And what can we do to fix it? And my immediate answer was anhedonia. An utter inability to feel pleasure. That, and sheer exhaustion. The only thing that can get me off the couch is fear. So I thought why don't we try something to pep you up? I'm not abusing more drugs, I'm just treating the symptoms of dopesickness.

Getting a script for an amphetamine, something like Adderall, would be too tricky. So I simplified it and went with Phendimetrazine. It's a diet pill, but it's a stimulant, very much like an amphetamine. It's controlled, so I can't write it for myself, but there are enough weight loss clinics around that it's easy to get. "Gee doc, I just can't seem to lose these last ten pounds…" And the pills help like I'd hoped, if I take eight or ten of them at once. At least for those first couple of days when withdrawals are mostly in the mind. But try adding a stimulant to the second part, when the fight or flight nervous system comes screaming back to life, and well…it's a mistake you won't make twice. Or at least I didn't.

So the diet pills could help me survive a weekend, but anything more is out of the question, there'd be no way I could go on a vacation. I needed something better. And that something turned out to be Kratom.

The first time I saw it mentioned on a message board, some guy said it was about like taking two Vicodin. And I was immediately hooked. This stuff is legal? And it's not a prescription? You can just buy it, or order it online? It sounded too good to be true. So I looked it up, everything I could. Kratom comes from a plant, an herb I guess, and is native to Southeast Asia. It's not an opioid, it isn't a relative of the poppy, but it does act on opioid receptors in the body. Just not all of them. That guy might've been exaggerating to compare it with Vicodin, especially in someone opioid-dependent enough to get dopesick. But it does act on enough receptors to prevent withdrawals. Or at least it does for me. With Kratom, I can go where I want, when I want, with who I want. Just so long as Kratom comes along, too, of course.

So that's the good news. The bad news is, all it does is postpone the inevitable. But I'm an addict, I'm all about that. At first I thought all I had to do was take Kratom for a week or so, while my body adjusted itself to life beyond morphine, and then I'd be back to normal. No more withdrawal. But it doesn't work like that. Those opioid receptors, they're still getting stimulated, and they don't really give a crap if it's Kratom or OxyContin. So long as you keep feeding them, they stay hungry. I knew this to be a fact, of course, but it didn't stop me from hoping.

But the Kratom *has* been a lifesaver. It's allowed me to have a somewhat normal life. I never would've been able to keep this up for well over four years. Without it, I would've almost certainly been caught by now. Ok, I actually have been caught, sort of, three and a

half years ago. But it wasn't because I didn't have Kratom. It was
because I did.

"You've got a package."

Tami has picked up the mail on the way in, and she hands it to
me. I've ordered Kratom before, but I was always able to intercept it at
the mailbox. This time I hadn't.

"What is it?" She asks, clearly expecting me to open it. I don't
want to, but I hold my breath, and I do it anyway. I pull a nondescript
sealed paper sack out of the box. On it is written "2g". As in two
grams.

"What is it?" She asks it again. A little more concerned than
curious.

"It's an herbal tea. I'm hoping it'll help me sleep. Supposed to be
from Thailand or something. It's better than taking an ambien, right?" I
put the sack in the pantry, like that's where it belongs. Like I don't
have anything to hide. Then, I throw away all the packaging in the
outside trash can. Like I do.

—"Come home before you go pick up the boys. We need to talk."

Tami's texted me, and it doesn't sound good. We're supposed to
go to the Alabama beaches on vacation in about two weeks, and my
swimsuit from last summer is way too big. After tossing out the Kratom

box, I came to the store to buy a new one. I'm standing in the dressing room about to try one on when her text comes.

Shit. Shit shit shit. It's the kind of request that strikes fear in the gut of a guilty man. I wish there were something else it could be about. Anything but what it is. She knows. I'm not sure how, but I know she knows.

—"Ok"

From here on out, everything between us is about to be different…

When I come into the kitchen from the garage, she's sitting at the bottom steps of the staircase. Just sitting there, like she hasn't moved since she texted me. She won't look at me. I do my best to appear relaxed, like I've got no idea on earth what this conversation is going to be about.

"What's up?"

After a few seconds she fixes me with a stare.

"Do you have something you need to tell me?"

"What do you mean?" But my blood is cold. I sound guilty, even to myself.

"Do you…have something…you need to tell me." It's not a question. It's a demand. She can't say it, she needs me to do it. Wants to make me.

"What are you talking about?" I know I'm just buying time here, delaying the inevitable, because there's no way out. She knows, has known since she'd wondered why I'd immediately taken the Kratom packaging outside instead of just throwing it in the kitchen trash. So she went to find out why. I'm sure she'd thought "Kratom, what's Kratom?". But since she can google stuff too, she wasn't wondering long.

"Come on, Tom. Just tell me."

I take a seat on the kitchen floor, fold my knees into my chest. It's going to take me just a minute. I've never done this before.

"I'm...I'm a drug addict."

She knew it was coming, but I can still see all the air go out of her. It's devastating. It feels like a form of violence, when all it is, is the truth. I guess that's how it is when what you used to think was true turns out not to be.

"How long."

"How long?"

"How long have you been using drugs!" She is no longer contained.

"Eleven months." This doesn't include the months spent stealing from my mom. It's just since I started injecting. And I know this with near precision. It's not the sort of thing you forget.

"You've been lying to me for eleven months? What, are you stealing them from work? Why?!? You just went to work one day and decided to shoot up with...with...   what?!? What are you on???"

"No...yes...what?" I just want this to stop but I know it can't, no matter how much I shake my head and rock back and forth. "I'm so sorry. I'm sorry."

"Did you do it here? In this house?"

I look at her like are you crazy or something? "Yes."

This she can't bear sitting down, and she paces the kitchen. "You did it here. Was I here? Were the *boys* here?"

"I don't know..." I know, but I can't see why it matters. It's not like I brought home a hooker. Is it?

"I can't live here anymore. I can't be in this house. You've destroyed it."

She goes to the garage, gets into her car, and I get in the passenger seat beside her.

"You can stay here, I don't care what you do, but the boys and I are leaving. You have a nice life. I'm sorry we weren't enough for you, that you had to go and do this to yourself, to US! You're so selfish! Good luck with your next family, Tom."

And for the first time, it occurs to me what I've done to her. I've become her father. I've told lies that make her feel four years old, second best, and abandoned. I'm no psychiatrist, but I'd have to be blind not to see it. Even if she can't.

———————

I know that it's devastating to Tami to be lied to. But I also know that what I've been lying about is devastating, too. Both are a betrayal.

I have this dim awareness that we're supposed to be responsible for each other's happiness. It's like an unspoken promise we had when we got married—"marry me…and I'll make you the happiest person in the world." As if that were even possible. The fact that I'm not…it feels like a failure. And it makes Tami feel like she's not enough, that if she were, then I wouldn't have had to do this to myself. It's the only thing she can come up with when she asks herself why I would do something so stupid.

"Why???" I can tell her what, when, and where. But what I can't answer, at least to her satisfaction, is why.

"Because if I don't, I get sick. If I could just get back to normal, believe me, I'd stop."

"Believe you? I'm never going to believe anything you say ever again. But at least things make more sense now. Like why you never seem to be interested in me, in any of us. You're just there. Even when you're here, you're not here. How could I be so *stupid*…You did this right under my nose and I just kept telling myself it was just me. But it's not me, it's you."

"I know it's not you, none of this is your fault. I did it."

"Were we not enough for you?" Her voice shakes, and the vitriol is about to give way to the fear that is beneath it.

"Of course you were. That's got nothing to do with it." She's calmed down enough to come back inside the house, and she almost lets me get close enough to touch her if I stretched out my arm. But then the rage returns when we circle all the way back to the one answer I can't give her.

"Then *why*?!?"

"…I don't know…" And I realize I'm telling myself as much as her. I really don't know why. And I don't know why I can't seem to quit, but I promise her that I will. Now that my secret is out, I'll have to.

"I'm this close to being completely clean," and I show her the distance with my finger and my thumb. "I am almost there. That's why I got this Kratom. I was going to take it for two weeks, get all the opiates out of my system, then we go on vacation for a week, and then I'll be back to normal. I never wanted you to find any of this out. I never wanted to hurt you."

If it seems to her like I believe it, it's because I do. I mean it with every fiber of my being.

"You think you're going on vacation with us? You really are crazy."

———————————

But I do. For the next week, she can barely stand to look at me. But after that, she begins to soften. It's a pattern I'll come to recognize, but a week seems to be about what it takes for her to get over the trauma of being deceived. And just before we leave for Alabama, she puts a picture down in front of me.

"I want this back. I don't know where it went, or if it's even possible for you to get it back, but if we're going to be able to stay together, I have to have it back."

The picture is over a decade old, and it's of me. I'm lying on a park bench in Barcelona when we visited a few months after we met.

It was the trip when we fell in love for good. And I'm brushing away the camera like I really don't want my picture taken, but my happiness, it can't be misunderstood. It's what she wants back.

"If we're going to make it, I want this man back. I want to see your Spain smile."

All I can do now is nod. I know she's right.

I assure her that "I don't know where it went either…but I'm gonna find it. We'll find it together. Maybe we'll find it on the beach."

————————————

I'm not sure why Tami stayed after I lied to her. Not necessarily this time, it was just the first, and maybe everybody deserves a second chance. But a third? Fourth? A fifth? She couldn't stand the thought of being a constantly suspicious person, so she just wasn't. She didn't go through my bags. Didn't snoop through my phone, didn't demand I ever take a drug test. She just did her best to believe me, and I suppose I could be convincing. It wasn't hard. When I swore I'd get straight, I meant it. I believed myself, too. I'd just happen to change my mind about it later and not bother to tell her.

Some people say that a person with emotional or mental health won't stay through that kind of deception. Won't sit around and watch a person they love destroy themselves. They'll set healthy boundaries, and eventually say "Enough! This I cannot abide." And I suppose that's probably true, but I also don't know too many people I'd describe as the picture of emotional health. Most people I know feel like they have something to prove. They want to get what they've got coming to them. Maybe they know how to hold a grudge, if only privately, and it spurs them on to success, even to greatness. The same tools people use to survive, can help them thrive.

Like I say, I'm not certain why Tami stayed, and it's not my story to tell anyhow. It's hers. Maybe she just didn't want her own boys to grow up without a father, like she had, regardless of what a fuck up I was turning out to be. At least I still loved our boys, and she knew that. Or maybe she had some of the same problems I did. Maybe she was just too proud, afraid that people would wonder how she could've been so stupid not to see it sooner, and the longer it went on, the more afraid she got. Or maybe she just thought if she stuck around long enough, she'd finally get an answer to that question—why?

I never asked her to keep my secrets. It was just assumed. But she would, she'd put on a smile and pretend to everyone on the outside that things were just fine, all the while wondering when everything at home might all just go straight to hell. But there's a thing about secrets—keeping them will keep you sick.

XXII

Steven and I, we got through the rest of that conference in Vegas just fine. We brought the high points back to our practice, including our take on the pros and cons of going with one of the big corporate buyouts. The vote was a solid "No", and hopefully we've put that topic to bed for a couple more years. I shouldn't have to address it again during my term as managing partner, which starts soon.

But there's one thing I know I do have to address—this fucking drug addiction. I've been on many trips like this before with the Kratom. And even all the way back to that first one to the beach with Tami, I always think I'll slow it down towards the end, and by the time I get back I won't go into withdrawals anymore. But it's just a pipe dream, and after Vegas, I go right back on the needle, as always. I'm not giving up on medication assisted treatment, though. The thought of not having anything to kick with is too terrifying. I've got severe symptoms, and I have to treat them. I've just accepted that if I really want to get clean, it can't be with Kratom.

I've added a couple of other options, including Ambien, which I used on a family vacation last summer. Only I have to take it round the clock to stave off the anxiety, and I kept nodding off on the LA freeway, and practically got us all killed. Oh, and I got caught, Tami couldn't help but notice I was dopesick. So it's just a supplement.

But lately I've been thinking about another medication, one that's recently become legal in Colorado—marijuana. My best friend,

Randall Wayne, the one I wrote the Clonidine for? He lives in Denver now, and better yet, he knows. Tami, she's kept my secret, but I haven't always been able to. When I'm in withdrawal, on an occasion or two I've confessed to a close friend. When I'm using I could never do that, I wouldn't need to, I'm invulnerable. But when I'm dopesick, it's different. The hopelessness is hard to bear alone. So I told best buddy Randall maybe two years back, and of course I swore to him afterwards that I got clean. Couldn't have him doing something stupid, like trying to help me. So I basically unloaded my suffering onto him for a brief moment, said "here, you hold it," and then left him to forever wonder if I was going to be ok. Might go to prison, who knows, might even die. And then how would he have felt. But I'm a drug addict, and we'll do that sort of thing to a friend.

Anyways, now that I've got the idea, I can't wait. I want to see if the cannabis comes through for me. People want to claim it's a gateway drug, like it'll lead to worse things, but I'm thinking it'll be more like a bridge. A bridge back to some form of sobriety. Because it's not addictive, right? Or I suppose what I mean is it doesn't cause physical dependence, and that is what I'm struggling so hard to overcome. Afterwards, when I'm finally clean, I'll just burn the bridge down, and who knows, maybe it'll light the way for somebody else.

But it's not legal in Oklahoma, and I really have no idea how to buy it. I know a few people who smoke, but I'm afraid it might be a red flag if all of a sudden I want to, too. I saw my friend Billy buy it once in Taos. Just said "See those hippies over there? I'm gonna see if they've got any pot." Walked right over to them and asked if they knew where we could play some disc golf. They said they didn't. "Don't know anything about the kind green, either, huh?" Billy asked them. Well, "why didn't you just say so", they said, and next thing I know, we're smoking a bowl right in the middle of Kit Carson Park with a bunch of vagabond teenagers with names like Apple Butter, and Open Smile.

But I don't think that's gonna work here in OKC, we don't have a Kit Carson Park, so I go try the next best thing—the bus station. I don't really have a plan, I just figure I'll do it like Billy did, walk up to the first folks I see and ask them. And that happens to be an African American couple sitting on a bench out behind the bus depot. They could be coming or going, it's hard to tell, and I can't tell at all how old they might be, but if they're cops, they're spectacularly good. And if I'm one, well I'm spectacularly bad.

"Excuse me, you all wouldn't know where I could find something to smoke, would you?"

They look at each other. "Smoke?", like are you stupid or something?

"Yeah…something to smoke. You know where I could find some…" I pause, look around. "Weed?"

"Ah, you lookin' for weed, are you?" The man says it. The woman says "white boy lookin' for weed," like she's seen it all.

"What you be askin' us for?" the man says, suspicious..

I just shrug. "I dunno. Thought maybe you'd know is all."

I'm illegally parked, right behind the rear exit of the bus station, and a uniformed man comes out, tells me I can't park there. Asks me if I'm taking the bus.

"Yes," I lie.

"Where you going?"

"Albuquerque." It just comes out, like I'm Bugs Bunny, or maybe because I'm thinking of Billy and New Mexico. But the uniformed man, he doesn't buy it.

"You need to move your vehicle."

I figure I'm finished, that this was an entirely stupid idea, but the couple, they get up, the man says "We'll go with you."

I think to myself, right on, like I've already succeeded, and we all pile into the minivan and I wave goodbye to the uniformed man.

_____

"So you guys can help me out?"

"Yeah, we got you," the man says. The woman, she doesn't say anything, just listens while the man gives me directions to an apartment complex maybe five minutes away.

"Park here. We'll be right back." And they are, except it isn't the man and woman anymore, it's the man and a friend of his, I guess, and I'm assured that "he can hook you up."

They give me directions to another apartment complex in a part of town I'm unfamiliar with, and it takes a little longer to get there.

There's some small talk, the new man tells his friend about a job opportunity he's heard about, a warehouse job with good pay, but you gotta pass a drug test. So shit.

We get to the new complex in about fifteen minutes.

"How much you want?" the first man asks.

I'm not sure how to answer. I don't want to say a dime bag, maybe it's too small, and maybe it's another kind of dope altogether. Or an ounce, maybe that's too much.

I settle on "A hundred dollars worth."

"Ok cool," the man from the bus stop tells me. "Here…you can keep my phone. So's you know we coming back."

I hand him the hundred and he gives me his phone, and I watch while they disappear around the corner of the building. I've got nothing to do but wait anxiously, while my first illicit drug deal goes down. And I guess it's gonna work, holy shit.

And I'll be damned, but it does. Ten minutes later, they're back, and once inside the car, the man with the connection slides me a big plastic baggie full of bud. I immediately reach inside, and start to pull some out.

"The fuck you doing?" It's the first time I've seen either of them agitated, and they glance around like we're under observation. And for the first time it occurs to me that what I'm doing might be dangerous.

"I just want to give you guys some. Show my appreciation." I'm grateful.

"Well get the fuck outta here first."

I do, and drop them off at yet a third apartment complex a couple of minutes away. I share my score, and they seem grateful, too. This wasn't an ordinary day for me, and who knows, maybe it hasn't been for them either.

After I leave, I think that maybe I should've gotten their number. Maybe I'll want to try this again. And perhaps pot wasn't all that was to be had from the apartment. Maybe I could've gotten more. Pills, or powders. But I'm not here for that shit, I'm not trying to abuse more drugs, I'm here to get clean. This marijuana, it's my new medicine.

XXIII

The pot's not perfect. But it'll do. I didn't want to come home smelling like I'd just left a Todd Snyder concert or something, so as soon as I got a chance, I tore off a sizable chunk, and I just ate it. I figured if you can cook it into brownies, chewing it up should work just as well. And this led to two serendipitous discoveries—One, it lasts a whole lot longer than simply smoking it. And two, it works a bit more on relaxing the body than the mind. These are highly advantageous traits for the type of treatment I'm looking for. Now I just need a one week window of time to use it for a thorough detox.

And I don't have to wait long. Spring break is right around the corner. The boys are already five and seven, it's so hard to believe, but now we have to plan vacation time around their school schedules. The gulf coast of Alabama has remained our go to place. Tami has already started hinting about wanting to get an investment property there. Our place in Medicine Park, it was fine while it lasted, it served its purpose, but in the long run it just didn't make any sense. Not much of a rental market there. That, and I'd spent so many weekends there trying to kick cold turkey back before I found Kratom, that I wanted to burn the place to the ground to scorch the memories. I sold it instead, but I can't ever go back. Fuck Medicine Park.

The boys are excited about all of us finally taking a vacation together. We haven't attempted anything like this in almost two years, not since LA, and LA had not gone well, what with the Ambien, and

Tami discovering that I'd been lying to her for yet another year. She'd been about to give up, convinced that when I was using drugs, she couldn't tell. And now with the Kratom, she wouldn't be able to tell when I wasn't, either.

But this time is going to be different. I've assured her. Things have changed since then. She knows all my secret tricks, or most of them. She knows about the triple sneezes, that only happen when I'm withdrawing. That the dark blue scrubs are to hide the blood. And even that a home drug test from the pharmacy she works at won't detect fentanyl. It's synthetic. Not that she ever asked me to take a drug test, I offered. To prove that I was "clean", even when I wasn't. But I've traded all those secrets away for one more chance to earn her trust.

And this trip is it. Tami is happy too, I can tell. She's been optimistic, but cautious, for a week, and now that we've got all the luggage checked at the airport, she's starting to relax. Even takes my hand as we walk towards the security checkpoint. And I wonder if she can feel it. Surely she can feel the sweat.

I've read about whether I can get away with this, convinced myself that the TSA is charged with looking for weapons, not weed, and if I can just keep my cool, I should breeze right through. I debated whether to pack the pot in my backpack, or in the luggage, but since Tami insisted we could get everything packed into one suitcase, she made my decision for me.

Since we have smaller kids, we get to skip to a side scanner and pass through quickly, but I'm about to shit myself waiting on my backpack to go through the X-ray. The belt slides back and forth a few times, but I can't tell which bag has drawn the interest of the bored TSA agent. I'm terrified that my boys are about to see me taken away in handcuffs, but eventually my backpack slides through, and I finally exhale. We made it. Holy shit.

———————————

It'd be a stretch to say I enjoyed myself the first couple of days. There's no easy way to detox from opioids, outside of being completely anesthetized, but there's definitely worse ways than with weed. It's bearable, and I'm at least able to sleep.

But on the third day, things change. Tami, she's having a great time, and the boys are too. They all want to live here, "can we daddy, pleeeease!" There's no way that's happening, but Tami is giving me the hard sell on the vacation home idea.

"It's an investment. This place is a hidden secret about to be discovered, and it'll appreciate faster than anything in the stock market." And she's pretty convincing. I'm too tired to put up much of a fight, and besides, maybe she's right. What harm could it do just to contact a realtor and go see what's available.

———————————

"So this is our model unit. Yours would be pretty much like this, and of course you could choose your colors, and fixtures, and what not. It's not on the water, but the development does have beach access. There's a bike path right down to the sand."

194

The realtor's voice is soothing, it's like a balm on my seared soul. It's the sound of Alabama and it reminds me of better days. I like listening to her.

"There'll be a community pool, with a clubhouse, and a lovely playground for your little ones. They're just so cute." She smiles and squints her eyes towards the boys. "This place is perfect for families like yours."

Families like ours? What, does it come with a marriage counseling service? On-site rehab? She has no idea. Still…it's tempting. I can tell Tami is imagining herself here.

"Now, if you decide a place like this would suit you, just remember, construction is anywhere from six to eight months. That's what we're looking at right now. If you'd like to have something sooner, I've got a couple of places I've just listed that you'd love. They're less than five years old and really nice."

Tami and I look at each other and shrug. Why not? I could listen to the realtor's voice all day.

———————————

The realtor unlocks the door of the condo, announces herself. "Hello? Anybody home? Realtor for a showing." She turns to us. "Nobody should be here, but you never know what you may find."

The place is beautiful. It's on the water, with gulf views from the living room. It's also way out of our price range, but it can't hurt to look. They say put your money into the kitchen and bathrooms, that's what counts, and that's exactly what they've done here. The kitchen is amazing and Tami heads straight for it. I wander upstairs, to check out the bedrooms, and the master is impressive, with a luxurious bathroom attached. I can still hear Tami and Stacey the realtor, they're like friends now, chatting it up in the kitchen. It looks like an older couple lives here, or at least owns the place, who knows how long it's been since they've been here. The place is kind of dusty. There are creams on the countertop, anti-aging agents for the skin, and some brand of cologne that hasn't been fashionable since the seventies. These people are old. Which means…maybe they've got meds.

I quickly slide open the drawers of the vanity, but don't find anything of use. Still, I know it's here. I can somehow feel it. It's like I've already scored. There's a medicine cabinet above the toilet, and when I crack it open, my heart rate jumps twenty beats. There are pill bottles here. But unfortunately, it's all over the counter crap like glucosamine and chondroitin. It's such a disappointment. But for no particular reason at all, I open one anyway, and it's clearly not just a supplement. It's full of pharmaceuticals. But what kind is anyone's guess. It'd be great if I could holler down to Tami, "hey babe, what kinda pill is an M523?" That's what is stamped on these, and there's gotta be fifty of them. I reach for my phone to google it, but then I remember…I gave it to TJ. Had to keep him entertained and right now he's still downstairs. I can already hear the realtor saying "let's check out the upstairs," and it's now or never, so I pour a quarter of the bottle into my pocket, because sometimes you get lucky, and I pop two of the M523s into my mouth. What's the worst that could happen? Maybe I'll get a boner, or my blood pressure will drop.

———————————

"What do you think?" Tami is sold, but I haven't said much since we left the realtor's office.

"Well, what do *you* think?" I answer. "There's no way we can afford a place like the one on the beach. But....the one in Providence...we could probably make it work...if it's really what you want."

Tami breaks into a big smile. It's what she wants, alright. And making her happy, it makes me happy, too. It makes me feel like we're still a couple. She works hard, she sacrifices, and maybe she deserves something like this. I've never thought I'd be one to want to vacation every year in the very same spot, but maybe I could get used to it. Besides...I'm liking it here more and more. This trip, it's turning into quite the surprise. You never know what you might find, indeed. Like those M523s....by the time I got my phone back from TJ, I didn't even need google to show me what I was holding. I already knew. I got me a pocketful of oxy.

———————————

I didn't make any decision to steal. It never even occurred to me not to. There wasn't ever a debate. My spirit, that side of myself that considers others, that can be thoughtful, even kind, has lost. It lost to survival, so far as taking drugs is concerned. It's not necessarily so in all other aspects of my life, but when it comes to opioids, I've no patience left whatsoever. It doesn't feel like I'm faced with a choice between right and wrong, it feels like there's no choice at all, and if there is, there's only one right answer—just do it.

I chalk all this up to my dependency, my physiologic need. You'd steal too, if you were starving, and way too proud to beg. And if we just hadn't gone inside that last house, this week would've cured me. But no matter. I'm almost out of the weed I bought, but I know where I can get more, anytime I want, and I won't have to worry about getting arrested doing it. I just need a chance to get up to Colorado, where the Green Rush is booming.

XXIV

According to Weed Maps, eastern Colorado might as well be Kansas. The closest towns in the southeast are only a six hour drive away, but evidently they don't want to be part of the Rocky Mountain High. It looks like the nearest dispensary is in Pueblo. And it's probably an eighteen hour round trip.

I need an alibi, so I invent an overnight call on the obstetrics service, tell Tami I won't be home until sometime tomorrow afternoon, and I head off to "work". I've loaded my car with essentials—a couple of backpacks, a tent, and a Coleman stove that I've never even used. It's all conspicuously laid out in the backseat to give my story some verisimilitude. I even thought about renting a jeep, but thought it might be too much. It's a Thursday morning, and counting today, I'll have four days clean from opioids when I have to face my demons again on Monday. Four days should suffice.

A lot of people think the drive across western Oklahoma, through the Texas panhandle, and up over into New Mexico is boring. And it is desolate, no doubt. But I think it's beautiful, too. It'd be damn near as close for me to just drive to Denver, but I like this route a lot better. Well over a hundred years ago, this was Comanche country, part of their vast empire, and their mounted warriors lorded over it all. It wasn't always this way, before the Spanish came, the Comanche had no horses, but once they did, they were unstoppable. You passed through here at your own peril. Nobody fucked with Comanches.

I'm not Comanche, but I am part Cherokee, and I imagine my Mazda is a little Spanish Mustang. Out in the middle of nowhere, it's easy to feel small and insignificant, isolated. Even with a tankful of gas and a cell phone to get back to safety. I can't imagine the courage it took to venture across this country just relying on the rivers. It will fill you with awe.

As I pass through the little towns, like Borger, Dumas, and Dalhart, I wonder what it'd be like to live here. I wonder what people do. How do they spend their days? This is dust bowl country, and if anyone knows about survival, it's the grandparents and great-grandparents of these good folk.

_____

I make it to Pueblo and the dispensary before three. Local time it's only two, but since I'll be headed back to central time almost immediately after my purchase, I don't even consider it. I'm not in any particular hurry, I'm well ahead of schedule, but as soon as I approach the dispensary, I just want to get in and get out. Immediately. And the fucking bud-tender…he doesn't seem to be operating with the same sense of urgency.

"Heeey man. How's it going?" He greets me with a broad smile, like I'm an old friend he hasn't seen in quite awhile. Like we're going to take some time to catch up. But I have no interest in that. Still, I don't want to be discourteous. This isn't a crack house.

"Oh, I'm good dude. Thanks."

"Can I see your ID real quick my man?" I have it at the ready and I hand him my driver's license.

"From Oklahoma, huh? Niiice." He nods his head, gives me a knowing smile. "So what brings you in today to our fine establishment?" He gestures grandly to the broad assortment of cannabis products for sale. Things I didn't know existed. They've got candy bars, flavored drinks, gummy bears and other assorted drops. Creams, lotions, candles, oils. Waxes, dabs, and vape pens. And of course, they've got flower. Lots of it, in various strains that come with names straight off the Woodstock set list. I don't think just telling him "I'd like some marijuana, please" is gonna cut it.

"Well, I think I'd like to get some edibles." My experience chewing up the pot leaves has taught me this is the way I want to go. And now I won't even have to wonder how much I need to eat. It's got the dose mapped out, down to the milligram. And it'll taste a helluva lot better.

"Right on, right on," the bud-tender approves. His name is Jacob, and he looks exactly like a stoner straight out of central casting. He's in the right line of work. "Well, we've got the gummies, those are really nice, very popular these days. Several types of hard candies. Some watermel..."

"Just gimme some gummies." I can't take this shit anymore.

"Ok. Ok cool. Well what flavor you leaning towards? Personally, I like the cinnamon, but we've also got..."

"Cinnamon is fine." I'm running out of patience with Jacob. I want to scream at him, 'do you actually think I give two fucks what flavor the gummy bears are, Jakob?!?' He prolly spells it with a K.

"Alright, alright, alright. So one cinnamon gummy bear."

"No. I'll take four."

"Oh, ok. Well, it comes ten to a bottle. Each one of those guys is 10 milligrams. If I were you, I'd start out with one, two at the most. Three will put your ass out for good, yo, like for the rest of the night. You know what I'm saying?"

I try to exhibit a bit more patience. These are things I need to know.

"So you wanna take one, wait maybe half hour, forty-five minutes, and then if you need a bit more effect, take another. Cool?" Jacob instructs me.

"Yeah…cool." I plan to start out with four.

"And gimme a couple of those candy bars, too."

"Ok, so we've got…"

"Any flavor is fine."

"Cookies and creme it is," Jacob with a K smiles. Must be his favorite. "Anything else for you, my man?"

"I tell you what, let me have a couple of your pre-rolls, too."

"Excellent choice. Now are you looking for more of the stimulating, creative type of high? Or you thinking more the mellow out and chill vibe. Because we've got both sativa and indica strains in our pre-rolls. It really just depends on what you're looking for."

I can barely restrain my impatience. This is not like running into the convenience store and grabbing a can of copenhagen. This is like trying to order off a menu in a foreign language.

"Jacob?"

"Yeah, bro."

"What's your favorite?"

He smiles. Big. "Sativa all the way, bro. My favorite part about Sativa, man…it doesn't matter what you do next!"

"Sounds good, then."

"Alright, dude, is there *anything* else I can do for you today?"

I look at the beverages, and I'm thirsty. "Give me one of those drinks there. You pick."

"Cool. Now these are seventy-five milligrams, ok bro? It's like eating a whole handful of those gummies. Don't go chugging it on me, bro."

Now all Jacob has to do is sack up my purchase and I can get out of here. But it's not that simple. To supposedly protect children from accidentally ingesting these innocent looking candies, he has to secure each item in a zip lock bag that puts a child proof pill bottle to shame. It feels like it takes for-fucking-ever.

"Now you be safe out there, brother, you hear? We appreciate you coming in, and make sure you come back next time you're in town."

"Thanks man. I will."

But I know I won't. I have no intentions of coming to this dispensary, or any other one for that matter…ever again.

XXV

Another Long Ass Year Later…

I was wrong about never visiting Jacob at the Pueblo dispensary again. Within a month after my first trip, I was out. And yeah, I went back. I know…it's a shocker. But only a couple of times, three at the most, because within a few months, marijuana had made its way down to Trinidad. Shaved a couple of hours off the trip, each way, and now I can make it all in one day, easy. I can be back by 7 or 8pm, and for all Tami knows, it was just a long day at work.

I'm not sure how many times I've been to Trinidad, once a month or so, probably, and I've got the routine down pat. I'm still suiting up, either as a backpacker or a skier, depends on the season. But it's getting old. I've been trying to beat this morphine habit for going on six years now. Six. *Years*.

I've been considering this the whole drive up. It's not like I've substituted one addiction for another, it's more like I'm just supplementing the morphine and fentanyl with edibles and weed pens. But I'm still convinced it's helping, why the hell else would I drive all the way up here. I make the turnaround at Trinidad a little after noon. I still find the casual, semi-spiritual affectations of the dispensary staff to be irksome, but I accept it as my own impatience and I try not to be an asshole, but it's hard. I still want to get in and get out.

I'm particularly disappointed in myself on the way back, and there's a Denny's in Raton, so I figure I'll stop in for a bite. Maybe it'll be a comfort, or feel like the freedom I know I don't have. It's come to have a meaning for my kids like I'd hoped. I find the demeanor of the staff here to be much more in sync with my own spirit, like they don't want to be here any more than I do, and though the place is empty, they seat me directly across from a family of five, with three rowdy, unwashed kids of their own who don't want to eat.

The dad does, though. They're having some kind of all you can eat pancake special, and this guy is getting his money's worth. He was finishing up a plate when I sat down, and he's gone through another before I even need a refill on my coffee. By the time my food comes, he's on a third. Going for a grand slam.

I can't even eat, I'm so disgusted. There's pancake stuck in his bushy beard, and he keeps sucking syrup off his big fat fingers. It appears he hasn't changed his sweat-stained T shirt in about three days, and the evidence of what he's previously eaten is all over it. His wife is doing what appears to be her best to manage the chaos of the kids, but that doesn't mean it's very good. One has more food on his face than on his plate. Meanwhile, dad just keeps putting away more pancakes. He's oblivious, he gives zero fucks. The entire scene is repulsive.

Finally they finish up, and on the way to the door, dad is overtly probing his decaying dentition with a toothpick, like he's just finished a rack of ribs. I can't help watching them herd across the parking lot where they all load up inside a rusted green Chevy conversion van that looks like it rolled off the lot during the Carter administration, and it belches and smokes as they pull out into the street. I look back towards my nearly new Mazda 6, the silver shining in the sun, and I think to myself…I'd trade places with that fucker in a heartbeat. I envy him.

I'm serious. I don't care what that guy's life looks like on the outside. On the inside, where it counts, he can't possibly be in as bad a shape as me. At worst, we're even. I guess if there's a silver lining to all this, it's that my experience has shown me what's really important in life. Without my health—mental, physical, and spiritual—I have nothing. And it can't be bought. I thought I already knew this, way back when I first chose medicine. But I really had no idea. So thank you, drug addiction, for the lesson.

Something has got to change. I've even been having fantasies about quitting my job lately, even though it's really the only thing I have left. Work is my last sanctuary, the only place I can go and know I'll feel normal. But I wonder if it's worth it. If I can't get away from the drugs, maybe I just need to get the drugs away from me, and do something else. But what…? It's the only thing I'm good at, the only thing I know how to do.

I've read so many books, searched so many websites looking for answers, that it feels pointless punching "opioid addiction" into the search engine of my phone yet again. I immediately scroll over all the sites that say "Need Help? Call Us!", because all that stuff about reaching out and asking for help is bullshit. Another person can't talk me through the fucking detox, how's that gonna help? And if the first step in solving a problem is admitting one exists, then I'm already there. I admit it. I can't seem to quit. But that doesn't mean I'm gonna stop trying.

A few scrolls down I come across a familiar medication that has shown promise in ameliorating the symptoms of an opioid detox. But heretofore I've been much too terrified to try it. And despite nearly six years of evidence otherwise, I'm still pretty convinced that if I could just feel normal, for once, if I could only feel the way I used to before all this started, then my life can go on without the rest of it having to be defined by opioid addiction. I simply cannot let that happen. But it's obvious I'm going to have to try something new, I can't keep doing the same thing over and over, so maybe it's time I tried it out. If the scientists say maybe it can help, maybe it's time I tried ketamine...

I don't need to see anymore, I'm ready to go, and not more than a few minutes after the green Chevy has belched its way out onto the interstate, I signal for my check.

"You want a to-go box?" My food is still untouched and the sunny-side up eggs are staring at the server.

"No thanks." I leave her a $20 and she shrugs, like "suit yourself," and I follow a few minutes behind the Chevy. I can't get out of here fast enough. Denny's isn't comforting anymore, it doesn't remind me of home, like it did in Japan, I don't even know where home is. It's shaken me to realize that I'd trade away most everything I have just for the chance to feel normal in my own skin. For a chance to be free again.

———————————————

There are a lot of different ways to define insanity. The one it seems people like to trot out most is the one about doing the same damned thing over and over and expecting different results. Probably because it's often attributed to Einstein, so it must be genius. But the one I like to consider is just being out of sync with everyone else. Sanity is pretty much accepting a reality that everyone else agrees with. And if you're the only person who believes something, or who thinks something might be a good idea, well…you could say that's insane. Like to almost everyone else, a trash can is just a place to put garbage. But to a schizophrenic sleeping on the sidewalk, it can be an offering plate of the western heaven, and you can eat out of it. But with this definition, there's always just a bit of wiggle room. For instance, if everyone else believes the world is flat, but I'm convinced it's round, to them I'm insane…even though I'm actually right. And I like this aspect. Because even though I know that if I were to tell anyone else that "yeah, I think ketamine might be the key to conquering my opioid habit," their response would be "what are you, nuts???"—but that doesn't have to mean that I am. Because you don't know what I know. You haven't been through what I've been through. In my mind, I can still be right, even if nobody else would agree.

But there's another definition of insanity, and it's probably the one that people learn first. It's by far the simplest. It just means you're fucking crazy. And ketamine is about to teach me exactly what that's like.

XXVI

Ketamine is a dissociative anesthetic. It's got a few cousins, like the street drug PCP, aka Angel Dust, and the cough suppressant dextromethorophan. Ketamine has been used as a veterinary tranquilizer, a battlefield anesthetic, and a party drug of abuse for ravers. Recently, it's shown some real promise as a possible remedy for treatment resistant severe depression, and as an aid for opioid withdrawal. So I figure I qualify on two fronts. Although I'm not about to subject myself to formalized therapy, I'll handle my own experiments, thank you very much.

Ketamine use isn't terribly common in the OR, although it's probably underutilized. It provides powerful anesthetic effects through dissociation. What you might call, a trip. It does this by blocking certain receptors in the brain. These receptors form connections between the outside world, our sense of what is going on around us, with the world inside our mind, where we give this perceived reality meaning.

I say perceived reality, because that's really all our senses give us—a view of reality from a certain vantage point, that is really only a very small slice of the whole pie. Dogs can smell and hear things we can't. Eagles have visual acuity far sharper than ours. That doesn't mean those sights and smells don't exist. We just can't perceive them. Our sense of time and space is only a perception, too, but that's some quantum level physics shit that I can't understand, let alone explain.

210

But what I do know is that our human senses are elegantly adapted to our environment, and are finely tuned to promote our survival. Our adaptations are to our advantage. It's not all just some random coincidence, we see what we need to see. Hear what we need to hear. I knew all of this before using ketamine, of course, and it's probably plainly obvious to most anyone. But knowing it, and experiencing it are two different things.

I've never tried LSD, but I understand roughly how it works. It opens up the sensory pathways, so that the brain becomes massively overloaded with outside input. This is not the perceived reality humans are accustomed to. You don't see color, you see blazing rainbows. You don't hear a sound, you hear a symphony. And all of this sensory input getting to your brain has 'deep meaning, man!', because your mind assigns it that meaning. This isn't ultimate reality, the world as it exists outside the limits of normal human perception, they're just hallucinations. They're not real, or at least I'm pretty sure. You're just tripping.

Ketamine does basically the exact opposite. It blocks the outside sensory input, or at least alters it in such a way that it is not assigned its normal interpretation in the mind, its normal meaning. And instead of tripping on sensory overload of outside reality, you create a reality all your own from a hodgepodge of recent experiences, remote memories, or deeply held dreams. Or fears.

In the OR, ketamine is always given with an amnestic agent. Something that makes you forget, like versed. Because a ketamine trip isn't always good. But I didn't want to do it this way, because for some stupid reason, I thought it would prevent me from staying in

211

control. I thought if I knew what was going on, maybe I could keep a handle on things. Which in retrospect, was completely crazy.

―――――――――――

The time Tami caught me wasn't my first experience with ketamine. I'd used it before, a few times. And the results were astounding. Almost indescribable. It doesn't last long, maybe twenty minutes, thirty at most, and the vast majority of it is just kind of like la la land. It's like your brain is in a box, not connected to your body, or anything else that's going on around you. It's just your mind, or maybe what is spirit, floating on a tranquil sea in space. Like a place that doesn't exist. And when you're trying to escape the doom of dopesickness, that's a pretty decent place for your mind to be. But then, towards the end, it's like your brain sort of knows it's almost time to re-enter reality, and it struggles to get its shit together, just kind of throwing things here and there, but it's not as if you just got your shirt on backwards trying to get dressed really fast, it's like the pieces it puts back together are straight up fantasy, sci-fi, comic book shit. It's literally whatever you imagine it to be, because that's really all it is—a combination of your memories and dreams. It's like a dream, or a nightmare, come to life. And what's more, it feels every bit as real as any moment you can remember. Why wouldn't it? Your brain is telling you it's reality. If you'd like an example, just make one up. Anything you can conceive of will do, anything you've ever dreamed. Only it's not happening inside your mind, it's happening in the world around you. Or at least that's what your senses are telling you. Maybe you can fly. Maybe we're all just cartoons, or in a computer simulation of some sort.

212

This isn't why I do it, though. I do it because it helps. Or at least that's what I tell myself. The trips might last only twenty minutes, but afterwards it's like my nervous system gets a several hour respite from the opiate withdrawals. It's not perfect, nothing is. But it helps. The trips can be pretty spectacular, but they're every bit as likely to be terrifying. And they usually involve some sort of apocalyptic event that culminates in the afterlife or eternity. Once I was in a helicopter crash and my backyard was crawling with EMTs trying to rescue me from the wreckage. But they couldn't. It wasn't exactly a pleasant experience. But the time that Tami discovered what I was up to, that night was the second coming of Christ.

———————

I never saw Him coming through the clouds or anything…but somehow, I just *knew*. All that talk about Jesus coming back to see us, well it was real. And what's more, it's just happened. Can you imagine how spectacular it might be to believe not just in this possibility, but in its actuality? It feels like winning the largest lottery ever, but it comes with not only money, but an end to every problem in the world. "There shall be no more death, neither sorrow, nor crying, neither shall there be any more pain—for the former things are passed away." This…is very exciting news. Any description of the sheer joy I felt would be an understatement. And it had to be shared. We'd moved by this time, and I was no longer sleeping in an upstairs bedroom, but in a mother-in-law suite out off the garage. And with an evangelical zeal that would make any television preacher shout out an Amen, I came tearing into the house. Where Tami was unprepared.

"Tami! He's back! Jesus is back! Can you believe it???"

Tami doesn't look quite as joyful as I was at the news. In fact, she looks horrified.

"What are you *talking* about?"

"It's unbelievable, you're not gonna believe this, he's back! It's all true, Jesus is back!"

"Tom… what is wrong with you?!? You've got to be quiet. You're going to wake up the boys." It seems an absurd concern in retrospect, but then again, she's in shock.

"It's ok, it's ok, it's ok, we've got to tell them, too. He's back! He's alive!"

"Tom. *Tom!* What are you *on*?" There's no other explanation. I'm either on something, or I've gone completely mad. Or both.

"Nothing. I'm not on anything. Well, ketamine, but it's just shown me the truth, I'm awake now, and everything is gonna be ok!"

"Tom…come sit down, and let's talk about it."

She gets eerily calm. I'm not sure how she does it, but she does.

"Tell me…exactly what you took."

As she's speaking, my senses slowly stop spinning, and I start to understand what has happened. And the realization is crushing. I haven't awakened into an everlasting eternity of joy, I've been hallucinating. The reality is I woke up in hell. And I can tell by the look on Tami's face that I've taken her with me.

"Oh, God. Tami. Tami, I'm so sorry."

"I think we need to take you to the hospital."

"No, no, I'm fine now."

She's got her phone out, the 911 dialed in. All she has to do is hit send.

"I don't think you're fine. I think you've gone crazy."

I realize she can't tell any difference between what was happening two minutes ago and what's occurring right now, whereas to me, it's as plain as black and white. I need to give her some time.

"It's ok. I fucked up. I took too much ketamine. But I'm fine now."

"You what? You took what?" This is impossible for her to process. "Show me exactly what you took."

I feel unusually transparent, like I'm willing to tell her anything she wants to know. Because why not, there's nothing left to hide. I can't convince her the house isn't on fire when it's already burned to the ground. Might as well show her where the matches are.

"Here." I hand her the ketamine vial.

"What else." There is an unfamiliar steel in her voice. And also something shattered.

I tell her everything, about the trips to Colorado, how I've continued to buy Kratom from a head shop in town, everything I can think of. It's a lot. A lot for Tami to absorb.

"Why ketamine?"

"Because I read that it can help with withdrawals."

"You should have seen yourself. You were crazy. I was about to call the police. I was afraid of you. You can't stay here anymore, you know that right? I will take the boys to my brother's tomorrow evening, and I want you out. I don't care where you go, just go."

"Ok."

I know she's right. And she means it this time. She's kicked me out before, I've stayed in every hotel within a five mile radius over the years, but eventually it just felt like I was being punished for a few days until I came crawling back home. But this time feels different. Nothing else has worked anyway. Maybe moving out will.

"Tom, you've *got* to get help. You obviously can't quit."

"I don't need help. I just need to get back to normal, back to where I can actually sleep, where I don't have an anxiety attack every time I walk into the hospital after a few days clean. I know it doesn't seem like it, but I'm getting closer."

"Tom, what if you die? Where does that leave the boys? Where does that leave me?"

"I'm not gonna die."

"You could overdose. It happens all the time."

"People OD for three reasons—they mix drugs together, like with alcohol. Or they quit for three months and their tolerance goes back to normal but they still use their usual dose. Or they're using street drugs that aren't cut right and they get a hot shot. None of that is going to happen to me. I know what I'm doing."

216

"You're so…you're so arrogant. You didn't just see yourself. I did. You have no idea what you're doing."

"I won't use ketamine anymore. That was obviously a mistake."

"You could've done something crazy, you weren't yourself, Tom. What if instead of thinking Jesus came back, you thought something different? Don't you see that?"

I do. And it's terrifying.

"I don't understand why you won't just stop. Nobody is putting a gun to your head and making you do it. *You're* doing it. You're choosing to do it, instead of choosing your own family. You are just so…fucking selfish."

Tami, who never swears, is partly right.

———————————

Tami and I, we each hold two beliefs at once. I'm beyond believing I can stop anytime I want. I wanted to a long time ago. I just haven't been able to do it. But I also still believe that I can, eventually. I'm both the problem and the solution at the same time. Or rather, the opioids are the problem, and I just haven't adjusted the circumstances exactly right to solve it. Haven't read the right inspirational book. Haven't approached the hospital on a Monday with the right number of days clean, or with the right attitude. Or most importantly, found the right alternative chemical to compensate. Which, not coincidentally, must be another mood or mind altering drug. But I'll get there. What other choice do I have?

And Tami, she knows I'm arrogant for believing I'm the solution. For believing that I can do things other people can't, things I obviously can't do either, like quit on my own. She's got six years of evidence to prove it. But she also seems to believe, maybe needs to believe, that if I just wanted to a little bit more, that if I just loved her more than the drugs, that I'd choose her over them. I mean, she's right—nobody is putting a gun to my head. So what else could it be, if it's not a choice?

———————————

Sometimes a physiologic answer won't suffice. At least not for me. I can understand how, but still wonder why. Especially when science doesn't offer me any solutions. There seems to be no way that my neurons can ever remember how to 'just say no'. My "No" button is broken. My off switch is short-circuited. It's why so many addicts just substitute one substance for another. It's why former smokers get fat. Maybe someday the scientists will invent a pill that can undo all the damage, and alcoholics can go back to enjoying a glass and a half of good wine with dinner, and all the families will rejoice. But so far, there's no such thing.

There's an old joke among health professionals that's short and sweet. A patient holds his arm in a certain position and says "Doc, it hurts when I do this. What should I do?" And the doc says, "Well…stop doing that." Seems logical. But addiction isn't logical. It's baffling. Nobody's putting a gun to my head. So if there's no chains, then why don't I have a choice? Why can I not simply stop doing the thing that is causing me and everyone I claim to love so much misery?

—Jesus answered, "Truly, truly, I say to you, everyone who practices sin, is a slave to sin."

219

XXVII

Rockville, Virginia

Missionary Orientation

1992

"So here's Jesus…and here's us."

The man speaking is a cultural anthropologist from New Zealand, and he's tasked with helping us future missionary volunteers expand our worldview just a bit. Most of us are Bible Belt Christians, fresh out of college, and we'll soon be traveling to foreign countries to share our Christian beliefs. A little widening of our worldviews couldn't hurt.

"So what does a person have to do to go from here…to here?"

He's got Jesus in a box on his whiteboard. And the question he wants us to consider, is what does a person have to do to move from outside the box, to inside the box with Jesus. Because from our perspective, that's what a person has to do to receive salvation. To be saved. To be born again. Inside the box there is grace. And outside it, condemnation.

This question, it's right in our wheelhouse. I mean, if you can't answer it, you're probably bound for hell yourself. And that's why we're going overseas. Because our belief is that Jesus is the one true way to salvation, and everyone must call upon Him in order to receive it. But how can they call upon Him if they don't believe? And how can they believe if they have not heard? It's pretty much straight out of the Bible.

—"You have to accept Jesus as your personal Lord and Savior."

—"You have to ask for forgiveness from your sin."

—"You have to believe that Jesus is the Son of God."

—"You have to believe in his death on the cross for your sin, and that he rose again from the grave."

—"You have to repent."

We've got lots of answers to this question of what a person has to do to get inside that box. Because everything outside it, all that's going straight to hell. These box walls, they are sturdy. Certain. They are the very basis for our faith.

But there's always that one guy who's got to mess it all up for everyone. The one guy raises his hand, hesitates. It's not easy to be a heretic.

"Um, I've kind of got a big problem with all of this," he says.

"Oh yes? How so?" asks the kiwi cultural anthropologist. But there's a new lilt in his voice. As if this is the response he's been waiting for, and the lesson is about to begin.

"Well…who am I to say what a person has to do to experience Jesus. I don't really think that's for any of us to decide."

"Interesting. Tell me more."

"I guess what I mean is, I don't think it's my job to come up with a list or a few criteria that a person has to meet in order to have an encounter with God. We don't save people, God does."

It sounds pretty obvious when he says it out loud, and it makes me feel a little sheepish for not thinking of it myself. Interestingly enough, this particular guy has an actual skill, unlike most of us. He's going to Africa to work on water resources. But what about that box? It's built with our beliefs, it's got to mean something.

Our instructor seems to have anticipated this. "Well, what if…" He's back to drawing on his whiteboard, erasing those solid square walls, and replacing them with something more…flexible. "Instead of having a box…we had…a blob. More like an amoeba. And in different circumstances, maybe it takes different shapes. Someone who has grown up like you all, in a Christian culture, might be incredibly close to Jesus with what's in here," he points to his head, "but still separated in here," and he presses on his heart. And the amoeba brushes right up against the middle where Jesus is, but a thin line still maintains a barrier.

"As opposed to someone who has grown up in a culture where Christianity is unknown…who may have very little comprehension of the gospel as we understand it…but Jesus…meets them exactly where they are." And the amoeba expands to encompass even the soul farthest away from the center.

It makes perfect sense to me. But not necessarily to all of us.

"So what are you trying to say? That all of those things we came up with don't matter? That a person doesn't have to necessarily believe that Jesus is God's son, sent to earth to die on a cross for the sins of mankind?"

"No, that's not what I'm saying. Is that what you heard?" the instructor responds.

"Well, it's got to be one or the other. All of the things we said are true. We are all born sinners, and it's through Christ's death and resurrection that we are forgiven. Jesus is either the way the truth and the life, or he isn't. This is an obvious slippery slope."

"Well, what I'm hoping that you will consider, is that you live in a specific time, and a specific place. And all of that influences your understanding of God. God may be timeless, but you are used to viewing him through a certain prism, which is your worldview. There's nothing wrong with that, it's inevitable. But If we were able to carry out this exercise with Christians in say, 6th century Lebanon, I suspect that their criteria would be somewhat different from yours. If they even understood the concept at all. You're from a time and place where the individual is everything. You're products of democracy, and individual liberty. But in the past, 'we' often counted for much more than 'me'. These days we view salvation as a 'personal relationship with Christ', and it's an exclusive club, you're either in or you're out, there's no middle ground. And everything in is the elect, bound for an afterlife in heaven, and everything out...well it's all doomed to hell."

The Calvinists in the room, well they're like "no shit." They're not going to some foreign land thinking they've got to save *everyone*. Only those who God, in His infinite mercy, has predestined to receive His saving grace. And as for everyone else, well they will rightly be the

223

recipients of God's mighty wrath. Maybe not in this life, but most certainly in the next, where an eternal lake of fire awaits. And if you've got a problem with this, well take it up with God. He makes the rules, not us. This isn't just their "worldview", that's almost an insult. And if it is, well it's correct. It's New Testament Christianity. To the Calvinists, this whole exercise with Jesus in the box is a bunch of BS.

But there are plenty for whom it's not. And for some people, it's a devastating blow. One young woman is near tears. "Are you trying to say that salvation can be different for everyone, like, depending on where you're from, or what you know? That just sounds ridiculous to me. I mean, if the things I believe aren't necessarily the way to lead someone to Christ…then…then *why are we even going*? If God doesn't even need us, if just what happens to be in their heart is enough, then why would Jesus even need to die on the cross? If they don't have to specifically place their faith in it? It doesn't make any sense."

There's another popular opinion voiced from someone else—"Well God doesn't judge people for revelations they did not receive. Luke chapter 12. If someone has never heard of Jesus, they won't be judged the same as those that have."

It occurs to me that if this is true, then ignorance is bliss. About the cruelest thing you could do to another person is tell them about Jesus, if they would've been better off never knowing in the first place. It seems like something the devil himself would do.

The instructor, he's not giving us any answers. We'll have to hash those out for ourselves. And if we can't do it here, among fellow

Christians, how could we ever hope to do it half a world away where people don't necessarily see things the way we do. And I suspect he also wants to teach us a little humility.

"Listen, these conversations can be uncomfortable, but they're necessary for growth. I would just encourage you to approach your experience with an open mind. Let God be God. Don't close him in a box, and don't close your minds either."

A fellow on the row in front of me takes mild offense. "I'm not closed minded. But I am narrow minded." He supports himself with scripture. "'But small is the gate, and narrow the road that leads to life. And few they are that find it.'"

"Ah, Matthew 7:14." The anthropologist has read it. "All I'm saying, is don't limit God. He may surprise you how He shows up. You may surprise yourself, as well. Who knows, in time, that scripture may become even more meaningful for you."

———————————

I can see why it's such a comfort to be a Calvinist. It's black and white, true or false, you're either in, or you're out. But I also get why the one young lady is so despondent. 'Why are we even going?' Because once you start sliding down that slippery slope, start to peck away at the foundations of your faith, who knows when the whole thing might just come crashing down.

XXVIII

The flight to Japan is a long one, and I've got a lot of time to think. And as I still do these days, pray. It was at the airport where my mom read me the quote from that book my campus minister gave me—"We lead limited lives until we step over into the concrete world of another culture, another tradition of worship." And I couldn't help but notice the similarities between that statement and what the cultural anthropologist had advised—don't limit God, or yourself.

I've been thinking about my college campus minister a lot, actually. When I first started college, I went through a miniaturized version of the Jesus in A Box exercise on my own. I grew up Baptist, but I really had no reason to remain one other than that's how my parents raised me. And besides, it worked. So why fix it? But I was curious, and after trying out all the campus ministries of various denominational flavors, I ended up sticking with the Methodists. And it was all because of Ben, the campus minister.

He was probably only in his late twenties, but Ben seemed a lot older. He didn't make any effort to appear otherwise, he wasn't trying to necessarily fit in with the college students, he just wanted to minister to us. He was an adult. And to me, he was way cooler because of it.

Ben hadn't grown up with any particular faith at all, and it wasn't until his early twenties that he became a Christian himself. This wasn't my experience, and so it interested me.

"You basically had your pick of denominations. Baptist, Nazarene, Presbyterian. Why'd you become a Methodist?" All I really knew about Methodists from my youth was that their church was a lot smaller than mine, and their spring break ski trips seemed to be a lot more wild.

He had an answer immediately. "Because I'm not really certain how my beliefs may evolve over the next thirty years. Ten years ago I could never have imagined myself here. And in Methodism, there is room for that growth. We have some theologians who are very liberal, who believe that the truth found in the Bible isn't necessarily dependent on a literal interpretation of its text. But there are others who are far more conservative, and right now, I'm one of them. But it may not always be this way."

I liked this answer. A lot. Although at the time, it didn't really occur to me why. I don't recall giving much thought to how it might apply to me personally. Most of my crises of faith had been minor. As in "Jesus said the mustard seed is the smallest of all seeds. But in actual fact, it's not. So did He just not know this, even though He was God? Or was he just dumbing it down for His audience? Or is this an example of how literally interpreting scripture can be (gasp) wrong?" But this kind of philosophical conundrum can be resolved fairly easily, because wherever you decide to come down, there's a soft enough spot to land. We can agree to disagree. If the parable of the mustard seed presents a paradox, it's a paltry one. It's not life or death.

Or heaven and hell. I'm not sure if I'm missing the trees because of the forest, but this is a huge deal for me. I can't get over it. The tension between God's mercy and his wrath is more than I can take, I can't resolve it. And something is going to have to give. Like I've said before, the church of my childhood was a place of refuge for me. It's where I went to feel OK. And the God of my understanding, He is like the shepherd who will leave the ninety-nine sheep who are safe, to save the one that is lost. My God is love.

But in Japan, it's going to be reversed. There's not one sheep that's lost, there's ninety-nine million of them. Only one percent of the population identifies as Christian. We could have church revivals every single night, convert souls by the thousands, and still millions upon millions upon millions of people are just...damned. And they're not just some nameless faces, foreigners, outsiders...they're people, just like me. Who happen to have had the misfortune of being born in a different place. But why should it even *be* misfortunate. Where is this Good Shepherd God now?

I want to argue that this all just seems so unfair. That if God is Just, well this just isn't. And any arguments about "well, they're sinners, see. It's not God's fault, it's their own," just doesn't make any sense to me at all, because best I can tell, very few of the ninety-nine million even stand a chance. The game is rigged. If God is love, then why? Why would he go to the trouble of creating souls with a predetermined outcome of damning them to an eternity of torture?

There is no soft spot to land here, whichever side I come down on is going to be very uncomfortable. But this plane, it's about to land, too. And pretty soon, all those thoughts about who's in and who's out, the tension between God's loving mercy and His righteous wrath won't be just a perplexing paradox, one of life's mysteries I can push aside

for another day. I'm going to have to look it in the eye, face to face.
Literally.

XXIX

Kobe, Japan

1993

"Moshi moshi"

"Tom-san. Amano desu. Sushi tabemasho ka? Konban?

"Amano-san, konbanwa. Sushi tabetakunai, yo. Yakitoriya wa do?"

"Ii desu yo. Itsumo no basho? Hachi-ji ni gurai?"

"Sounds good. See you then."

My friend, Mr. Amano, has called me on the telephone at my apartment, wants to know if I want to go eat some sushi tonight. I don't. But yakitori sounds good. It's chicken, grilled and skewered on a stick, and it's delicious. He's cool with that, and we're going to meet this evening at the usual place, around eight.

I don't really speak Japanese all that well, couldn't speak a word of it when I first got here. But I've been here almost a year now, and I can get by. Amano-san humors me every once in a while, and tries to speak to me in Japanese. But like almost everyone else here, he really prefers to converse in English. It's good practice. Not that he needs it, though. Amano-san learned to speak English when he was just a kid, sometime after World War II, during the American

230

occupation of Japan. I'm not sure exactly how he got the exposure, but his English is wonderful, not like a native, but close enough. Language acquisition is easy at that age, a lot easier than it is when you're in your early twenties, like me. I sound like a buffoon. I guess as you get older, the brain gets sort of set in its ways. Fortunately for me, the Japanese people have a lot of patience.

I'm not exactly sure how old Mr. Amano is now, but he's old. Probably at least fifty. I met him in my Monday evening conversational English class where I work, at Kobe Friendship House.

As far as job assignments go, well I feel like I hit the jackpot. Kobe is amazing. It's a fairly narrow city nestled in between Osaka Bay to the south and a green mountainous region to the north, and home to a million or so people. Friendship House is staffed by a missionary couple in their early forties who have made Japan their permanent home, and every couple of years, they get a new volunteer like me to help them in their ministry. Mike and Sarah are great, and they truly love the people here. Japan doesn't have any real humanitarian needs, so we offer what they want—English classes. That's my skill, being able to speak. And then after the conversational courses, we have tea and cookies, and the missionary couple will lead a short chapel service in Japanese, and share about the fundamentals of our faith. Occasionally they'll ask me to share at chapel, and either Mike or Sarah will translate into Japanese. When I'm asked what else I might be able to do, I tell them I can play guitar a little, and we sometimes sing a few tunes during the service. The chords to Kumbaya are pretty much the same in any language. Some of the

Japanese think the guitar is pretty cool, so I also teach a class for whoever is interested.

And that's pretty much my job. The missionary couple is great, but they've got a busy family with two kids to raise, and outside of Friendship House hours, I'm pretty much on my own. I can do whatever I want. I try to be a steward of my time, and I use it to develop relationships with the people who come to Friendship House. For instance, Monday mornings I play tennis with a group of middle aged housewives who take one of my classes later in the week. The Japanese are meticulous rule followers, and they always show up at precisely the same time, and after exactly fifty minutes of tennis, we spend the last ten minutes of our hour raking sand through the fake grass court to prepare it for the next group. Nobody makes us, but it's expected, and thinking of others is a matter of integrity for them.

Things like this make an impression on me. I've found the differences in culture and values to be fascinating. Stereotypes aren't always accurate, of course, but there's a reason they exist. And Americans can be stereotyped as assertive. Braggadocious. Brash. The squeaky wheel gets the grease. But in Japan, the nail that sticks up gets hammered down. They're much more interested in fitting in than in standing out. Both ways of being can be beneficial. In a homogenous country like Japan, where you've got over a hundred million people crammed into a space the size of California, harmony is very helpful. But in America, with our wide open spaces, we've got a lot more solo artists.

I love talking about all of this with Amano-san. He originally offered to pay me. He considered our semi-weekly meetings an extra

English lesson, and he felt obligated to compensate me for my time. I told him that wasn't necessary, of course, because what else do I have to do anyway. And I secretly hoped it would be an opportunity to practice my Japanese without being embarrassed. We rarely speak Japanese though, simply because the things we end up discussing are well beyond my limited grasp of the language. And besides, Amano always pays for dinner, so I figure he gets to pick who gets to practice.

I feel like it's me who always ends up learning the most, though. Amano-san is a professor of some sort at a university in town, and he's a good teacher, a real sensei. Soon after I got to Japan I had read a book about some of the cultural differences an American like me might encounter living in Japan, and one part that puzzled me was about an approach to conversation. It's the sort of thing I like to ask Amano-san about.

"So I read this book about adjusting to Japan when I first got here, and it said things like Japanese men might introduce you to their wives and say things like 'please excuse my wife, she is ugly' or she can't cook well. Do people really say that?"

Amano just laughs. "Not exactly. But something like that. In Japan we don't like to be seen as arrogant. We would not usually say something like 'Oh my wife is the best cook ever.' Or 'let me introduce you to my beautiful wife.' We think it sounds rude. But of course things don't always translate perfectly between languages. But you do kind of the same thing, Tom-san."

"I do? How so?"

"People ask you to play the guitar. And you say, 'oh, please excuse my lousy guitar playing. I'm not very good.' But your guitar playing is very nice. It speaks for itself, you don't have to do it yourself."

He's wrong. My guitar playing is only so-so, but I think I understand his point.

"Ah so ka." I see. It's a good opportunity to slip in a little Japanese.

"See, you are like a Japanese, Tom-san." He smiles, a bit red in the face from the two beers he's drank, and he offers me a toast.

"Kampai!" And I meet his mug of Kirin with my own.

"So Amano-san, I have another question. The book also said that in America our conversations are like a tennis match. I say something, and then you respond, and then it's my turn, and it's kind of a back and forth exchange. But a conversation in Japan isn't like tennis. It's supposed to be like bowling. That makes no sense to me. I say something, then you just say whatever you want, doesn't matter if it has anything to do with the topic at hand? I don't get it."

He thinks for a long time. Maybe he's showing me. I hit the ball to him, and he's just letting it sit there.

But finally he says "Like bowling. Interesting. I will think more about this." He taps his temple and smiles as he slides out of the booth. It's late, and it's time for him to go. It's a Wednesday night, but I don't have anywhere in particular to be in the morning. Thursday classes at Friendship House are for high schoolers and college students, and they don't start until five.

"Arigato, Tom-san." Mr. Amano bows deeply. "I enjoyed 'bowling' with you."

I bow to him as well. "Hai, domo arigato gozaimasu. Thank you sir. Matta Getsuyoubi?"

"Yep, see you at class on Monday."

"My name is Hannako Nakagawa, and I am twenty-two years old. I live in Takarazuka, Japan, with my parents, and my two sisters. I enjoy nature, going for walks, and visiting Japanese temples. Soon, I will graduate from university. I wish to continue my studies in the United States."

Hannako is another one of my students from Friendship House, and if there's anything wrong with her speech, it's my fault. I wrote it. She's quite an impressive art student, but her English, it's worse than my Japanese. And to pass an interview for art school in the US, she's going to have to fake it. I'm not sure how memorizing a short speech is going to help, but she asked me if I could coach her, and this is what I came up with. I've listened to her go over it at least ten times, and I think she's finally got it.

I'm not really sure how Hannako is going to get by the interview, but I'm pretty sure if she can, she's really going to love it in America. She's sort of like one of those nails that stick up, but so far, she hasn't let anyone hammer her back down. She does her own thing. And right now, her thing is banana trees. I have no idea why, Hannako doesn't either, but it's all she likes to paint. They're not even that beautiful, but somehow she makes them so, and I suppose that's what art is. Finding something meaningful in the mundane. And she's good at it.

I don't think Hannako feels very encouraged as an artist in Japan, which I suppose is why she'd like to continue her studies in the US. In her country, there's a right way and a wrong way to do practically everything, and I guess being passionate about tropical fruit at this stage of her career isn't exactly impressing her professors. But what do I know, I have no eye for these sort of things, and our mutual linguistic limitations prevent us from delving into it very deeply. But it does seem to me that most of the Japanese art forms I've been exposed to seem almost scientific. As if there are certain steps you have to master, and it must take years and years of practiced repetition. Things like calligraphy. Or origami. A Japanese tea ceremony. And a Zen Garden. The simplicity seems to belie the complexity. I don't think they have many one-hit-wonders here.

Not that art has to be wild and free. Or an accident. It's certainly not. But I just think that Hannako wants to be the type of artist that is perhaps…unexpected. Unique. I don't know any of this for sure, it's more just something I feel, an impression left after conversations that are more like playing a game of charades than bowling or tennis. I wish I could write her a little speech that captures this sentiment better than the short little biography I gave her. But I'm pretty sure that when the professors in Baltimore see her banana trees, they'll be able to hear it.

————————————

Hannako, she's definitely sure she wants to go to the US. But heaven she's not so certain about. She comes to our Thursday night college class, and afterwards the students sometimes hang out quite a while. On one particular evening I overhear Hannako and Sarah, the missionary wife, having a conversation about Christianity. Sarah's got her Bible open to Revelations and she's reading.

"…'There shall be no more death, neither sorrow, nor crying. Neither shall there be any more pain.' Doesn't that sound wonderful to you, Hannako? That's what heaven will be like one day. And all you have to do to go there when you die is confess with your mouth that Jesus is Lord, and believe in your heart that God raised Him from the dead, and then you will be saved."

I have to give it to Sarah, at least she's going with the carrot first. When I was a kid we weren't always so fortunate. But then my cynical side starts thinking maybe her husband Mike will come in later with some sort of good cop/ bad cop routine, and let Hannako know what's supposed to happen if she makes the wrong choice. It's a thought that immediately makes me feel guilty, I mean, this is Hannako's eternal soul we're talking about.

Of course Sarah offers to lead her in prayer if it's a decision she'd like to make, that's just how it's done. Hannako declines, but with profuse politeness and regret, she's Japanese after all. She doesn't want to offend. But it's not because she doesn't believe Sarah. It's because she does.

Her reasoning stuns me. Turns out, she doesn't *want* God to wipe away every tear from her eye. It's not an image of eternity that carries any appeal for her. No sorrow? No pain? Then how is what's left supposed to be beautiful? I guess to Hannako, the absence of pain and suffering isn't bliss. It's just...boredom. And an eternity of that would be terrifying. Eventually you'd scream out for something to make it stop.

"No, no, you're thinking about it all wrong. Heaven will be the opposite of boring, it'll be AMAZING! Can't you just imagine?" Sarah wants to rescue her from her thinking. I can't say I share Hannako's perspective. Freedom from worry and grief sounds pretty glorious to me. But maybe I've been limiting myself. Maybe without love you don't have hate, you just have apathy. And if the absence of God's mercy isn't wrath, then what is it...abandonment?

238

XXX

March 1994

Hiroshima, Japan

"Excuse me Sir...could you tell me how to get to the bus station?"

This is my first trip to Hiroshima, and I have no idea how to get around. I've only got something like three months left in this country, and for me, this city is a must see. I went to a conference in Nagasaki this time last year, and after this visit, I'll have been to the only two cities in the world to be obliterated by nuclear weapons.

Just walking around, you'd never know it. It's a thriving city, everyone looks happy and healthy, and the cherry blossoms are just starting to bloom. I suspect the ones in Washington D.C are about ready to do the same. The ones there were a gift from Japan in 1912, back when our two countries were on friendly terms. The man who made it happen was a Japanese biochemist named Takamine. He was also one of the first to chemically isolate epinephrine, which he called adrenaline, so anyone who's ever died and been resuscitated with epi, well they owe this man a debt of gratitude.

I suspect this little side excursion will probably be my last, though, and as I'm traveling by myself, I've had a lot of time to reflect on my time here. I love Japan. Not like 'Oh, this is a great place to visit, I recommend you put it high on your list of really cool places to see.' Although it is that. I love it because I've had a good life here. I've traveled, of course. The ancient capital of Kyoto is just a couple of hours away from Kobe, and I had a chance to visit all the famous temples and pagodas there. I got to train in judo at a real Japanese dojo. And although I didn't climb it, I did get to see Mount Fuji, which is an accomplishment in itself. It's often hidden in the haze, but I was fortunate to be there on a clear day, and its snow-capped peak was silhouetted against a crystal blue sky. It was beautiful.

But I've also done all the other things that make a life worth living. I've gained independence, I feel like I've grown up, I had meaningful work. I made a best friend, said goodbye to others, and even though I was told not to, I probably fell in love at least once.

My best friend was Junichi. He was one of the few people I didn't meet from Friendship House, just saw him strumming an acoustic 12 string Gibson guitar one afternoon outside the train station in the city center, and that was pretty much it. We were immediately friends. I'm not sure if it was a coincidence or not, but he was also one of the only Christians I would meet. It kind of makes sense if you think about it, though. If Junichi was a nail that stuck out, well he got hammered down so hard he came sticking out the other side. One look at him would tell you he wasn't going to survive as a salaryman, what with his long hair and overall scruffy exterior. I think he just never found the peace he was looking for on the eastern shore of the ocean, and so he sought it on the other side. It's not unusual at all, I know plenty of Americans who do the exact same thing.

240

I suppose the first thing about my country that soothed him was the sound. Man, did he love the music. It wasn't long before we would meet regularly at Suma Beach where he lived, and it was unbelievable how much he knew about American rock music, circa the early 70's. He'd want me to play Ry Cooder, Gram Parsons, just people I had never even heard of. I still have no idea where he learned it all, there wasn't any World Wide Web. The closest I could get to what he wanted was The Eagles.

Eventually, Junichi had turned to spirituality, too, and when I told him what I was doing in Japan, he just smiled and told me he was a Christian as well, and he went to a Japanese Baptist Church. Small world.

And then Miki, I'm pretty sure I was in love with her before I ever even met her. Her mom is the secretary at Friendship House, and I'd been hearing about her basically since I got here. Their family had lived several places overseas, she spent her childhood in Germany, went to high school in England, and these days she's studying piano at Juilliard in New York City. Even Sarah, the missionary wife, just gushed about her, how's she's *so* talented, and wears these big hoop earrings and her hair in long curls. She stands out. Of course I don't let on, but I secretly can't wait to meet her, and my first Christmas in Japan, she comes home.

"Miki to asobi ni iku, ne?" Her mom is telling me that Miki and I should go out and have fun, or at least that's what she means. What she literally says is I should 'go play with Miki.' And that sounds alright by me. Miki didn't grow up in Kobe, doesn't really have many friends here other than her family, so she's like "why not?" We basically spend the whole Christmas break together, going to movies, eating out. Playing, I guess. Everyone has been looking forward to her visit, and it feels like a privilege I get to spend all this time with her. Before she goes back to school, she puts on a mini-performance with the baby grand piano at Friendship House, and it's just out of this world. I have no appreciation for the classical music she plays, but it's like nothing I've ever seen or heard, being that close to that kind of mastery. She's truly gifted. Miki speaks German, English, and of course Japanese, but it's that piano in which she is the most fluent. It says everything.

Also before she leaves, we have the closest thing to a real date I've had in a long time. We hold hands during a movie, and after dinner, we go down to the harbor by the water. I place one ear bud from my headphones into her ear, put the other in my own, and we listen to a mix tape I've made full of songs by Journey and Queen. It's the best date I've ever been on. I hate it when she goes back to New York, but on all her other school breaks, we've picked right back up where we left off. She's never been far from my mind.

These are the kind of things I'm going to remember when I leave Japan. My relationships with Miki and Junichi, that move me, yeah. But also my connections with Amano-san, and Hannako. I guess the speech I prepared worked, because she made it to Baltimore, and I can't wait to hear how it went. And there are so many others it's hard to keep count. Relationships are what make life mean something, it's what we are here for, and I feel beyond blessed for the life I've had in Japan. I never could've made it if I would've felt isolated.

Not that it's all been easy. I buck up against some of the "rules" now and then, can't always be bothered to obey all the signs, and I still wear shorts when it's sweltering even though it's considered childish. And you're never completely sure that someone is telling you exactly what they mean. Not that they're being dishonest, but they'll go to great lengths to avoid confrontation. Sometimes yes, really means no.

But nothing about this is wrong, it's just different. And so far as the things that bothered me, well it was on me to adjust. I came to kind of like corn on my pizza. And the virtual silence on buses and trains stopped being unnerving and I learned to savor it.

———————————

Another great thing about Japan is that people are extremely helpful. That's why when I asked this man how to find the bus stop here in Hiroshima, I already knew he was going to help me.

"Sumimasen, basutei wa doko desuka?"

It's not a surprise when he answers me in English.

"Eh, bus stop. Let me see…"

It's also not a surprise when he can't quite find the right words to tell me, even though I'm sure he knows where it is. I almost expect it when instead of telling me, he just figures it'll be easier to show me. He's almost apologetic as he says "Please. This way," and beckons me to follow him. But after that, well that part is truly serendipitous.

Mr. Matsumoto, that's the man's name, he's quite familiar with the city. It's the only place he's ever lived. Not only does he know where everything is now, he also remembers pretty much where it used to be, too. When I told him I was looking for the bus to Peace

Memorial Park, he suddenly stopped, looked at me and smiled. Patted his chest and said, "I was nine years old." Out of a population of 300,000 people, nearly half were either immediately incinerated, or died within the year from the devastating effects of the most destructive bomb ever dropped. Mr. Matsumoto was one of the lucky ones.

If I thought that perhaps he was going to harbor bitterness, I was wrong. In fact, he insists on joining me as I tour the memorial. I don't know what else Matsumoto-san had planned for the day, he's dressed in a sport coat and slacks, but whatever it was, he shelves it and he literally becomes my guide. And what would've already been a most solemn experience seems almost holy, for here I am, walking next to someone who survived. Everything I see appears different because of it. Neither of us speaks the other's language well enough to give much of a voice to what is so meaningful, at least to me, but perhaps it's better this way. I don't need him to explain to me what it was like, the images are everywhere. Past and present. Silence fits.

———————————

Afterwards Mrs. Matsumoto joins us for tea at a little shop just outside the peace park. We enjoy one of those conversations that, due to our limited fluency, takes place very slowly, and with great deliberation. It takes patience, but it also feels like victory. They understand me, I understand them. It is not casual. This couple, of everything I have just seen and felt in Hiroshima, they will be my lasting memory. Out of all the destruction, they will be my image even thirty years later, and I already know it now.

Which is good, because the lasting image from my visit to the memorial in Nagasaki is rice. Black rice. On display there in the museum is a little bento box, like a child would carry to school for their lunch. Half of the box is empty, the rice is gone, eaten I suppose. Maybe at school they started lunch a little before eleven. Because at 11:02, the bomb exploded, and the remaining rice was charred and petrified right there in the bento box, but it's unmistakeable what it is. It's rice. Just unfinished, like all the hopes and dreams of whatever kid was eating it. It's sad, obviously, but the rice will be my lasting memory of Nagasaki, and I knew it as soon as I saw it.

I don't know if the bombs were a greater good or not. If lives had to be lost in order to save them. If Japan was never going to surrender without it being overwhelmingly obvious that they had to. I don't know how far back in time you'd have to travel to reach a point where there was a better alternative. Back before both countries were trying to establish their international influence. Before there were embargoes, and Japan was starved for fuel, ready to do something drastic when they felt like they were fighting for their own survival. Certainly prior to Pearl Harbor. But I don't think anybody is completely righteous here, both sides ultimately did things that could be considered atrocious, or depending on your perspective, necessary. Some things justified and rationalized, other things shrouded in shame. Never officially owned up to in the open.

But maybe 1912 would've been a good enough place to start. Back when we exchanged cherry blossoms instead of bombs. I'm grateful that I visited Hiroshima last, that my most recent memory will be the Matsumotos. I'll remember the rice, too, but it's always better to leave with some hope. And they've given me that. The Peace Park isn't about assigning blame. It's not about anybody being guilty or innocent. Mr. Matsumoto didn't deserve to survive any more than the little boy or girl eating rice in Nagasaki, but of course that child didn't get what they deserved either. Maybe none of us do.

I'm not sure I deserved Matsumoto-san's kindness either, but he freely gave it anyway. Because maybe he knows that peace requires something more than just the absence of conflict. You can't just lay down the weapons of destruction, something has to actually change. He may have had every right to be resentful, even if the extent of his anger was to simply ignore me. 'Find the bus stop on your own, foreigner.' He might've thought that's what I deserved, to be ignored, that I'd earned no right to even participate in the Peace Park. How could I even understand it? Nobody would blame him.

But he didn't. Instead, he showed kindness to a stranger. And patience. Goodness. He sacrificed his intentions for the day to ensure that I enjoyed mine just a little bit more. This is an act of genuine love. My Chrisitianity teaches me that these virtues are the fruit of God's Spirit. And if the Breath of God isn't in Mr. Matsumoto, I can't imagine where else his peace could have come from. Somehow, the God that I want to put into a box, that I want to define with my own beliefs, that I want to limit to a time and place that I can comprehend, has already been here. I'm not here to share the Gospel with Mr. Matsumoto, he's sharing his Good News with me. What do I have to tell him about heaven and hell when he's lived more of both than I could ever imagine. For him, hell wasn't any sort of destination after death, it was a literal place here on earth, and God didn't make it. We did. As a

246

punishment for pride and arrogance and an utter refusal to surrender even in the face of such obvious internal impotence. For that, you get hell.

Fortunately for Mr. Matsumoto, hell wasn't just an alternative to heaven, but maybe it was a path to it. Maybe in the end, it was necessary. Maybe losing lives really did save them. Perhaps that's the gospel I'm supposed to share, or maybe even learn. That the road to heaven may well seem to be upside down, or backwards. That when you choose to follow the way of Jesus, sometimes you have to lose your own life to find it. It's Good News that I hope I've been able to share in this country in whatever way I could. Maybe the seeds I've sown will someday do somebody some good, will blossom into something beautiful. But I know that whatever I leave here will pale in comparison to what I'm taking home. And someday when I need it most, perhaps I will find that something has grown in my own heart as well, like a little bonsai tree I never even knew was there.

XXXI

Kobe, Japan

June 1994

I'm doing a lot of things in Japan for the last time. My last conversational class, my last chapel, last time to sing "Amazing Grace" in Japanese. There's a phrase I've learned here–*mono no aware*. Literally it means the "pathos of things." But I think Dr. Seuss captured its sentiment better. It means "Don't cry because it's over. Smile because it happened." It's about joy and sadness existing at the same time. Everything is impermanent.

I'm saving my last night for Miki, of course, but I have to have one last beer with Amano-san before I go. It took me a while to get comfortable drinking one with him. Or two. He noticed. And he's wondered why.

"Short answer? Because it's a sin."

This surprises him, and his eyes get big. "It's a sin? Why?"

I laugh and give him a shrug. "I don't really know. It's just how I was raised. 'Don't Drink', it's a rule. At least for the type of Christianity I grew up with."

248

"If you think it is a sin means you think it is wrong then?"

"I don't think it's a sin. At least I don't anymore. Or at least not for me. In the Bible it says that the Kingdom of God is not a matter of what we eat or drink, but of peace and joy. The fruit of God's spirit. But it also says that it is better not to drink wine or anything else that may cause someone else to stumble. Like Mike and Sarah, they don't drink. Or at least I don't think so. And maybe if they saw me here, having a beer with you, it would be a problem for them. So I guess that's my reasoning now."

"So you hide it?"

"I'm not sure I'm hiding it, am I? I just don't want them to know." I laugh at the obvious contradiction. "I guess it's complicated."

"I thought sin is like the ten commandments. Same for everyone. Do not kill. Do not steal. Do not lie. But it's not a sin to lie about drinking, if the person you lie to doesn't drink, because drinking is a sin. I do not understand your sin."

We both laugh, a little bit drunk. It sounds absurd. This might be the last conversation Amano-san and I have about God, but it's certainly not the first. He's been coming to Friendship House since way before I got here, even longer than Mike and Sarah have been running it. Yet he's not a Christian, or at least that's not all he is. There are too many things he struggles with.

"Truth?" I ask. Amano nods. "I don't understand all of it either. There are things I struggle with, too. Like you do. I wouldn't want Mike and Sarah to know I'm drinking beer with you, but there are other things I was never comfortable talking to them about."

249

"Why?" He wonders.

"Not sure. Part of it is I don't want them to judge me. I want them to think certain things about me, even if they're not true. I don't believe everything they do, not anymore. And what if I'm wrong? What if I'm wrong about everything?"

"I don't think you have to worry about that, Tom-san. Whatever you believe, you're almost certainly wrong about some of it. Why do you worry so much about being right anyway? There is more to it than just being right or wrong."

"More to what?"

"More to *everything*. More to your life. How else would you grow if you're unwilling to be wrong? You should welcome it."

I don't know what to say to this, and we sit in silence.

Finally Amano-san breaks it. "I've been thinking about…bowling. You remember? You read in a book that conversation in Japanese is like bowling."

I do.

"I think that whoever wrote that meant we Japanese are perhaps more respectful. More patient in conversation. We allow each other to finish. We take turns. Whereas conversations in English may be a bit more lively. More assertive. But maybe whoever wrote it also hasn't been out drinking in a Japanese pub at the end of sixteen hour work days, eh Tom-san?" He laughs, and sips his beer, then gets serious again.

250

"I have a different thought that may just be my own, but what I've learned, at least from conversation at Friendship House, is this…In tennis we may banter about, enjoy a playful back and forth, but ultimately, there may be a point to be won. You try to hit the ball where I cannot retrieve it, or return my solid serve with a better one of your own. Somebody wins, and somebody loses. It is a view that is compatible with a western way of thinking. Of duality. Although I'm not sure this is what your book meant." He pauses for a moment, gathers his thoughts, and I don't interrupt. "Are you familiar with language branching, Tom-san?"

"With what?"

"Let's order another beer. You are going to need it." Amano smiles, signals the bartender.

Our beers come, and Mr. Amano begins.

"As you know from your study of Japanese, Tom-san, our languages are very different. Not just in the words, but also in the way in which they are arranged. In any language, a sentence has a center. A nucleus. A subject. And then all the words that describe it, or tell what it does, that paint the picture, tend to lean either to the left or the right of the center. If the subject is the tree trunk, the modifiers are the branches. English is more right-branching than left. 'Tom drank three beers.'" Amano laughs. "Japanese is almost entirely left-branching, however. As we acquire language in childhood, significant differences may develop in how we think, how we form memories, and even how we conceptualize the world."

"Somebody's been studying."

"I know, I know." Amano-san smiles. "It's just that your question is very interesting to me."

"I thought you'd forgotten," I say.

"Oh no. I have thought much about it. Now instead of tennis, where every play ends in a point one way or the other, consider bowling. It's not that our conversation has to be unrelated, that we cannot share a topic back and forth. But perhaps comments can be connected without canceling each other out. And it's something more than courtesy, more than just conceding a point. I can bowl a strike, and you can bowl a strike at exactly the same time. My being right, does not require your being wrong. We can be connected by what we have in common, not be defined by our differences. Your only opponent is the one within. Not everything must be a paradox. This is a kind of non-duality. I think we Japanese are more comfortable with it. At least with the Christians who come here, the way they present your religion is binary. God and the devil. Heaven and hell. Good and evil."

———————————

Well, he couldn't have described my perspective better if he tried. It's binary. Either everything is meant to be, or nothing has any meaning at all. There are either a few select souls we are meant to seek and find, or if not, why are we even going at all? But I'm gathering that this is not a tension that I'm supposed to resolve, but rather, learn to live with. Maybe this is growing beyond my previous limits.

Later, when I get home, I'll try and explain some of this to my mom. I could tell when she read that quote in the airport about

252

stepping into another culture, it meant as much to her as it did to me. She took it as some sort of sign, that her son was going to be okay. God had a plan, whatever it was. And that it would be for my good.

But when I get home and try to share my experience with her beyond what I've written in letters, I'm afraid that she's not going to see it that way. I have more questions than answers. I'm still not sure what all I believe, but in a sort of addition by subtraction, I know what I don't.

"But mom, I don't believe in hell anymore. At least not like I did before." I'm certain that this is going to break her heart, or at the least, disappoint her. Because the center of Christianity, it's nucleus, is the cross. In Latin, literally the crux. And this is kind of ironic, because if you look up the definition of crux, it's not a solution. A crux is a puzzling problem, an unresolved question. It's a central point, and understanding it is essential to everything else. So if there's no hell, then what else is left for the cross to even mean? Questioning hell is questioning the crucifixion.

But my mom, she's a surprise. "Your grandpa didn't either." It's that simple, and I wonder why she wouldn't have shared this sooner. My only memories of her dad are of him either lying in a bed, or sitting in his easy chair smoking Marlboro reds. The same ones that caused his stroke, I suspect. Which is why he was never anywhere but his bed or that chair. He couldn't even light his own cigarettes, and when I visited, he'd let me do it with his Zippo lighter. It's still one of my favorite smells. Well those last seven or eight years, I guess for him it was hell. It was a prison.

"I told him that I didn't agree with him," my mom says. "But I couldn't tell him he was wrong, either. And that's pretty much what I'd say to you now."

Turns out, my mom is a much better bowler than I'd given her credit for. She might not think I bowled a strike, but she'll let me figure that out on my own. Maybe the best teachers do.

The cross is a paradox of its own. It's a symbol of God's love for us, but one only made necessary by His apparent need to punish sin. It's a sort cosmic justice that can be very confusing. "This is how much God loves me...But only because I am completely unloveable otherwise." Or maybe...I'm just being self-centered. Maybe if I stopped making it all about me, I could find something more meaningful in between the two extremes. Perhaps the death of Jesus on a cross wasn't meant to change the way God is looking at us. It would make much more sense to me if that were the case. If the cross were simply meant to change the way that we look at God. If it means that no matter what, God is with us. That not even one of us will be abandoned. Even if the only sheep who is lost, is me.

XXXII

It's been almost a year since I moved out, a year since that time with the ketamine, and it hasn't been easy for Tami. Understandably so, watching me stay clean now that I'm out on my own. Away from her. Kicking me out set me free. Like maybe she was the problem all along, that I was just medicating myself to make a bad situation bearable.

Or at least that's what she thinks. None of it is true, of course. She wasn't the problem, and I'm nowhere near clean. But she thinks I am, because that's what I tell her, and it's hard to know any different. But I don't plan on lying to her forever, just until I can get my shit together, so what good would it do her to know the truth now? It would only hurt her more.

Tami's not the only person I claim to care about who gets lied to. My buddy Randall Wayne, he's on that list, too. I've been lying to him for almost as long, almost as often. He transplanted himself up to Denver several years back, and it's made for a convenient place to hide out every once in a while, trying to kick. Right now it's spring break, and Tami has taken the boys down to the Alabama beach house. She might've been willing to let me come along, but I'm not really in any shape to do it, and I can't let her know that. Randall, however, well I figure he'll understand. Maybe he won't even be able to tell I'm still using.

255

"You're still using." Dammit. He can tell. Well, he can't tell I'm using, but he can tell that I'm not, and it means the same thing. I've been lying to him. Again.

"How long has it been?" We're riding up the ski lift at Breckenridge, and I just told him this is my last run. Even though we've been on the mountain less than an hour. But I'm exhausted, I feel like I could pass out. Today I just can't fake it.

"How long has what been?" I ask.

"How long have you been trying to *quit*?" He says "quit" with such sarcasm.

"Well...I guess coming up on seven years or so."

RW, he shakes his head. "You know I love you man. But..."

I don't want to look at him.

"Aren't you afraid?"

I shrug. "Of what?"

"I don't know, of like, killing somebody? Of killing yourself? Or at least afraid of getting fucking caught?"

I think for a second, and my answer is certain. "Nope." And I'm not.

"Do you think maybe you should be?"

I'm not used to hearing him talk like this. He's not only always believed me, but he's always believed *in* me, too. If anybody can do this, I can. His shared belief matters, but this sounds like he's wavering. I look down at my skis and boots, dangling over the mountain, and my feet feel like they weigh a thousand pounds, like it would be so much easier just to fall off.

"I'm sorry, man. I hate lying to you, but I don't really know what else to do. You've saved my life so many times, brother. For real." And he has. There's no doubt about that. RW spent four days with me holed up in a cabin just this past New Years. I supposedly came up to ski but I was so sick I couldn't do anything but sit there and suffer. And RW, he fucking sat with me. We've been best friends since we were high school freshmen, and only a best friend would do something like that. And he's done that so many times I've lost count. Whatever I need, he's always there.

"What are you gonna do different? You've been coming up here for weed for what, two years? Three? It doesn't seem like it's made any difference. How does it even help?"

"It might not seem like it, but it does. It helps me sleep." Without cannabis, the insomnia…it's indescribable. Staying awake four, five days straight. A week. Some people say it can take up to three months to start to feel somewhat normal when you come off opioids, but I just don't have that kind of time.

I sigh. "The truth is, I dunno what the fuck I'm gonna do. I'm out of magic bullets. Keep trying pot and kratom I guess. Eventually I'll get it. I have to."

"Yeah, you do man. You don't have a choice."

257

RW, he has no idea exactly how right he is. It's time to get off the lift, and it's all I can do not to fall down. "I'm done, dude. I'm gonna ski back to the condo."

"You need me to come with you?"

"Nah brother. I'm good. Go ski with Brian and Chan. You guys enjoy. I'll be better by tonight. We'll go into town and get dinner." A couple of other guys we grew up with have come up for the week as well, and RW, he gives me a fist bump and skis off to catch them. I appreciate his offer to babysit me, but I'm not that bad. This week I don't need saving. But later tonight, I'm going to get a chance to return the favor.

_____

"Man, I'm bummed you had to go in earlier. You feel any better?" Brian asks me.

"Meh." Brian and Chan, they don't know anything about what's really wrong with me. Altitude sickness is my alibi, and I'm carrying around one of those portable oxygen canisters they sell in the souvenir shops for credibility.

"Come on brother, you gotta rally," RW tells me. "We're going to Eric's to eat. Get your ass ready." He claps me on the back and his enthusiasm is just contagious enough to get me going.

"Alright, alright." And I am hungry. One of the benefits of eating ganja gummies all day, I guess. And Eric's, it's a place, not a person, and I have fond memories of going there when I've come to Breck in better days. "Let's do it."

"Hey brother, you got any of those drinks left?" RW's not whispering, but he's not announcing it either. Brian and Chan, it's not that they're Puritans, but they just say no to pot. And RW wants to know if he can have one of my infused drinks.

I smile, or try to, and hand him one. "Go easy. They're seventy-five milligrams."

"Shit. I *live* here, brother. I'm a local."

I shrug. "Suit yourself, motherfucker."

We're not the only ones who love Eric's, the place is packed, and we've got a while to wait for a table. The other three, they get beers, including RW, but I figure he's done this before. He's a big boy. Downstairs at Eric's they've got some games, pinball machines and shit to pass the time. You wouldn't really think that something as stupid as skee-ball would be do any good for opioid detox, but I'll be damned if it doesn't. I learned this way back at a birthday party for one of Tyson's friends at a Chuck-E Cheese or some other such miserable place. But something about scoring, all those lights, bells, and whistles going off, it does something to dopamine. Ask the casino designers. It works. Not great mind you, but I feel just a wee bit better than before.

But RW, he must not, because he's kind of being a dick. Which is highly unlike him. I sneak a peek at his bottle, some kind of hard cider type of thing, and it appears to be at least half full. Maybe he's just tired.

"Wanna hit?" I offer him my oxygen.

259

"Those things are a waste of fucking money," he grumbles.

"Alright man, let's just go sit down. I think Brian and Chan are still in the bar."

The bar's not that busy, and we all four find stools up against the wall to wait. RW, he's over in the corner off to my right, like he doesn't really want to be here. Chan looks at me, like 'what's with him?' and I just shrug, like 'who the fuck knows.' I'm not sure how long we sit there, but it isn't long, nobody even has to buy another round, before they announce "Brian, party of four. Brian, party of four." It's a relief. I'm ready to eat, and three of us, we start to head on over to the seating area. But RW doesn't.

"Randall, let's go. Hey. RW." But Randall, he ain't saying shit. It's kind of dark in here, and all I can really see is that he appears to have leaned back into the corner. Like he fell asleep or something.

Chan shouts at him, "Hey Wayne, let's go, man. Table's ready."

I'm closest to him, and I step over to try and maybe shake him awake or something, but it doesn't look like he's asleep at all. It looks like he's fucking dead.

I should know. I've seen every stage of cyanosis at one time or another, from the pale pallor of mildly low oxygen levels to the ashen-shade of death. And right now, RW's face is completely gray and his lips are blue. It's surreal, seeing your best friend like that, when ten minutes ago, you were just talking, even if he was kind of being an ass. I think I holler for someone to call 911, or if I didn't, I should've, but the first thing I actually do is try to feel for a pulse. He's kind of slumped back into the corner with his chin in his chest, and to get my fingers into his neck I have to lift his chin up, and I instinctively reach for the back of his mandible and thrust his jaw forward like I'd do in the operating room. And the huge rush of air that comes out, it's a relief. Both for him and for me. I think I understand what's happened here.

For whatever reason, RW passed out. Who knows why, but the cannabis and cider combo couldn't have helped. If he would've wobbled off his bar stool, we would've noticed, but instead he got stabilized in the corner, with his chin tucked into his chest, and he obstructed his airway. Like a severe example of sleep apnea. Once I relieved the obstruction with a jaw thrust, he can breathe again, and the initial rush of relief is followed a few seconds later by inspiration. He's breathing again. In a few breaths his color begins to return, but I continue to render medical aid. Which according to our buddy Brian, consists of slapping him upside the head telling him to wake the fuck up. And within two or three minutes, he finally does.

"What? What's going on? What are you doing?" He's confused, not quite certain where he is.

"Man, you were passed *out*."

We finally all get over to the table, and as might be expected, inappropriate hilarity ensues.

"Dude...you were fucking dead! You were gray!"

Chan and Brian, they're still trying to figure out exactly what happened. "I just saw you jump over there real quick, and next thing I know you're beating the shit out of him, hollering 'Randall! Wake up!'" Brian says.

"Whaddya mean I was dead…?" RW is still a little confused.

"Well, you weren't," I say. "But you were well on your way."

"What if they wouldn't have called for our table at just the right time?" Chan says.

"I guess we woulda said, oh well," Brian thinks. "Make it a party of three."

And this is just the funniest fucking thing I've ever heard. I can't stop laughing. It's like I've saved up seven years worth of chuckles and they're all coming up at once. But then I start to notice Randall, he isn't really laughing. He's sweating. His bald head is beaded, and he doesn't look so hot.

I try to get serious. "You ok brother? Seriously…"

"Yeah, yeah. I'm fine."

"Ok, for real. Do you have any chest pain? Do you feel short of breath? Any numbness, tingling, anything at all?" This could've all been started by something more than just a marijuana drink, maybe it was an MI or something. Randall is pushing fifty.

He just shakes his head. "No…I feel fine. But maybe we should get this shit to go."

———————————

I'm not certain what would've happened to RW had we not gotten him breathing again exactly when we did. It's possible that his inspiratory instincts would've overcome the obstruction, and he could've revived himself. But I doubt it. By this time his blood pressure had undoubtedly dropped, his brain wasn't getting much blood flow, and the little it did get had no oxygen in it. Without oxygen, his heart rate would've slowed, and eventually it would fibrillate, not really beat at all, just sort of flail about like a bag full of worms, until everything finally just…stopped. If only he could've just fallen it would've fixed everything, relieved the obstruction, restored blood flow to his brain. But instead, he stayed propped up in that corner not making a sound, just slowly dying.

Not that I'm blaming it all on the cannabis, there must have been a lot of factors involved, including bad luck, but the infused drink I gave him certainly didn't help. And truth be told, it's not helping me any, either.

_____

People don't just pick their drug of choice at random, there's a reason. Stimulants, depressants, hallucinogens, they all have a certain appeal, an ability to fill a void, to act as an artificial substitute for something the users lack, or think they do. Need power? Here's cocaine. Need love? Have some heroin. And it works, at least for awhile. At least until it doesn't. I'm generalizing here, I know, none of this is black and white, but that doesn't make it untrue. So other than help me sleep, what exactly is the cannabis contributing?

Everybody has naturally occurring cannabinoid molecules, and the prime time for their receptors to proliferate is during adolescence. That time of life when you're a teenager, and ready to break out on your own. When you need to believe in yourself, like never before. Normally when our sensory neurons get stimulated, either through sound, sight, whatever it is, the level of stimulation is precise, finely tuned to create that perceived reality. LSD and ketamine corrupt this precision in opposite directions. But so do cannabinoid receptors. Not to the extent of acid, but sensory information coming in is amplified, the neurons don't shut down quite as soon as they normally would, and the meaning the brain assigns to that altered input, well it's grand. When you're a teenager, responding to just that little extra confidence that naturally occurring cannabis-like chemicals offer, that's helpful. You can't rely on mom and dad forever, which is ok, because now they suddenly don't know shit. It's the dreams dancing in your head that matter, and it's a clever little aid to independence. It basically makes you a believer.

But grandiosity isn't always beneficial. Sometimes what you believe is bullshit. Especially when you're not a teenager, you're a middle-aged man, and the cannabis concentration swimming through your bloodstream isn't an adaptive advantage, it's not natural at all. It's just more drug abuse. And everything you plan is just a pipe dream. All the pot is doing is propping me up in the corner, and what I'm sustained by is pure stupidity, a certainty that this time will be different, even if it's all a delusion. So I just sit there, not making a sound, surrounded by my secrets and an assurance that nobody knows, while my spirit is slowly dying. And that's where I'll stay, until I either fall off that stool, or something knocks me off. Something that comes along with sirens, to save me.

XXXIII

A MONTH LATER…

"Well, I've got some good news, and then I've got some bad news."

"Well, we've got like eight hours. Lay it on me."

Tony is driving us to St. Louis to see this band he just loves—Guided By Voices. Apparently the people that are into them are really into them, and Tony, he's like that. Obsessed. I've known this since we shared an apartment back in medical school. He was another one of my classmates, and he's a close friend. Or at least he used to be. I haven't really been a good friend to anyone in the last few years, and almost everyone I've told about my drug problems lives out of state, like RW, where they can't check in on me. But I'm about to tell him about getting arrested in Pampa earlier this week. The sirens are a secret I won't be able to keep, I'm going to have to tell someone. Might as well start with Tony.

"Well, this past Tuesday I spent the night in jail in Pampa, Texas, after getting arrested with a trunkful of pot gummies and vapes and stuff…"

Tony just kind of looks at me, then chuckles. "You serious?" I nod. "Well then, what's the good news?"

265

"That *is* the good news."

"This is gonna be good…"

And for the next several hours, I tell Tony the story of the last seven years, one that starts with hydrocodone, and ends up pretty much on this highway, up into Missouri, me popping kratom capsules every couple of hours to keep from getting dopesick. He even makes a couple of appearances in the story himself.

"So when you came to my office, complaining you couldn't sleep…"

"Yeah…the Ambien. I'm sorry man." I'm getting good at apologies, even if they don't mean much.

I've told a variation of this story to five or six people over those years, but this is the first time it's been from beginning to end. Because it's the first time it's actually had an end, or at least I think it does. I mean, it has to, I'm not going back to work on Monday. I just can't do it, and I'm finally admitting it. I admitted it to myself lying on that concrete slab in the Pampa jail cell, admitted it to Tami after I got out, and I'm telling Tony, right now. I don't bother trying to shore up his secrecy by swearing that I've cracked the code, that I finally know what I have to do different this time. I finally get it—if my job involves drugs, I can't do my job without doing the drugs, too. I'm just…fucked.

"What are you gonna do now?" Tony wants to know.

"Not sure. But anything'll be better than what I've been doing. Maybe I'll teach again."

"I thought you said they were going to charge you with a felony."

"Oh...that."

The truth is, I have absolutely no idea what I'm ultimately going to do. But I know what I have to do first—I've got to kick. One last time. So as soon as we get back from St. Louis, I toss out what little kratom I have left, tell Tami not to expect much of me for several days, and I resolve not to leave my little rent house until I can look myself in the mirror and stand on my own two feet.

Tami's got concerns, and rightly so, that I'm going to do something stupid. Something desperate. Like drag my raggedy ass up off the couch, head down to some place like the bus station and try to score. It's what drug addicts do. But she also still sort of thinks I kept doing drugs on purpose. That I wanted to. She didn't get it, *nobody* gets it unless you're in it. But thank God I don't have a connection, somebody I can call to hook me up. A dealer saying "Hey buddy, haven't heard from you in awhile." I do my best to explain this to Tami, I tell her, "this is the whole reason I have to quit my job."

I accept it as a price I have to pay. It's what freedom costs, there are just places I can't go, things I can no longer do. This isn't the way I originally planned it, but this is how it's worked out. And I still get to walk away, before they make me run. And that's the only thing that matters. My secrets will still be safe. I might've had to admit to getting caught with pot, but that shit's going to be legal any day now, right? It's a shame I can live with. I was a good doctor. I was a good person. At least that's what most people will think, even if I don't.

I do, however, have a connection at the liquor store. Who doesn't? And right now, I need it. Even with it, I don't sleep for a week. I buy rum, the biggest bottles I can find, and sip myself into a stupor. But it isn't the kind of drunk I'd grown accustomed to. That sweet spot, with serenity and ease, seems to have just evaporated. The rum doesn't seem to do much of anything except relieve me of the need to drink it. But as soon as I do, I just want more.

For a week, I don't sleep at all, just drift between the bedroom, the living room, and the liquor store. But I tell myself this is temporary. It's just until my nervous system can realign itself. I might be drinking like an alcoholic, but that doesn't mean I really am one. I'm just a morphine addict, and the booze is just a short term necessary evil. Besides, nobody can keep drinking like this forever. I'll eventually have to stop so I can...so I can...do what? What the fuck am I going to do, even when I can function? I don't realize it yet, but work was my last tether to society, it was the only thing I could keep together. I've isolated myself from friendships, my family is in shambles, and my only purpose was my profession.

It's not that I don't have any other options. I'm not the first doctor to develop chemical dependency, I'm not even the first anesthesiologist to divert drugs. It happens. It's an occupational hazard. It's just that it's not supposed to happen to me. But every once in a while, I wonder what would happen if I just admitted everything. Back in med school, we sat through a presentation where a few doctors who were participating in a recovery program for physicians shared their stories. Maybe just calling someone isn't the worst idea in the world.

At about five AM, on one of the last mornings that I can't sleep, it occurs to me that this is exactly what I should do. I'm even more convinced when I climb into my car, and out of the hundreds and hundreds of songs on my music player, "Why Don't You Look Into Jesus" pours out of the speaker. It's by Larry Norman, one of my favorite artists as a teenager, and for a Christian song, its lyrics are radical. It's about shooting drugs, catching the clap.

"Sippin' whiskey from a paper cup,

You drown your sorrows 'til you can't stand up…"

Holy shit. This must be some sort of divine providence, I haven't heard this song in years and it just happens to play on this, of all mornings? It's meant to be.

Tami and the kids, they live just a couple of miles away, and I'm still all like "why *don't* I look into Jesus" when I slip my spare key into the lock and let myself inside, well before anyone here is even close to being awake.

"Tami. Wake up. Tami. Tami!"

"Tom? What's wrong? What are you doing here?"

"Nothing. Nothing's wrong, I mean." My speech is a shouted whisper, and it doesn't even occur to me that maybe this is eerily similar to the last time I rushed into the house to preach to Tami about Jesus.

"I think…I think if I just admitted everything…I think things might be ok. Now just listen to me, if I got help, I think things might somehow work out. What do you think?"

Tami can't trust what she's hearing. How could she? For all she knows I've found some ketamine I had stashed somewhere and I'm straight tripping. And even if I'm not, aren't I the guy who's been telling her for years that admitting anything to anyone is absolutely the worst thing I could ever do??? And get help? From the guy who has sworn on everything holy that the only person who can help me is me? That treatment is a bunch of bullshit where all they can do is tell me stuff I already know? No, she can't trust any of this talk. How could she?

She sits up, puts her head in her hands, overwhelmed. "I don't know Tom. I don't know what you should do. I can't tell you what to do. You never listen to me anyway." Tami is going to take care of herself, as she should. It's not a coincidence that she's kept her career on track. She's going to survive this. Even if I don't.

"Ok," I sigh. I'm sleep-deprived, drunk. A little delirious. And it's not nearly as abrupt as coming off ketamine, but my faith still fades. I walk outside to the backyard I don't belong in anymore, look up at the sky. I don't remember the last time I prayed anything and meant it. Or believed it. But I'm desperate and I don't know what else to do, so I pray, "Please God, help me. I don't know what to do here. I just need to know if everything is gonna be ok...or not?" I want to know if I should tell someone. And I stare up into the sky like that's where all the answers are, where it's starting to get light, but not nearly as bright as it would be if clouds weren't covering the dawn. But just up above them I can clearly see the shadow of a bird. It's most likely a hawk, but to me, it's an eagle, and he's soaring like a beautiful bird should. He's free. And it's just as obvious to me what it all means as if it weren't even overcast. It means it's all going to be ok. Dawn is coming...

But not yet.

XXXIV

I took that bird silhouette above the cloud cover to be a promise—I didn't need to do anything just yet, simply hang in there, and everything will be ok. But maybe I just saw what I wanted to see. Maybe instead of a sign, it was just another excuse, because a month later, morning still hasn't broken, and I'm not soaring through the sky. I'm in Birmingham, back where my whole story started, staring at that skeleton of what was once a great hospital. That burned out building with all the broken glass.

It's too late for that building. It'll never be a hospital again. But it's not too late for me. My medical career might be over, but I've got a lot of life left, I've got these two boys to raise, and a marriage to save. I can't just sit around feeling sorry for myself, and I certainly can't keep soaking my soul in whiskey.

I intended to accomplish two things on this final trip to the beach house. I needed to get it sold, and it's on the market now with an agent who is certain she can move it. And I hoped to quit drinking. Unfortunately there's no one who can do it for me, I'll have to do that one myself, and so far, I'm failing. But I'll get there. It's been a month since Pampa, a month without morphine, and at first I just lived on hard liquor. On this trip I've got that down to wine, and the next step is going to be beer. Specifically, this twenty-four pack of Natural Light I'm loading into the trunk for the drive back home.

272

"You boys ready to find a hotel?" I ask TJ and Tyson when I hop back into the car.

"With a pool!" Tyson says.

"Of course buddy."

"Dad…when are we gonna go home?" TJ wants to know.

"We'll go in the morning, son. It's too late to make it tonight." The boys have been great on this trip, but I can tell they miss their mom. They're ready to go home. I miss home, too. And if I ever want to have a chance at going back, then I'm going to have to pull myself together.

———————

I'm giving myself a week. That's what the twenty-four pack is for. A beer every six hours ought to be plenty, and after it's gone, I should be back to my old self. No more morphine, no more marijuana, just me.

It's our last morning, and for breakfast TJ wants Dennys, of course. These days it's nothing but a reminder of misery for me, but I'll go for him. Besides, I won't be eating anyway. After I get the boys loaded up, I pop the trunk in the hotel parking lot and guzzle my breakfast. That's one. I'll have another around one o'clock when we stop for snacks.

Except as soon as the boys have eaten breakfast, I figure everything'll be better if I have just one more beer, and I'm down two before we've even left Birmingham. And then about an hour later, when we're on the open highway, of course I need to pee, so I find a discreet place to stop off, and I sneak behind the car to relieve myself. And chug another beer.

And that's pretty much how it goes the whole way home, almost every hour. That's what it's come to. I'm drinking with a desperation I've never known. Guzzling hot beer just as fast as I can get it down behind a dumpster at some abandoned rest stop, while my children wait in the car. I'm a fucking disaster.

When we get back, I attempt to get it together. The next morning I go for a jog. Or at least I try. Exercising went out the window several years ago, and I haven't had an honest sweat outside of being dopesick in forever. But I manage to make it a mile, and even though I follow it up with the last two Natty Lights, it feels like a victory.

But it doesn't last. I've got a lot of free time on my hands, too much, and nothing to occupy my mind but fear of the future. I need to get out of town, and I ask Tony if he'll go up to Tulsa one evening so we can hang out with wake and bake Billy. They became friends back when Billy would come hang out at the apartment Tony and I shared in school. Tony says "yeah, let's do it."

"So what have you been doing, man?" Tony asks me on the drive up.

"Drinking…"

"Besides that."

"Nothing. Just that."

I'd called Billy on the drive home from jail in Pampa, told him what happened. He knew about the drugs by then, but maybe not how

bad it was, and he was a little concerned when I told him I was quitting
medicine. This is the first chance I've had to see him since, and the
three of us meet up for dinner.

"So what are you gonna do now?" Billy wants to know. "How are
you gonna get by without a job?"

"Well, believe it or not, the only thing in my life I didn't fuck up
was my finances. Tami and I have always done a good job of living
well beneath our means, and it's the only aspect of my life that's not a
train wreck." I can't quite tell if Billy is a little envious, or thinks it's all
bullshit. But then again, I've been working longer than he has, I don't
have three ex-wives, and Tami has contributed a lot. We're not rich,
but we've invested well, saved as much as possible, and we'll be ok.

I go on. "Tami's never been one to buy into the typical
husband/wife stereotypes. She says she's fine being the one to bring
home the paycheck for a while. We never even fought about money at
all back in Birmingham. It wasn't until I actually started making more
than she did that it sometimes became an issue."

"So you're just gonna be a bon vivant," Tony says. "Kick back,
enjoy the good life for awhile. Eat, drink, and be merry."

It doesn't sound half bad when he says it.

"Yeah. Yeah, maybe so. Who knows, maybe I'll home school the
boys or something. Wouldn't that be cool? Study the Civil War by
actually going to Gettysburg? Shit like that?" But for shit like that, I'd
need to be sober.

275

"We're just gonna simplify things, you know? All the other stuff, it never made me happy, anyway. Big house, fancy car. A mansion with a huge mortgage is just a prison, man. None of that can ever satisfy you. It's just greed."

It's not necessarily that I'm wrong. It's just that my motives are. And motives matter. But it's so much easier to just question everyone else's so I don't have to think much about my own.

"Well, man. I'm happy for you. It sounds like you just might have it made," Billy tells me. "But some of us gotta work tomorrow, you know?"

"Yeah, no shit," says Tony. "I've got clinic at eight in the morning."

Now it's my turn to be envious. I've got nowhere to be til ten, when the liquor stores unlock their doors.

———————————

"Man, I'm kinda scared. I have to quit drinking, but I don't know if I can," I tell Tony on the drive back.

"Why?" he asks.

"Well, I guess I haven't really tried yet, but…"

"No. Why do you have to quit?"

"What do you mean? It's not normal to be going to the liquor store every day as soon as it opens, drinking a liter of hard liquor a day. I don't have a choice, I have to quit."

"Sure you've got a choice."

I just look at him, like, "how?"

"Stay thirsty."

Now I look at him like I want to punch him. "I can't do that."

"Look dude, you think you're an alcoholic? I don't even really remember you drinking all that much when we were roommates. You always had your shit together, coming up with a study schedule, all that. I don't know if I would've made it through without you."

Tony's smart. A lot smarter than I am. He would've made it just fine.

"I can't be a bon vivant, Tony. I'm fucking miserable." Tony is one of these assholes who can smoke a few cigarettes at the bar on the weekend, then either throw the pack out or save it for next time. He's not a drug addict, he dabbles. And he figures if he can do it, anybody can. Just cut back. Just stop for awhile. Not that it's easy for him, sometimes it takes will power. It takes work. So maybe he thinks I'm just being weak.

"Alright, alright man," he tells me. "If you really want to quit, let me help you. You know the saddest part to me about your whole opioid story? It's that you had to go through all that alone, basically. When I was right here. You were an army of one. Just be honest with me. I'll help hold you accountable."

It sounds just like something I need.

"Alright man. I'll be honest with you. No matter what."

———————————

I'm not honest with Tony. Every time he asks me if I've had a drink, I lie. "Nope. Not yet. Doing good." When I always lied to Tami like this, I had a reason. I was doing it for her. I assumed the truth was just too awful to take, and I wanted to shield her from that sorrow. Or at least that was my excuse. But Tony doesn't give a fuck if I drink or not, sometimes I think he wants me to, to be his entertainer. But still, I lie to him anyway.

I'm ready to stop lying to Tami, though. And in a rare example of honesty, I level with her.

"Look, I've been drinking. A lot. And I'm not sure if I can quit."

"Okay," she draws it out, like it'll delay whatever is coming next.

"I want to try something…"

XXXV

"What are these for?" Tami asks me. I've just opened up my wallet, and I'm handing her my ATM card, and all my credit cards. Well, all of them except one.

"I need this one, just to buy gas," I say. She's confused, I can tell, so I explain.

"I'm a little worried, okay?" It's an understatement, but it's a start. "I can't quit drinking, and I dunno what else to do. But if I don't have any access to money, how am I gonna buy alcohol?" I spread my hands, wait for an answer that doesn't come until I supply it myself. "I'm not." I've thought this through, see. "The only access to any money I'll have is this one credit card, and we'll set up alerts to go to your phone every time it gets charged. And the only thing you'll ever see on it is a charge from 7-11 or something when I get gas." In Oklahoma at this time, the only place you can buy anything stronger than low point beer is the liquor store. And without money, the only way I'd be able to get any liquor would be to rob one.

"You think this is going to work." It's not a question, it's a statement, like what I've proposed is stupid.

"It has to."

"And what if it doesn't, Tom? What are you going to do then?" I notice there's no "we" in that sentence. She might be willing to help me here, but if I blow this, fuck her over, I'm on my own.

279

All I can do is shake my head. "Well…if this doesn't work, I guess I'll have to go to rehab. I don't know what else I could do." The thought of going to treatment is inconceivable. I can't imagine anything more humiliating.

"It's going to work. I realize I can't really say no anymore. What I have to do is eliminate alcohol as an option. It'd be nice if it was just illegal." We each manage a half smile at that, which together makes a whole, so I guess we're good, for now.

"Like that would stop you," Tami says.

———————————

My first test comes quickly, as in right when I leave Tami's house. I have an old Ford Bronco that I'm probably going to have to sell, it's worth a bit of money, and it has a big ashtray like automobiles used to have. But the ashtray isn't full of cigarette butts, it's full of quarters. A lot of them. Must be ten or twenty bucks in there, at least.

"I'll take a pint of that Smirnoff." It's time to switch to vodka. It's economical, and efficient. I stack up the quarters in piles of four, count off eight of them, and the cashier never even blinks. It appears I'm not the first alcoholic to buy booze with spare change.

I convince myself the quarters won't last long. I'm only putting off quitting for a couple of more days. What's the hurry. But the ashtray of my bronco isn't the only place I've stashed spare change. I've got a big jar of it at home. Well, it's a house, but it's hardly home. It's a place to sleep, or sit on the couch. There's nothing to eat here except store brand potato chips, and nothing to drink, but vodka.

280

What I should do is take that big jar of coins straight to Tami's, say 'here, I can't keep this. Let's fill up the kids' piggy banks.' But I don't. I can't. My stash of coins stays secret, and I stay sick. I spend them in little stacks, piled up to pay for little airplane-bottle sized booze, at a dollar a pop. It's humiliating, walking into the liquor store for the third or fourth time in a day with another handful of nickels and dimes, so I frequent every liquor store within a five mile radius to save face. 'Just getting rid of some more spare change I found in my car. It's such a hassle having it around, don't ya know.' And whoever is manning the register just nods, like they could not give a fuck if I paid in pennies. I exist hour by hour, and each day, the jar gets emptier and emptier, and I anticipate the day when it's gone with both prayer and dread.

Tyson and TJ, they're seven and nine now. Of course they haven't been completely shielded from the collateral damage my addiction has caused. TJ learned to swim at the swimming pool of a cheap hotel I was staying at during one of the many times I'd been temporarily evicted. They've both overheard shouting matches carried on through closed doors. They've experienced their share of chaos. But my addiction has largely been something hidden beneath the surface, where they couldn't see it, or smell it. But they're older now, and harder to fool.

"What are you drinking, dad?" Tyson wants to know.

"It's water." I finish guzzling on the pint of vodka and toss it in the glovebox.

He's only seven, but he's skeptical. I'm not sure if he believed my red wine was really juice or not back in Alabama, but he's not buying it now.

"That's not water."

"Yes, son, it's water."

"I've never seen a water bottle like that."

They're old enough to know what booze is, and I don't know if Tami and I directly told them or they've figured it out on their own, but they also know I'm not supposed to be drinking it. You'd think it'd be easy to hide from them, but it's not, they'll sneak up on you.

"Don't drink anymore of that, Dad." TJ tells me.

"Ok buddy, I won't." But what I mean is after I finish this bottle, and I can't erase the look on his face when he walks into the garage not two minutes later and sees me draining it down my throat.

"Dad! Don't!"

But it don't help.

When the jar of coins runs out, I pull all the cushions off of the couch, all the floor mats out of the car, looking for anything silver. Nickels and dimes will do, but a quarter, that's the real treasure. You'd think if I was this desperate I'd just give in and use the credit card, make a purchase at the liquor store and pray Tami doesn't notice, but I won't. I'm too proud to get caught in the light, no matter how much garbage I might dig through in the dark.

Eventually I've scavenged all the silver coins, so surely this is it, I'm not going to resort to robbing a liquor store. But it's not stealing if the money is already mine, and I figure that's sort of the case with all the coins that are in my kids' piggy banks, right? I mean, they might've lost a tooth or something for it, but they don't need it right now, and I swear to myself I'll put it back before they even know it's gone.

Tami was right. Even if they made liquor illegal, I'm not sure it would stop me. But I wish they would. I wish it were hidden, with wherever they're hiding the heroin and everything else illicit. If everything were just somewhere I couldn't find it, maybe it would save me. Or maybe it's me that needs to be removed. Locked up. At the gas station a few weeks ago, a man with a look of being formerly homeless walked up to me at the pump, told me he was raising money for a good cause and handed me a pamphlet.

"I don't have any cash, man. But if you'll go inside and buy me a six pack, I'll fill your car up with gas on my credit card."

The man just laughed. "I don't have a car. Read the pamphlet."

When I got home, I did. It was for some outfit called "My Brother's Keeper", and it was kind of a sober living facility for alcoholics and drug addicts. People exactly like me. At the time I didn't give it any thought, but that was then. Before I'd emptied my boys' piggy banks. Stolen money from a Starbuck's tip jar. Before I'd drank two dollars and twenty-nine cents worth of bottom shelf vodka so fast I barfed it back up, and would've drank it a second time if it weren't splattered all over the sidewalk.

But now, having my brother keep me wouldn't be so bad, if he could keep me locked up. If he could do for me what I can't seem to do for myself. It wasn't supposed to be this way. By quitting my job, I was supposed to be getting my life back. I was supposed to get my freedom, not more restraint. I didn't believe any of that bullshit about swapping out one addiction for another. Certainly not alcohol, hadn't I drank it for a decade? And it was nothing like this. If I wasn't experiencing it myself, I wouldn't believe it. I thought my problem was morphine. But maybe my problem, is me.

XXXVI

It's Independence Day. Not mine, the nation's. It's the Fourth of July. There's no better time in summer for a kid, and Tami must be thinking of ours when she decides to invite me to join her and the boys for a late afternoon pool party with some of her co-workers. Of course I say yes, what else would I have to do, but first, I'll have to run a quick errand. Out to my mom's.

My mom…She doesn't know every dirty detail, but I've given her a rough description of what's been going on. She knows about the beginning, with the boxes of wine. How it progressed, with the pills pilfered from her kitchen. And she knows that when the next step was needles, things became terminal. None of it was easy to tell her.

"It was…hell." I wasn't trying to be overly dramatic, it's just the only word that came to mind. The only one adequate, and inescapable. And a thoughtful look crossed her face.

"You've put your whole family through it, Tommy." She wasn't scolding me, she was just sad, and I know she included herself on that list, too. But she also couldn't help blaming herself, at least a little. If only she hadn't had those damn pills, maybe things would've been different. Of course it wasn't her fault, she wasn't the one abusing them, I was. And there's no possible way she could've known it then, hell, I don't even know it now, but those pills…it's possible that they might've turned out to be a blessing in disguise.

285

My poor mom, she thinks things are better now, that it was just that job and the access to drugs it afforded that was the issue. It's what I told her, of course. Which is why I can't let her know that I'm coming to her house. Fortunately her door is unlocked, and the television is blaring, so she'll never even know I was here. I didn't come for her hydrocodone, though. Whether it was to protect me from myself or out of her own guilt, she got off of it. She switched to another drug called ultram, and I think they classify it as an opioid these days. It certainly is adequate for relieving her pain, but it doesn't do shit for mine. I know because I tried it. No, I'm here instead for her Ativan.

Ativan is a benzodiazepine. Like Valium, or Xanax. It's for anxiety, but it can also be a substitute for alcohol. Unlike opioid withdrawal, acute alcohol withdrawal can be fatal, and benzos can be used to treat it. I don't really know if I'm physically addicted to the booze yet or not, I haven't gone long enough without it to know. But that's not why I want the Ativan, anyway. I want it to keep me from crawling out of my skin in front of Tami and her friends at the pool party. Because there's no way I'll be able to drink.

———————————

Although it doesn't take long to be offered one.

"You want a beer, man?"

Dave, one of Tami's co-workers at the pharmacy, is a generous host.

"Nah, I'm good man. Thanks." I don't look at Tami, but I can feel her looking at me as I say it.

"You sure?" Like it's abnormal not to be drinking on the 4th.

"I'm sure." And with the Ativan swirling in my brain, I'm surprised at how comfortable I am saying it. This might turn out just fine.

"We should take the boys to watch fireworks downtown after dark," I tell Tami.

She nods. "We'll see. I have to work early tomorrow. You can come over and stay with the boys, right?"

"Of course." It's not like I'm tempted to drink right in front of her, but all the conversation with her colleagues isn't comfortable. I don't have anything to add. I'm not even sure if they know I'm "retired", that I'm a bon vivant now, and I'm afraid it'll somehow come up.

"I think I'll go swim." I tell Tami.

"Take the boys with you. I think they're getting bored."

Dave has a nice setup, an in-ground pool surrounded by a stone patio. Lush landscaping. Very private. And hidden around a hedge, he's got a fucking bar, all stocked for when the party makes its way outside, I suppose. And so far as I'm concerned, it just did. I glance back towards the porch, but I can't even see it, which means nobody can see me, either. I grab the nearest bottle, which is some kind of spiced rum, and without bothering to pour it into a cup, I take a long pull straight from the bottle. I'm certain I do it once or twice more, but that can't have been it. Even though it's all I can remember until morning.

―――――――――

Zeus is with Tami and the boys.

P.S.—call us and we will tell you where your keys are! Tami got a sitter for the boys tomorrow, so do not try to go over there.

Tony and Kate

P.S.S…and there's blood on your couch. Blood everywhere!

When I wake up the next morning and put my feet on the floor, I find this note. It's written in crayon on a sheet torn out from a coloring book, something I must have had lying around for the boys. But it takes me a minute to figure out what it means. And when I do, I know it means I've fucked up. Big time. Tami doesn't want me around the boys, and she's taken the dog, my little schnauzer, Zeus. He's the boys' dog, really, we got him last Christmas, but he stays with me. And he's saved me in a way. He just sits with me on the couch, keeps me company, and now he's gone. But why are Tony and his wife telling me all this with a note in crayon? So I follow the instructions on the note, and I call him.

"Dude, don't go anywhere. We'll come over."

"What happened last night?" Tony asks me.

"Um….I don't know." Not only do I not get hangovers, but I've never blacked out. Until last night.

288

"Did you take anything last night? Go inside with somebody and take a Xanax or anything?"

"No."

"You sure?"

Now I remember the Ativan, but I'm not about to tell him about it. I'd hide the fact that I was drunk, if I could.

"Yeah, man. I guess I drank too much though. What were you doing here, anyway?"

"Tami called us. Said she didn't know who else to call."

"Why?"

"You should've seen yourself. In fact….here." And he hands me his phone. He's taken photos, or Kate did, because Tony and I are both in them. He's smiling, posing over me, my lifeless body facedown on the living room floor, my swimsuit still on. It's like one of those bonus scenes at the end of The Hangover films, when they finally get to figure out what the hell happened. Only none of this is funny. Tony, he's smiling now, too, but I'm pretty sure I know what this means. It means my life is over.

"How's your head?" Kate asks me.

"My head?"

"Yeah. You were bleeding. It's all over your couch, all over your bedroom, too."

"Oh." I had no idea. But upon further inspection, my hair is all matted. I've got a bruise coming up on my left flank, and all the skin is gone from my right wrist. I have no explanation for any of it.

"Tami is *pissed*, dude. She said you were throwing TJ and Tyson in the deep end of the pool, trying to jump on them."

I have a vague memory of being in the swimming pool. I thought we were having fun. But it doesn't sound like it.

"You guys had to leave early, you humiliated yourself, and her too. She could barely get you in the car. She asked us to meet her here so we could stay with you, make sure you didn't pull a Jimi Hendrix and choke on your vomit or something. You fell over in the street and hit your head when she was trying to get you inside."

"How long did you stay?"

"Til midnight," Kate says. "We kept trying to get you to bed, but you just kept saying, 'no *you* go to bed.'" She can't help snickering a little bit at the memory. "But finally you went."

"What are you going to do?" Tony asks me.

—————————

Why the hell do people keep asking me what I'm going to do? Isn't it obvious that I don't know? That the more I try to fix things, the more I fuck them up? I wish instead of asking me, somebody would just tell me. Tell me what to do.

—"You're going to rehab."

290

Tami texts me, she doesn't want to talk, and that's all she has to say, anyway. I know I'd said it might come to this, back when I tried to make her responsible for my actions by giving her all my access to money, but I'm not sure I believed it would actually happen. I know on television when they stage interventions, people often put up a fight. But if she thinks I'm going to do that, I already know I won't. It feels like she's giving me permission to do what deep down I know I should've done a long time ago. Might've done three months ago if it wasn't for that stupid bird. Lot of good praying did me.

A few minutes later my brother calls me, tells me he'll be over soon. Tami's already called him, told him she's done with me, and that if he wants to help me, he should make sure I go to treatment. When he shows up he's got a list with like five places on it and tells me to choose, and that I have to leave today. He'll take me to the airport. He's not waiting around for me to change my mind.

"I'll go, I'll go. I promise I'll go. But just let me think a minute, ok?"

He doesn't want to hear any of this, there's no other alternative, so what is it exactly I need to think about?

"Just give me a second," and I scroll back through my texts until I find one from almost three months ago, right after I quit my job. It's from one of my older partners.

—"Hey Tom. Hope you are well. Listen, I hate to see you make such a hasty decision. You're still fairly young and you've got a lot of life left. Maybe you just need a little time away. I'm not sure what all is going on with you, but we all face hard times and challenges. We can get

291

through them if we have a little faith. If you're convinced you're making the right decision, then I'm happy for you, and I wish you and your lovely family well. But if you change your mind and decide you'd like to talk to somebody, give Dr. Evans a call. He's there to help. 664-5623"

At the time, this text infuriated me. What exactly does he think is going on with me? Who does he think he is? He doesn't know shit. Isn't this the guy who's always smiling to your face, but will try to steal cases behind your back to make more money? What the fuck would he know about faith. And to prove I knew exactly what I was doing, I'd burned down all the bridges. I didn't just quit my practice, I resigned my hospital privileges, suspended my malpractice. I cancelled my whole damned career. But thankfully I kept the text. Dr. Evans, he's the director of the state physicians health program. I'm too ashamed of myself to even consider the possibility that I could ever be one of those doctors like I listened to back in medical school, who talked about their story of recovery. And I'm simultaneously too proud to ever want to be. I will not be that guy from the video in residency. I'm too proud to admit that I need treatment, too ashamed of myself to believe that I deserve it, and too hopeless to trust that it will do any good. All at exactly the same time. But still, I call Dr. Evans.

The call lasts all of about five minutes, most of it with me crying, and that's all it takes—"I'm a drug addict and an alcoholic, and I need help." That's all Dr. Evans needed to hear, and he knows exactly what to do, he's got connections, and he'll take it from here. Twenty minutes later he calls me back, asks me if I can get myself to the airport in the morning, and tells me to buy a ticket to Florida. Not to Miami, or any place beautiful near a beach. I'm going to Gainesville, to a residential drug and alcohol treatment center affiliated with the University of Florida. I thank him profusely, as alcoholics are prone to do in fits of emotional instability. He says no problem, and get better. Tells me I won't want to leave, once I get there.

That's how quickly it can all come to an end, once you decide to try something different, something that doesn't involve a drink or just a different drug. Maybe it all started with a feeling I can't forget, one that I've been chasing and trying to recreate for seven years. And maybe, just maybe, it can end with a night that I'll never be able to remember.

I tell my brother, "I guess I'm going to Gainesville."

XXXVII

Atlanta International Airport

If I want to back out, now is the time. I've got a two hour layover before I board the last flight to Florida, and though it's not even nine AM, I do what I assume you're supposed to do before you show up at rehab—I drink. Four shots of Jager. And I think.

If I wanted to, I could get on a plane and go anywhere in the country. But I'm not backing out, that's not what I'm thinking of. I'm trying to decide what to say when I get to Gainesville. I'm trying to get my story straight. Because I just figure what difference does it make what drugs I was on or where I got them. The "treatment" is the same, right? It's not like they put all the alcoholics on one side, and all the junkies on the other, and dole out different medicine to fix them. I don't know much about what treatment will be like, but I know it won't be like *that*. So what's the harm in just telling them I'm an alcoholic? Because it's true enough.

"Well…if an alcoholic is the moral equivalent of a wife beater, then you're an axe murderer."

That's how Tony put it to me when I sort of ran this idea by him last night. He was getting sick of me referring to myself as an 'alcoholic' anyway, he thought I was just saying it because I think it's more socially acceptable, and I guess it just gave him a chance to say what he really believes. He thinks I'm full of shit. And not that I blame him. I am, and I lied to him repeatedly.

Kate, his wife, was kinder. "But don't you kind of have to tell them, you know, the truth?"

I don't know, do I? I sure as hell hope not. The truth is terrible. I'd like to be able to stay on the right side of the law, if I can. There are certain secrets I'd prefer to carry to the grave. And since I'm never going to practice medicine again, I see no reason I shouldn't. Kate was super sweet, and she reminded me to pack some sweaters and stuff, because even though it's still summer, I'll probably get chilly sitting in those rooms where we talk about our feelings and such. She and Tony have watched a lot of television shows about rehab, I guess, like Intervention.

Tony predicts, "You're going to be like one of those guys they interview two weeks later, you'll be all on cloud nine, talking about how close you feel to God and shit. And then after a couple more weeks, you'll be gone. '*Tom relapsed, and no one knows where he went.*'"

Tony doesn't believe in God, not in any meaningful way, at least. And he knows that if this is all up to me, then I'm fucked. And he's probably right about that.

Not many people know I'm headed to rehab. My family, of course. Even Tyson and TJ. They know dad is headed to a place that will help him not drink, and they're happy about that. Relieved. And I told three or four of my childhood best friends. It seems I need the people who knew me when I was young more than ever, and though they're surprised, they're also supportive. But I'd be mortified if anyone else knew. Especially anyone I worked with. Or any parents of Tyson or TJ's friends, good grief, can you imagine? They'd never let their kids come over again.

But then my mind starts to kind of drift, and I wonder what rehab is going to be like. I know there'll be some other doctors, it's one of the reasons I'm being sent there, but I wonder if there will be anyone famous. Someone like Josh Hamilton. I think that would be kind of cool, you know? And it dawns on me that I wouldn't think Josh Hamilton was a piece of shit if he showed up in rehab with me, I'd think it was awesome. So why do I think *I'm* such a piece of shit. Is it because I think I'm so much worse? Or maybe it's that I think I'm better? That a guy like me, I shouldn't even be here? I'm not really sure.

But thinking of Josh gets me to thinking about that time the boys and I saw him play, how he ended up winning with a sacrifice, and that every time he stepped up to the plate he announced to the whole stadium through song, that if you surrender, you will live. I just hope to God he's right.

XXXVIII

Gainesville, Florida

Those shots I had in Atlanta? Along with the beer I had once I got to Gainesville, they're ultimately going to run me about $1200 a piece. If I would've showed up sober, I could've gone straight to the residential treatment center. But since I blew a 0.16, I got to come to detox. And since it's a Friday, I'll be here for seventy-two hours, or six thousand extra bucks. And my insurance isn't paying.

But it's all for the best, because I'm not ready to start treatment yet, not really. I'm still full of too much bullshit. As part of my intake, a physician finishing up his fellowship in addiction medicine takes a thorough history of my drinking and drugging. I tell him about the booze, and the marijuana bust, but as far as he knows, I was just traveling back and forth to Colorado because I really dig cannabis. And I do, it's true, but when he asks me if I've ever taken an opioid, I've decided that I'm mostly keeping my mouth shut.

"Well, I have a couple of times. I got a prescription for hydrocodone when I broke my jaw in my twenties, but I never even finished it." And I decide it'll look a bit fishy if that's all there is to it, I'm so used to being manipulative, I can't help it, so I add that I might've taken a couple of my mom's pills once. But only because I didn't have any alcohol. He looks at me for an extra beat, seems satisfied, and moves on to other topics, and I assume that'll be all there is to it. I'm officially an alcoholic.

_____

And it is all there is to it, until I see him coming through the double doors on Sunday evening.

"Say, Tom, could we go sit in your room a minute and chat? I want to go over a couple more things."

And I immediately know why he's here. I've worried about it all weekend, wondered whether I'll be able to pull off this charade for another thirty days, or however long rehab is supposed to last. I can tell him I stole money to buy booze. I can tell him I got arrested with marijuana. I can even tell him I drove drunk with my kids in the car. But the thing I can't admit, is the thing I know he's going to ask me about.

"You know, I want to go back to those pills you say you took at your mom's."

"Ok..."

"Well, as you know, that's diversion of a controlled substance. And it's just not something most people would do. It's certainly something *I* would've done at one time, but most people wouldn't."

And for the first time I realize this doctor is like me. He's a drug addict, too, or at least he was. But now he looks respectable, professional, like people trust him. Maybe, just maybe, he's someone I could actually trust, too. Maybe if I just surrender, things will start getting better instead of worse.

298

"Alright," I throw up my hands like I'm frustrated, but really I'm just letting go, and it's scary as shit. "I've been injecting myself with opioids for seven years." Just like that, it's all out.

And now that I've answered his question, I've got about a dozen of my own. All of the awful things I used to tell myself would happen if anyone ever found out, I want him to tell me if they really will.

"Am I going to go to jail?"—Well, I wouldn't think so.

"Am I going to have to tell everyone? All the people I used to work with?"—Well, at some point you might want to do that.

"Is everyone going to hate me?"—Some people might. But that's probably more about them than you.

"Am I going to get sued?"—I really don't know. Did you have a bad outcome on a particular case?

"Well, no. Not that I know of."

"I did."

"Man, I'm sorry, I didn't mean to…"

"No, no. It's fine, Tom."

I figure this guy must have really fucked up, and I kind of feel sorry for him. He looks older, late fifties at least, and I assume he must have just wrecked the end of his career, and the only option he has left is to get this certification in addiction medicine so he can get some sort of job. But really, I don't know shit. The truth, as I'll find out later, is that he's been a very successful cardiologist for years, and has over a decade of sobriety. When he was ready to retire from his practice, he decided to spend his last productive years doing what he really loved—helping other addicts. Addicts like me.

"Man, I'm so sorry I lied to you."

"It's ok." He smiles and shrugs. "It's what we do."

He didn't come back to this detox center on a Sunday night to judge me, or try to catch me in more lies. He came to give me the chance to tell the truth, an opportunity to be honest. Because he knows something I don't—unless I'm willing to get honest, I have no shot at getting sober.

XXXIX

Detox sucked. Not for me, exactly, although my blood pressure was a little elevated, as were my liver enzymes. And they wouldn't let me have any Copenhagen, but I wasn't exactly withdrawing from anything. I wasn't really detoxing. But I was drawing my first completely sober breaths, free from any mood or mind altering chemicals whatsoever, in years. And I was doing it in an insane asylum. There were people around me going nuts.

Most of these people, they aren't going to make it. They've spent a few days, maybe a week, detoxing from various substances under medical supervision, but when they're deemed stable, they'll go right back to whatever circumstances led them here in the first place. And almost without exception, the first thing they'll do is fuck it up. I should know—I've done it myself dozens of times.

But now I'm one of the fortunate ones. I get to go to treatment. There are about eight of us, who have spent the weekend in this hospital, and are headed over by van to the residential rehab center. And still…over half of them have done this exact same thing before. And we're the fortunate ones. It's why I was skeptical of going to treatment in the first place—it doesn't work, right? But every solution I came up with on my own landed me here, so I figure what do I have to lose. At least I can say I tried.

————————

The treatment center used to be an extended-stay hotel. It's got a main building, with both large and small conference rooms where we will attend group sessions, and we will have an apartment on campus to share with another resident. I'll be meeting my roommate later, but first we have to fill out various forms in a conference room off the main lobby.

It's been a very long time since I've felt anything remotely close to hope, but when I walk into that conference room, I get just a glimmer. A poster hangs on the wall, and on it is the face of the medical director, Dr. Steven Hobaugh, and he's smiling in a rather self-satisfied way. We spoke on the phone the day before I left, and it's good to put a name with a face. But what gives me that ray of hope is what's written beside it—"*This is what recovery looks like*". And beneath that is a brief synopsis of Dr. Hobaugh's story. And except for the fact that he'd practiced internal medicine, his story sounds remarkably similar to mine, all except for the ending. If my story ended right now, the title would be "this is what wreckage looks like". But I allow myself to think, just for the briefest of moments, 'if it can happen for him, then why not me?'

'Because, asshole, don't you remember everything you've done? You're the worst of the worst, people trusted you, and you betrayed them, betrayed your partners, your patients, your family, and your friends. About all you deserve is to get out of this place alive.' That's the sort of thing I'm telling myself, and it quickly extinguishes the fragile flame of hope. But for just that brief moment that I held onto it, the hope helped.

———————

302

The rest of the first day is a whirlwind. We aren't allowed to go anywhere on our own, for obvious reasons, and the rest of the newbies and I get taken to the grocery store. I have no idea whatsoever how to plan a menu, I wouldn't even know where to start, but I figure I can survive for the first week on cereal, sandwiches, and soup, so that's what I buy. Oh, and snuff. I buy a lot of snuff. I won't be alone, coffee and nicotine is the breakfast of champions around here.

As soon as we get back from the grocery store, I have to rush to my apartment and put away all the stuff, because I immediately have to catch yet another van with all the other doctors in treatment here to a weekly Monday evening meeting we are required to attend. It's some sort of recovery organization for physicians, and in addition to the fifteen or twenty of us being transported from the rehab, there will be local folks from Gainesville who attend regularly. We are basically their guests. Several of them were once in treatment at the same facility we are from.

Other than a couple of meetings at the detox center, where everyone was essentially a zombie, this is my first ever real recovery meeting. And I feel like a complete imposter, both because I don't have any recovery whatsoever, I'm not even sure what recovery is, but also because these people are doctors, and maybe I used to be but I'm just not, not anymore. And I don't really intend to be. I don't belong here. I don't deserve it.

The meeting is quickly called to order, and begins with a moment of silence, and then everyone recites something called the serenity prayer—"*God, grant me the serenity to accept the things I cannot change, the courage to change the things I can, and the wisdom to know the difference."* Next, we begin going around the circle introducing ourselves—'I'm Bob, I'm an alcoholic'—that sort of thing, and thankfully I'm seated about halfway around the circle because it gives me a moment to decide what to say. Steve goes, he's an alcoholic. Then Dave, and he's an addict. And then a couple of people are 'alcoholic/addicts', and before I know it it's my turn, and I decide that's what I am, too. "I'm Tom…I'm an alcoholic and an addict." Nobody is shocked or even gives a shit, they just say 'hey Tom', and continue right around the circle like it's no big deal. But to me it is. I've just admitted to about forty other men and women, and most importantly to myself, exactly what I am. And it's just a little bit, but my sense of shame, shrinks.

For some reason, I had it in my imagination that I'd start and finish rehab with the same group of people. Like we were going to boot camp together or something. But that isn't in any way practical, people come and go all the time, and although there's a definite structure, everyone is kind of going at their own pace. 'Some are sicker than others', so they say. So it's a bit of a surprise to me when I finally get a chance to sit down in the apartment and talk to my roommate.

"You've been here how long?"

"Seven weeks." That's Rob, and he's evidently been stuck here almost twice as long as I've been expecting to be here my entire stay. Rob is a family practice doctor from Tennessee, and although I had a lot of trepidation about who I'd be sharing an apartment with, I'm relieved to find out that Rob is pretty cool. But seven weeks? He must be really fucked up.

"You might as well just relax and get comfortable. You're going to be here ninety days, give or take a few. We all are, it's just the way it works." I wonder how he knew what I was thinking. "Well, unless you decide to walk across the street to the convenience store and buy a bottle of wine or something. Did you see that quiet skinny guy at the meeting? Henry? He's been here almost six months. He keeps drinking."

It occurs to me that not once have I considered doing this all day, and I'm pleasantly surprised.

"Ninety days, huh?" I think of Tami, and the burden I've left her with. I wonder how she's going to manage her job, getting the boys back and forth from school, all her responsibilities, without much help. And again, it's like Rob is a mind-reader.

"I know it seems like a long time, but you need to just focus on yourself, worry about what's going on here. I know it seems selfish, but the best thing we can do for the people back home is get better. We sure as hell weren't doing them any good before, or we wouldn't be here."

He's right. I wasn't. It's weird, Rob seeming to know exactly what I'm thinking, what I'm worried about the most. It's almost like he's done this before. But I'm not really interested in hearing much about his story, I'm in too big a hurry to tell him mine, and for the rest of the evening, I just blurt out as much of it as I can. It feels good to just unload all that shit, and Rob, he just listens and lets me.

Every Tuesday, I'll have a standing appointment with my psychiatrist, Dr. Philips. And as it turns out, it's my first appointment, on my first full day of treatment. And I'm nervous as hell. I've been lying so long and so often, I'd just assumed that twisting the truth to suit myself here would be the same. But obviously after my experience lying about opioids in the detox center, I'm struggling to believe that. And there's still shit inside my head that I'd rather this shrink didn't know about, but it feels like he already does.

"So, tell me about your visit with Dr. Stanley." Stanley, he's the one doing his addiction fellowship, the one I lied to about being an opioid addict. I explain it, but it seems like Dr. Philips has already heard it. They're both part of the same treatment team.

"And how long were you using intravenous morphine?"

"Seven years. But it wasn't IV. I gave it to myself IM." I don't know why this distinction is important to me, but it is. As if it keeps me one rung lower on the ladder of shame.

"You never used IV?"

I did. Five times at least, but not more than ten. But how am I going to explain that to him? 'See, a hundred mics of fentanyl was all I had, and that would be just a waste to inject IM, so…' It just seems like too much of a hassle to explain. The simple answer is…

"No."

He just nods. Nothing I say seems to either impress or disappoint him, and it's unnerving.

"How much would you use in a day?"

"Well…it depends. Depends on how busy I was. I guess the answer is as much as I could get."

"I see. Did you ever leave the operating room to use? Just slip out to the restroom real quick during a case?"

His expression doesn't change, but mine does. I look surprised. "No. No, I never did *that*." As if it never would've even occurred to me.

"How about in the operating room itself. You ever use there? Up under the drapes where nobody could see what you were doing?"

When I was in high school, before I ever had any inkling of becoming a doctor, much less an anesthesiologist, I remember seeing a story on one of those tabloid television shows that included "shocking video" of a nurse anesthetist, a CRNA. And she was doing exactly what Dr. Philips has just described. Some kind of hidden camera had caught her, and the hosts of the show were just aghast.

And I'm aghast that he's asking me this. "No! Of course not." I don't say it, but I want him to think it—"I'm better than that."

"How did you handle the cravings, then?" he wants to know.

"I don't know…I just waited, I guess. Anybody could wait a couple of hours. Maybe my cravings weren't that bad."

My guilt is, though. It's awful. You'd think I'd be used to it by now, walking around with one version of my life on the outside, and an

307

entirely different one internally. I used rationalization, justification, and outright denial as tools to ease the tension this kind of discord inevitably creates. But something about being here has rendered my tools ineffective. The guilt bothers me the rest of the day, and all throughout the next.

There is a recovery meeting of some sort every single day, and on Wednesdays there is a large one on campus that's open to the community. And I'm surprised to see that Dr. Philips is here, or should I say 'Anthony, alcoholic' is. That's how he introduces himself to the group. I'm fortunate that no one calls on me to share anything, because the only thing I'm able to think about for the duration of the meeting is 'Just fucking tell him. Get it over with.' And for no other reason but to make the voices inside my head shut up, after the meeting, I do.

"Say, Dr. Philips, I'm sorry. I don't mean to bug you. I know this isn't the time or the place, but my appointment with you isn't for another week, and well, if I don't tell you this right now, I'm not going to be able to sleep."

He never smiled once in his office, but I detect the makings of a grin, and although I'm certain he's just going to laugh at me, I go on.

"See, when you asked me all those things, I didn't want to tell you, but I did it. I left the room to use in the restroom. I even used right in the OR behind the screen where nobody could see. Those things you asked me…I did it."

His smile is genuine now, and it's warm. He says, "I know. It happens to all of you. *And now you know why I asked."* I can almost return his smile, and he assures me, "You're in the right place."

When my secrets started to come apart in the detox center, it felt good. It felt like a little candle came to life in the dark. But this...this feels like the fucking sun just came up.

XL

As I've said before, I grew up Baptist. And Baptist's don't go to confession. Why would we? God forgives our sins, what's the point in telling some priest about them? The priest doesn't have any power to forgive, so what's the purpose of his absolution? We don't sin against each other anyways, right? We sin against God Himself, they're His rules we're breaking, the Law is God's. At least this is how I grew up seeing it.

Dr. Philips' subtle attempts to tease a confession out of me in his office felt much more like an interrogation at a police precinct than a church parish. But that was just my inevitable perspective. I was paranoid and didn't understand what in the heck he was doing. And though there was obviously no religious intent whatsoever, the result was profoundly spiritual. Telling the truth to the right person, at the right time, set me free.

Or at least it's a start. Honesty is just the very beginning, but if I can't do that right, nothing else is going to stick. It wasn't Willie Nelson that said it, I know that now, it was Bob Dylan who said if you're going to live outside the law, you have to be honest. I'm sure that means different things to different people, but when the sun started shining on my soul again, I understood exactly what it meant for me.

This rehab, it's not religious, although it's possible to find one that is, or one that is decidedly not. But this one *is* spiritual. It's true enough that I've got problems with my body and my mind. But my trouble is also in my spirit, and I'm asked early on if I'll be willing to accept spiritual help. I don't really know what that means exactly, but I'm willing. I've done a lot stupider things to try and get sober than get on my knees and say a few prayers, if that's what they expect me to do. And that serenity prayer I heard at the first meeting, it sounds like exactly what I need.

But any time you start talking about spirituality, eventually somebody gets squirrely and screws it all up. Ultimately somebody starts talking about God. And that's dangerous. For some people, any mention of God is grounds for outright dismissal. There simply isn't one, and they seem to have found some sort of proof. And for others, unless you can agree with them on the specific details, well you're wrong. They seem to have some incontrovertible evidence, too, but best I can tell, both are just going on faith. Maybe it doesn't feel like it though, because something about the certainty is a comfort. It relieves the tension. But sometimes, the most difficult place to be at home, is in the middle.

———————————

"You ever heard that before?"

Rob, my roommate is asking me a question. I hadn't realized I'm just standing in his bedroom staring at a poster he put on the wall, but I guess I am. To get to the bathroom in our apartment, I have to walk through his bedroom. Which can be awkward, but not nearly as awkward as if we were two grown men sharing this bedroom like Bert and Ernie or something, so I just sleep out in the living room.

311

"No. No I haven't. But I like it."

The poster has two prayers, one on either side, and on the left it says this—"*You are a meaningless speck of dust in an endless universe.*" And on the right side it says "*The entire world was created just for you.*" And right in the middle…"*NOW BALANCE THE TWO*".

"It's kind of based on the teachings of this Jewish rabbi from a couple hundred years ago," Rob tells me.

"You Jewish?" I ask him, interested.

"No…but whatever works, you know? And what I tried before didn't."

"What's that?"

Rob is pretty private. I knew he'd been to treatment before, but not really any of the details. Maybe it's because I never shut up about myself, but now it's his turn to tell me the rest of his story. At the few meetings we've been to it's always been "Rob, alcoholic", so I'm a little surprised to hear that the first time he was in treatment five years before, it wasn't for booze. It was opioids. He's divorced now, but back then he was married to a nurse, and it seems like they had a real prescription writing scam going on at pharmacies all over town. This was in the bad old days, when writing bogus scripts for things like oxycodone was a lot simpler, but eventually they were caught, and the DEA got involved.

"I was scared shitless. I was willing to do anything to keep my medical license, or stay out of prison even, so when they said you're going to treatment, I went. And I needed it of course, I mean you know

312

what it's like when you're hooked on that shit. It's the definition of being a drug addict. But the spiritual aspect, all that God stuff, I just didn't buy it. Didn't think I needed it. I signed a 5 year contract with the physicians health program, they drug tested me all the time at first, and for a while, that's all I needed. It worked. I was just so relieved to be back to work and out of trouble, I stayed clean out of fear of getting caught. I thought working a spiritual program could maybe supplement all the testing, but I didn't think it was really necessary. But I completely had it backwards. Eventually they start testing you less frequently, and by the fifth year it's only like once a month. And I started doing the math, you know. Figured if I tested like on a Thursday, I'd be good for a while and could quit before I got tested again."

"Where'd you get the pills this time?" I ask.

"I didn't. I drank. See, the first time in treatment I totally surrendered to opioids. I knew if I ever used them again, I'd be hooked. But I never surrendered to alcohol. Before the pills, I drank, you know, but it was never really a problem, at least not like the pills. So I assumed it would be the same, that I could still do it. I mean, they tell us we can't, but I never believed it. But turns out they were right." Rob shrugs. "Once I started drinking, I just couldn't control it, and eventually I got caught, even though I knew I'd be tested sooner or later. That's why when I introduce myself at meetings, I just say I'm an alcoholic. I never want to forget why I had to come back a second time."

———————————

Rob's poster isn't the only one I've seen hanging around this place. They're all over. They usually have slogans I try to ignore because most of them just seem trite, even irritating, like "One Day at a Time". It sounds like how you serve out a prison sentence. But there's one I just keep coming back to in my mind. It says "Trust the Timing Of Your Life". Dr. Philips told me directly, "you're in the right place," and I believe him. I'm sure Rob doesn't know it, but he's indirectly telling me that it's also the right time. His story could have just as easily been mine, it *is* mine in so many ways. It's just that the timing is different. I have to believe that the previous three months taught me the lessons that I still needed to know, that I'm not just physically addicted to opioids. And if not for that overcast sky, telling me it just wasn't quite time to soar like the bird up above, maybe I would've never figured it out. I thought I could drink again, too. Definitely would've thought I could smoke pot. And if I would've come here because Tami kicked me out of the house…or because I'd been arrested…or because I wanted to somehow hold on to my job…Just like Rob, I would've confused the relief I felt for sort of getting my life back with genuine gratitude. And once that relief wore off, I would've had to replace it with something else. I wonder how long I would've lasted before I drank. Or worse.

I'm not going to tell Rob any of this. Hell, I'm not going to tell anyone, because I'm afraid it'll sound too much like I think that the entire world was made just for me. But for this moment, just between me and a God of my own misunderstanding, I'm grateful…for that bird, the overcast sky, all of it. I'm going to trust in the timing of my life, even if sometimes the answer I need, is not yet.

XLI

Every Friday afternoon at treatment, we have an hour of music. It's meant to be a form of therapy, I suppose. And everybody hates it. I'm not sure why, because I'm kind of looking forward to it myself, but I hear people grumbling about it all morning. "Oh great, we get to listen to Linda play us more folk songs." Accompanied by an enormous eye roll, this seems to be the prevailing attitude towards Friday music hour.

Linda, she's Dr. Hobaugh's office assistant, and if I had to guess, I'd say her primary vice had been marijuana. Or grass, as she probably would've referred to it. She's not fantastic or anything, but she can strum an acoustic guitar and carry a tune, and it soothes my sadness. I'm not sure what everyone else was complaining about, would they rather sit through another hour of "process group"? Linda does a version of Neil Young's "Helpless" that's just fantastic, and those of us who know it sing along.

Some of the other residents here have brought their own instruments with them to treatment, which amazes me. I could barely get it together enough a week ago to pack adequate clothes, but after Linda plays, anyone who wants to can sing a song themselves. A guy from my small process group who happens to be an engineer of some sort gets up, and evidently it's not his first time, because I swear a small buzz goes through the crowd of forty or fifty of us. I guess he's pretty good.

"And it's been awhile

Since I could hold my head up high…"

He's singing a song I'm familiar with by Staind. And yeah, he's pretty good. I don't think about singing along, I just close my eyes and listen.

"And it's been awhile

Since I can say that I wasn't addicted.

And it's been awhile

Since I can say that I love myself as well…"

It's also been awhile since I experienced anything like normal emotions, it's all just completely overwhelming, and I feel joy, hope, fear, and regret all at exactly the same time. I'm just so thankful to finally be here, I think I've wanted to come for years but I just had too much fucking fear, buried beneath my massive pride. But I'm also regretful and sad about all the hurt I've caused, and I just curl myself around my knees and let myself weep. Tears of both joy and sadness are all mixed together and it is just the most immense relief and I do not give a shit if anybody sees me.

————————————

It might be a relief, admitting the truth. And in only a week, I've made a good beginning. I'm open to spiritual help, and I'm willing to try something different. And it feels great, being hopeful. But if I really want to stay sober, and feel comfortable doing it, I'm going to have to do a lot more than that. It can't all be just frothy emotion, it won't last. Because Tony was right—if it's all up to me, I'm going to fail. For over two decades I've been self-reliant, and I depended on my own will to attain what I thought would be success. You can't get to medical school, let alone through it, without a certain amount of pride and ego. And if my ego got a little greedy, well sometimes it was good. What's wrong with wanting to be the best you can be, to reach for the stars, if you can? Pride and ego not only helped me survive, but to thrive even. If I work hard, make sacrifices, and delay gratification, is it entitlement to have certain expectations of being rewarded? Wouldn't anyone feel the same? Isn't that what I should be teaching my kids? That if you want something, you've got to work for it?

Self-reliance, it works…until it doesn't. Until you're standing in your backyard surrounded by "success", but you're staring up into the sky wondering is this all there is? What next? There has to be something more than just passing gas in the galaxy. This is the moment of danger. It's not when you pierce your skin with a needle, it's before that, when your discontent tells you that you need to, your entitlement gives you permission, and your pride convinces you that you can get away with it. When your mind starts creating an environment where it's ok to do what you know you shouldn't—it's ok to use. You can do things other people can't. It's both a blessing, and a curse. It breeds both success and failure.

It's not really much of a surprise when I'm told early on that if self-reliance has failed me, then I'm going to have to find something greater than myself to believe in. I've read enough books, seen enough movies to know about finding a "Higher Power". And I also know that this is where a lot of people balk. Maybe it's because they weren't raised with a belief in God, or maybe it's because they were. Or maybe I just grew up with more naturally occurring cannabinoid receptors and it makes me gullible, but I'm grateful for it, because I'm not creative enough to find purpose and meaning in a world that isn't inherently enchanted. And as I'm discovering, purpose and meaning are the vitamins and minerals of the soul. They have to be part of my culture, my medium for growth, because without them, I am clay but no breath. I may survive, but just barely. I cannot fully live.

So for me, it's not a matter of finding some sort of belief. It's more in trying to understand why I'm so disconnected from it. I'm never going to be able to fit God back inside of the box I grew up with, the one I took with me to Japan. He's far too big for it. I have a great deal of respect and admiration for some of the philosophies and ways of being that I learned about in Japan. Even envy, sometimes. But I'm not spiritually fluent. None of it comes naturally to me, my mind gets in the way.

My spiritual native tongue is Christianity, but my ego attempts to get in the way of that, as well. Sometimes by telling me that people will think I'm foolish, that we're all just dust in an infinite universe, and if there's a God at all, he'd have to be so big and non-specific to belong there that he could never be concerned with something as small as me. And other times by telling me that "real" Christians will think I'm a heretic, that spiritual food isn't served in some kind of cafeteria, where I get to pick and choose what I find palatable. A specific meal is served, and how can I have any pudding if I won't eat my meat? Any God I claim to believe in is a corruption, a well-intentioned but erroneous alteration.

But fuck all that. Because my life depends on it. And if I really want to understand what's been separating me from God, I'm going to have to keep my ego in check, and balance the two.

XLII

During the first few weeks of treatment, one of the exercises they assign us is called a timeline. It's supposed to be a graphic illustration of our drug and alcohol use throughout our entire lives. Nothing is to be left out, we are to be thorough and honest. Usually when a doctor asks a patient 'how much do you drink', whatever the answer is, the doctor automatically doubles it. People tend to minimize that sort of thing. But here that's not going to do us any good, and it's obvious when everyone shares their timeline that for the most part we tell the truth. If anything, I'd swear some people must be exaggerating how much they used.

Pinpointing the precise moment when we lost control isn't the purpose of this exercise. The point is the progression. Some people started earlier, some later. Some only drank alcohol, a few never touched it, and for most of us alcohol was just another drug. But despite these differences, without fail, everyone's use got worse over time, never better. Some people may have had some brief success cutting back, but nobody ever thinks "well, I'm down to four drinks or pills a day now, maybe I'll go ahead and check myself into rehab to finish the job." No, we all come in on a losing streak.

The timeline isn't supposed to show me how to get better, it's meant to convince me that I need to in the first place. It's not just that things got a little out of hand, I don't just have a bad habit to break, I'm actually ill. Or if you prefer, unhealthy. There shouldn't be any debate about *that*. But what I'm looking at on my timeline isn't the sickness itself. It's actually just the symptoms.

All this makes me a little impatient. I didn't come here to have them tell me what I already knew, I want them to tell me what to do about it. I want that "spiritual help" they speak of. But the treatment team, they know something else that I don't—I'm not ready yet. You can't just go into a group of people who are starving and thirsty and say "I've got the Good News!" First you better dig a well and give them some water. Physical needs come before spiritual ones. And even if it's not overnight, I'm physically healing. I'm sleeping better, going to the gym, I'm not drinking ninety percent of my calories like I did for the last three months. My brain is healing, too, my neurotransmitters and receptors are resetting. I'm starting to feel better than I have in years. And the worst thing that could happen during all of this progress would be for me to conclude that 'things weren't really that bad. All I really needed to do was get clean, and now I am.' So while I'm physically healing, I've got this timeline staring me in the face, as a graphic reminder of exactly how unhealthy I was.

Most religious people I know, they wouldn't refer to all these examples of drug and alcohol abuse as "symptoms". They'd simply call it sin, and their solution might be to "stop sinning!" Only I can't. I'm what the poet Robert Browning called a "half-man", and 'the things that I'm actually able to do, I will not. And the things that I want to do, I cannot. Life itself is a struggle.' Not in these exact words or anything, but this is pretty much straight out of the Bible. For some, that might make them believe it even more, or it might make others disregard it as complete bullshit, but I don't really care where it comes from. I just know it's the truth.

A gazelle doesn't have to worry about things like sin. A "bad" gazelle, well there's just no such thing. He does have to worry about survival, though. And if he's lived long enough to be a full grown gazelle, he's got a set of skills for that. He's got a good nose, and he's fast, and when he smells a lion nearby, he knows to run. And if he's lucky enough to escape, I'll tell you what he doesn't do—he doesn't stand around thinking to himself, 'That fucking lion…I was having a perfectly good Tuesday afternoon until that asshole came along and ruined it.' I don't know this for certain, mind you, I'm not a gazelle. But I suspect instead he just keeps on keeping on in whatever way gazelles do.

But not me. Some surgeon steps in and interrupts while I'm interviewing a patient and I immediately think 'Hey jackass, you can wait your turn can't you?" But I only think it of course, I don't say shit, on the outside I stay polite—"No, no, you go ahead…" I'm not going to tell on him, or push him in the back like I might if we were kids and he cut in the cafeteria line at school. C'mon, I'm an adult. I know how to act like a grown up, even if I'm convinced that surgeon just doesn't, he's selfish, and every once in a while I'll remind myself, 'that guy is an arrogant asshole.' It makes me feel a little bit better about his insignificant slight. And none of this is because I'm smarter than the gazelle. I do it because I'm spiritual. Even if my spirit isn't healthy.

At first it's a bit of a surprise when the treatment team tells me that yeah, maybe the surgeon in my example is being self-centered. But so am I. And that's the only thing I should be concerned about, because what it means is, I'm not really acting like a grown up after all. It means I'm not being honest.

———————————

"What is your purpose in life?"

Dr. Gardner asks us this in a larger group session. If there's a guru here, it's Dr. Gardner. He's at least eighty, and it seems like everyone here is simultaneously both drawn to and terrified of him at the same time. Because he knows how to help us get better, but he's also got a bullshit detector like I've never seen before. Anything that comes remotely close to rationalization or justification is immediately called out. 'You used drugs because you couldn't not use them!' It's as simple as that, nothing else matters. 'You were powerless not to!' And for Dr. Gardner, nothing is more powerful than brutal honesty.

It's why I'm afraid to answer his question, because I know it'll be wrong. But the first answer that pops into my head is the first one I ever learned—to glorify God. That is the purpose of life. But I know that's not what he's looking for. Dr. Gardner doesn't talk about God, at all.

"To pass on your genes. To reproduce." One of the other doctors says it, and biologically speaking, from the standpoint of survival of the species, he's right.

"No." Dr. Gardner says it with finality, like he's mildly exasperated that nobody gets it, surveys the room to see if anyone else is brave enough to venture a guess. And no one is.

"Growth," he growls. "Your purpose in life, is growth."

Per Dr. G.'s criteria, I have evidently failed at my purpose, and he's not shy about letting me know it. "You're not acting like a grown up, you're not being honest with the people around you, and more importantly, with yourself," he tells me. And it's mildly offensive. 'Whaddya mean I'm not a grown up, I've got a mortgage!' But he's referring to the incident when the surgeon so rudely interrupted me and pissed me off. It was just some random example I came up with when I was asked to identify a time when I was angry at someone. It seems so small and insignificant, but Dr. Gardner assures me that it's not.

"Ok, so what, I should've just told him to wait his turn?" I ask.

"Don't use words like should've. We're not trying to judge ourselves. We're trying to learn from our patterns of behavior." He's talking to me, but looking at the rest of the group in the room. This is how we learn—from other peoples' experiences, as well as our own. Because we have a lot more in common than just how we drink and take drugs.

"Well, I was being polite. I didn't want to make a scene in front of the patient. Should I have," I stop myself. "I mean, would it have been more grown up to throw a fit about it? And since when is being polite dishonest?"

"When it doesn't reflect how you really feel," Dr. G. replies. And it sounds so obvious it's irritating. "When the surgeon interrupted you, how did you feel?"

"I thought he was being selfish, and rude."

324

"Those aren't feelings, they're thoughts. About him. I'm asking you what you felt."

"Um…irritated. Disrespected." I suck at this, identifying my feelings, and it's uncomfortable.

"Why?" he asks me. And all I can do is look at him like I suddenly don't remember that one and one makes two. So he answers for me, in a way I recognize, but either don't want to know or can't bring myself to say.

"You felt angry and afraid, because your pride was wounded, and you felt insignificant. And you think that just because you don't say anything, because you're "polite", that you aren't being prideful. But you just don't want your colleague to know how you really feel, so what seems like courtesy, is actually manipulative, and dishonest."

"You think telling him how I felt would've helped?" I reply, like I don't think so at all.

"Maybe. If you could've done that it might've prevented you from becoming resentful. But I suspect you would've done what you did today—told him what you thought. About him. It would have been your pride speaking. I don't suppose you would have said anything about how you felt hurt, or insignificant." He doesn't even need to look at me to know the answer to that.

"And you don't really know how to tell the truth to yourself, either. Instead, you remind yourself, 'That guy is an arrogant asshole,' right? Because it feels so much better than admitting the truth, which is that deep down, you're afraid that your colleague might be right about you. What if you really are just as small and insignificant as his actions seemed to show?

"So what kept Tom, here, from being honest with the person who offended him?" Dr. G. asks the group. And it's obvious to them all.

"His pride," they say.

"And Tom, what kept you from being honest with yourself?"

"Fear," I say, like it's some kind of pleasant surprise.

Dr. G. nods. "Self-centered fear controls us. We are afraid of not getting what we think we want, or of losing what we already have. This fear, along with other defects of character like pride and anger, keeps us from being honest. And without honesty, we have no true fellowship with others. Now I'm not suggesting you should go up to everyone who steps on your toes in some way and tell them how you feel about it. It's usually unnecessary. But the one person with whom you must always be transparent, is yourself. Your whole recovery depends on it. Because spirituality is having an honest relationship with yourself. Most of you weren't honest enough with yourselves to acknowledge that you'd become powerless over drugs and alcohol. And dishonesty with others kept you from asking for help."

This isn't the only interaction that ever left me angry or hurt, of course. I have others that aren't nearly as innocent, as do all of my fellow addicts here in treatment. Some are resentful at parents, who got divorced, big brothers who bullied them, employers who didn't hire them, police who arrested them, spouses who left them, adults who abused them, institutions that oppressed them. And all of us, are angry at ourselves. For the things we did and wished we hadn't, and for what we might've done but didn't. We are angry simply because we are here, in treatment. But *here*, could be anywhere.

It doesn't make it any easier to be told that we're responsible. Not for what happened to us, we didn't have any control over that. A lot of it happened when we were young, vulnerable, with no set of skills to defend ourselves. We didn't know what the lion smelled like, much less to run from him. Didn't know that the lion could smell like Brut 33 aftershave that your best friend's older brother wore when he was sixteen and you were what, six?

No, we are not responsible for the lions, even if some of them are sick themselves, doing the only thing they know how to do to survive. Sometimes hurt people, hurt people. But for us, surviving requires us to learn a new way to live, and for that, we are responsible. We have to learn what it truly means to turn the other cheek, because like Martin Luther King, Jr. said, we don't have a choice. It's not violence or non-violence, the only people our resentment continues to harm is ourselves. "It's non-violence, or non-existence."

XLIII

Addiction is hell. I don't mean that in a sort of "scariest environment imaginable" type of way. At least from what I experienced, as awful as it was, it could've been much worse. But it's not a description I take lightly, either. For me, it's actually not a description at all. It's a definition. I may struggle to wrap my head around the concept of hell as a destination after death, designed as an eternal punishment to satisfy God's wrath, but that doesn't mean I don't believe hell exists. And wherever it is, it seems not to be opposite from heaven, but tantalizingly close. That's what intensifies the suffering, knowing how close I am to salvation, but through my own efforts, am powerless to reach it. That's hell. It is separation from God. And what is separating me seems almost too simple to stumble upon.

Pride. Envy. Anger. Greed. Per the terminology of treatment, these are a few of what we call character defects, and they are fuel for my dishonesty and fear. But I have another name for them as well—they're also a few of the seven deadly sins. Not that anybody uses the word sin here. They'd probably scoff if anyone said it, so I don't. And it does sound rather religious and judgmental, I admit. But it's not baggage for me, and having a broader vocabulary to explain a truth, well I just find it helpful. So I still use "sin", if only in my own head, because it doesn't detract from my understanding. If anything, it enhances it. Because if I've got a new way to consider sin, I've got a new way to consider the God I grew up with, as well. Because in my mind, God and sin are intimately intertwined. Or rather, they're not. God and sin are separated.

Sin isn't something I do. It's something I am, spiritually at least. And I have to think that's the way Jesus might have seen it too, or why else would he have suggested that you didn't need to actually kill anybody to face the fires of hell. You just had to want to. You're already outside the law before you've lifted a finger. What separates me from God isn't an action. It's arrogance, the attitude that I am self-sufficient. That I myself can provide everything I'll ever need or want, only to find that once I have it, I cannot escape it, nor is it ever enough. I fear that the feasts will never last, and the famines will never end. I am a hungry ghost. This is a Buddhist term, by the way, and I'm almost certainly using it wrong. But sometimes things get found in translation, and to me, it says everything. The only spirit that can satisfy me, comes from God.

It's not easy to let go of pride and ego. They're as hard to let go of as a drink or a drug, maybe harder. I'm as dependent on them to make me feel the way I want to feel as I was on the chemicals. And just like with alcohol, my usage of them wasn't always pathological. It wasn't until I got too much of a good thing, and my assets became defective. When healthy pride became selfish arrogance. Sin is nothing more than corruption of a good thing, an unintended alteration that spoils so slowly I can't tell it's gone bad until it's too late. Until I've crossed that thin gray line of the yin and yang, and the only thing that

329

can put me back on it, is wisdom I don't know I need, until I've fought battles I've already lost.

I can't do it from here in treatment, anyway. It's not real life, it's a cocoon, and hopefully, I'm having a metamorphosis. But to test our wings a bit, before our ninety days are up, we start going home on weekends. It's not just a reward, it's a requirement. We've got training wheels on, of sorts, we pee into a cup both before we leave and the day we get back, and every eight or so hours, we blow into a breathalyzer. It's a safety net, of course, but if I stare at it too long, I'll fall right into it, and it'll be a trap instead. Drug testing is not the solution to my sickness. It just lets everyone else know when the symptoms are back. So for the most part I pretend the safety net's not there, and I keep my eyes focused on where I want to go.

The first time I went home was almost overwhelming. It was great to see TJ and Tyson, of course, and we tried to squeeze as much fun as possible into the three days. I also attended my first ever recovery meeting in Oklahoma City, which was a little surreal. I would've almost rather died than do this not even two months ago, but if somehow I had, I would've picked one just as far away from my house as possible to avoid the remote chance of seeing someone I knew. But now for convenience, I picked the one closest to my house, and turns out, it's less than a mile away. And though I was still a little anxious, I'm far enough along to understand that anyone I might happen to know, well they'd be happy as hell to see me. Especially if they're serious enough about sobriety to be at a meeting at seven on a Saturday morning. I didn't go because I had to. I could've not gone and no one at treatment would've known. I went because they told me to, and I've decided that I'm going to follow the instructions. Even when I don't want to. Even when it seems stupid, and sleeping in sounds better.

But that first trip home, it wasn't all easy. After a day or two, I began to feel irritated, to lose patience. A couple of times I got short with Tyson, who had a ton of questions, and if I didn't know better, I would've sworn I was in the early stages of dopesickness. It almost felt the same.

"It's spiritual fatigue," my therapist suggested, when I'd returned to treatment and told her about it. "It'll get better if you keep doing what you're doing. Spiritual fitness is your goal. And there's no better indicator of it than patience."

Love, joy, peace, patience, kindness. I recognize these things, too, just like I did the seven deadly sins. They're the fruit of God's spirit. I still get tripped up trying to conclude exactly what spirituality means, although Dr. G.'s definition of an honest relationship with myself seems sufficient. I just have trouble accepting that it could be that simple. I don't have any trouble deciding what it looks like, though—it looks exactly like these virtues. And if God and I have been separated, I've been cut off from their source. I don't know that God needs any other names, he just *is*, and "I Am" sort of says it all. But if I was pressed to make one up, that would be it—God is the source. Of everything good.

On my last trip home, I have an assignment that goes beyond just going to a recovery meeting—I have to actually meet someone.

And not only that, I have to walk up to them, and ask for their help. Because I can't do this by myself, I need fellowship, an honest relationship with another man. Because sometimes I'll still buy my own bullshit.

"How do I pick?" I ask my therapist, when she tells me I need to do it.

"Just find somebody who has what you want," she tells me.

"What if they say no?" I laugh, but I mean it. I'm nervous about it.

"They won't," she says. "But if they do, be grateful. It wouldn't have worked out anyway."

I assume it'll be hard, but meeting Ryan is ridiculously easy. That's the guy's name, the one I'm supposed to meet, and he's nothing like me. He's younger than I am, and better looking, thought he could be an actor or rock star or something, so he moved to California years ago. But turns out, he liked meth more than auditions, and he got more DUIs than actual roles, and when he finally came back from Cali, he had a record alright, but not the kind that you listen to. I won't know any of this until much later, and none of it really matters, anyway. All I know right now is that when he shares in the meeting, he sounds like a guy who has found a better way to live, and that's exactly what I want. And it's even more obvious when the chairman of the meeting says, "anybody willing to sponsor somebody, raise your hand," and Ryan does, so I figure that's it. I'm not even nervous at all when I walk up to him after the meeting and ask him if he'll be my sponsor, and just like my therapist promised, he says "when you get back from Gainesville, gimme a call."

———————————

"Do you think I could ever do my job again?" This is a question that does make me nervous, I'm much less sure of the answer, and it takes all the courage I can muster to even ask. But I know the only thing stopping me is my pride—'What if the answer is no? I'll look like a fool for even thinking it. Me? Go back to the OR? What are you, nuts?' But I was told early on by the medical director, Dr. Hobaugh, who's picture gave me my first glimpse of the goal—ask for what you want. And what I want, is to go back to work. I want to be useful. Oh, I had my moments of thinking that this recovery thing, it's the greatest thing in the world! *Everybody* needs it, not just drug addicts and alcoholics. I should do a fellowship in addiction medicine, imagine how many people I could help, people who really need it! If not me, then who? But I recognized that as just my ego talking. Another delusion of grandeur. More missionary zeal. Not that there's anything wrong with that, and maybe that could be in my future, like it was for the former cardiologist I met in detox. But TJ and Tyson, they're the ones who need me most, and they don't need more change. They need stability. And maybe it's just a way of avoiding disappointment, of the embarrassment of being told no. But before I ask if going back to the OR is even possible, I check my motives, as I've learned to do, and I decide that if the answer is no, then that's ok. It's for the best. It wouldn't have worked out anyway. If that's really the answer, then I want to know now, not after I've returned to the hell I came from. I don't ever want to go back to that. So the person I choose to ask, is the one I think I can most rely on to tell me the answer I don't want to hear. I ask Dr. G. And I'm a bit surprised when he doesn't really answer at all. Instead, he lets me do it for myself.

"You can do anything you want," he tells me. "If you can do it without fear." And I immediately know what he means, it is beyond a simple yes. It is the best possible reply.

XLIV

How do you know when you've been in rehab long enough?—When it no longer matters when you go home. I'm not sure if I buy that, but it's what Dr. G. would say. At least I'm not in a hurry, I'm being patient, and I'm trusting the treatment team to tell me when it's time, and maybe that's all that's meant by "it no longer matters" anyway. I'm not trying to control it. Still, I'm thrilled when I'm told that I'll be discharged in two weeks. After ninety-five days, I'll be going home.

That means two more appointments with Dr. Philips, my psychiatrist.

"Did you get your first Vivitrol shot yet?" he asks me.

"Yep," and I rub my right buttock, where I can still feel a small lump, and it's sore from the injection yesterday. Next month, I'll get another shot on the left side, and I'll continue like that, alternating ass cheeks every thirty days, for the next two years. In addition to random weekly drug and alcohol screening, it's another layer of my safety net. Vivitrol is an injectable form of an opiate blocking drug called naltrexone, and each shot lasts a month. I have an appointment scheduled with a doctor in Oklahoma City, who will administer my next one, and send documentation to the physician's health program so they know I've taken it. Naltrexone blocks opioid receptors, so that supposing I do get squirrelly, and find myself tempted by a syringe full of fentanyl or something, using it would be pointless. All my opioid receptors will be occupied, too busy to respond. Which will suck if I'm in an accident and break my leg, because it would take enough morphine to kill Keith Richards to make a dent in my pain. But if I'm a recovering opioid addict returning to an environment where handling the drugs is part of the job, it's fantastic. It's a necessity. Not only for my patients, but also for me. Sometimes the first sign of relapse in an anesthesiologist returning to the OR, is death.

But death isn't the fear I have to overcome. It's not what Dr. G. meant when he said I'd have to be without fear in order to do anything on earth that other free men and women can do. I immediately knew what he meant because I'd felt the fear he spoke of myself a thousand times. Felt it every time I'd vow to get clean on my own. That today, I will not fail, only to watch my resolve melt like a single flake of snow upon a bed of hot coals, for underneath all the fight songs and fist pumps, I was just a scared little kid, whistling in the dark, hands stuffed deep into the pockets, holding on to nothing. Except when I held a vial of morphine, my heart would race, my saliva would dry, and my mind could focus on nothing but escape, until a voice, soothing and soft, would say it's okay…there is always tomorrow…and nobody else will know. *That's* the kind of fear I'm talking about.

But it doesn't respond to confidence. It responds to acceptance. Not of the fear itself, but of whatever it is that I'm afraid of. The only reason I was willing to ask Dr. G. the question in the first place—to be willing to ask for what I want—is that if the answer is no? It's ok. It's no longer my will that matters. Because "all things work together for good for them that love God, for them who are called according to his purpose." All things. Even failure. That, especially.

When I was younger, and deciding whether I really wanted to be a physician or not, I read a book called *The Prophet*, by a Lebanese poet named Khalil Gibran. And best I can remember, it's essentially about an older man, the Prophet, I suppose, dispensing advice to a young man about how best to live. Most of the chapters I don't specifically recall, but one I do is about work, and how to make work meaningful. And like most useful answers are, this one is simple—whatever you do, whether you choose it or it chooses you, do it with love. If you are a baker, bake bread as if it will be eaten by your beloved.

I wonder if the Prophet knew the young man would likely fail. Almost certainly he did, because elsewhere in the book, he tells the young man to expect pain, but that it will uncover understanding, and be a means to healing himself. And, that the pain is self-inflicted. It is the inevitable result of relying on pride and ego to survive, as it seems that young people must as they make their way in the world, to get what they think they want. To succeed. If the young man did indeed become a baker, I have to imagine that he at first worried whether his business would survive, so he worked harder. And when it did, maybe he thought 'well now I have to get bigger, because that's how you grow,' or at least he thinks it is, so he opens up another store, and then another, and before you know it, he's got an empire, and he's not a baker anymore at all, it's been a long time since he actually baked any bread, let alone considered who might be eating it. The only thing that really matters is that they eat more, whether they need it or not, because that's the only way he can ever be satisfied. Even if it doesn't last.

Then, if he's lucky, he realizes that the prophet told him all this was going to happen, in one way or another, and he also told him what to do about it—whatever you do, do it with love. Now, if that's not God's purpose I am called to, then I can't imagine what is. I'm not sure if it requires failure to find it or not, but why bother saying that 'all things work together for good,' if they haven't fallen to pieces first. When asked what the greatest commandment is, Jesus said it's to love God above all else. But I like to think he assumed his audience would be as dumbfounded as I am about how to go about doing that, or what it even means, so he immediately followed it up with love your neighbor as yourself. Now, it might not be exactly the same thing, but for me it's close enough. It's as near as I'm ever going to get.

———————————

"How many of you all have been in treatment before?" Friday nights are for speaker meetings, and for the last forty-five minutes or so, our speaker Darren has been entertaining us with tales of what his life was like before he got sober. And he's good at it. He's hilarious. We've all been through experiences similar to his or we wouldn't be here, and trust me, none of that shit was funny at the time. But sometimes you just have to shake your head and laugh. Darren's question, though, it's serious. He wants to know how many of us are here because of a relapse. And I'll remember very little about the funny stories, but what he's going to say next, I'm going to burn into memory.

338

"So if you've been in treatment before, raise your hand." And I'm not counting or anything, but in a room full of fifty or so people, it seems like more than half stick their hand up. Some people are raising both arms, as if to say this is my third time, at least. Darren nods, as if this is not a surprise.

"So for those of you who raised your hands, before you came back this time...how many of you had a regular recovery meeting you attended, you were working on steps with a sponsor, you were praying or meditating, and you were doing something to help the next alcoholic or addict who was still suffering?"

And not one hand goes up.

Darren pauses, lets it sink in. Like I said, he's good at this. "You know, I've probably asked the same question ten thousand times, and every single time, it's just like this. Not one person says they were doing all those things before they relapsed. You can't just go to meetings. You can't just pray. You can't just be receiving all the time. Sobriety is a gift, man. It's an amazing, mysterious gift. We've all got a second chance at life. But if you want to keep it, you have to continue to give it away."

This isn't exactly what I wanted to hear. What I want is to be an artist, to be unique, to take a little of this, and a little of that, and come up with a creation that only I could conceive of, that would be just a little bit different from the next guy. Something that would be an original. I want to make my own path. And that might work in the regular world for regular people, but when it comes to getting sober for a drug addict like me, it just doesn't. I'll come up with an original result, alright. But it'll be a disaster. It'll sound like I was up all night smoking weed, writing music to a song that no one will ever hear, with lyrics that only I could understand, and my altered senses will tell me that it all sounds just so *amazing*, only when I wake up to the reality of day, it all just sounds like shit. Really, all I want is a shortcut, I'm just being lazy. It's sloth. And all it ever led to, was here, on a losing streak.

The drug testing, the Vivitrol, the support from the physicians health program, it's helpful. But it's compliance, it's not recovery. It's a safety net, but if I rely on it, it's already too late, I'll be off balance, and it'll be a matter of time before I fall. If I want what Darren has, I have to be willing to do what men and women like him do. I want to be able to look at my past without regret, to look towards my future without fear, and to be able to enjoy each day without thinking too much about either one. And he's told me exactly how to do it, that if I do a few simple things, follow certain steps, and maintain an attitude of service and humility, I will get the same result as he. So instead of trying to be an artist, it's time to start acting more like a scientist.

XLV

The life I once had, it's gone. I suppose that's what happens any time you leave home, even if you don't think it's for good. Because once you try to go back, things are different. Time passes. Even if nothing there changes, you have. I'd been trying to go back for years, to unwind the damage and just be the person I was when I was twenty, but of course I couldn't. Back home, "the chains are locked and tied across the door", it's a place locked permanently in the past. It's good to hear Linda sing "Helpless" one more time, but it doesn't make me sad like it did on that first Friday. I don't need to go back anymore. I'm at home today, and I'm at peace.

———————

At my last appointment with Dr. Philips, he smiles more than I've ever seen him before. He's happy for me. This is why he does his job, this is what it means for him to love through his work.

"So what are your plans for the future?" he asks me.

"Not sure," and I shrug. "Stay sober, try to be a good dad, see if Tami and I can work things out...and look for a job, I guess." And I smile, too. I am not afraid, no matter what the answer is.

"Good." Dr. Philips says. "I'm glad you're going back to work. We don't shoot our wounded. You can do it."

"Thank you," I tell him. "For everything."

"That doesn't mean it's going to be easy. Some people may not want you back."

I don't know if he means at home or at work, and I don't suppose it matters. He might as well mean everywhere.

"Some people just don't like drug addicts," he reminds me. "It doesn't really matter what their reasons are, they're on their own journey, and it's not your job to change them." Dr. Philips pauses. He wants what he's about to say to sink in.

"Wherever you go, you're going to encounter signs. Some will be stop signs. And some will be welcome signs." He smiles, and though it doesn't need to be said, he says it anyway. "Go toward the welcome signs."

I smile, too. "I will."

"And don't fuck it up."

Laughter. "I won't."

He shakes my hand, gives me a firm grip on the shoulder. "Good luck, Tom."

"Thank you sir."

'God grant me the serenity to accept the things I cannot change

The courage to change the things I can.

And the wisdom to know the difference.'

Going towards the welcome signs, it's going to be a lot harder than Dr. Philips makes it sound, I think. But he probably knew that. I've discovered I'm more of a people-pleaser than I would've ever wanted to admit. I have a hard time saying no sometimes, and my 'yes' is too often dishonest. But I also like to prove people wrong, and the stop signs he mentioned, they're a temptation to do that. I want to take the tools I've learned in treatment, turn them into a hammer, and walk across the street and start bashing the shit out of the stop sign. Not in broad daylight or anything, I don't like confrontation, and I'd probably be just as polite about it as possible, maybe even offer to replace the rusted sign with something better. But my motive would be the same—don't they know that sign shouldn't be there in the first place? Don't they know they're wrong?

But I'm not supposed to stay away from the stop signs just because I'm not welcome there. It's not only that it's hard to be successful in a place where you're not really wanted. I need to stay away to protect myself from the sin of self-righteousness. It's another one of my character defects, it will separate me from God, and if I want serenity, God is my source. My only real competition is with myself. Trying to prove people wrong, trying to do what they say can't be done, it never works out in the long run anyway. It's a young person's game, played with pride and confidence, and all the pats on the back, all the prizes, they fade like a dying round of applause that leaves only echoes of what you really wanted.

The welcome signs, they're for people like me, whose reach has exceeded our grasp, people who have fallen down trying to reach for the stars and into what was behind the blue, blue windows beyond them. We thought maybe it might be heaven. But had we never reached, how would we ever have known, that it's in the falling that we find it, in the last place we would have ever thought to look. How mysterious God must be to hide beneath desperation, to exist outside the box I've built, to be breath beneath the water, or wind across the sky. To be in a room full of outlaws, whose only virtue is having the honesty to admit it. And I am humbled and grateful to have a seat among them.

EPILOGUE

Five years later...

"You boys want to eat at the Big Texan?" It's hard to believe sometimes, but TJ and Tyson, they're teenagers now, fifteen and thirteen, and I'm taking them up to Taos to ski for Thanksgiving. It's opening weekend, and there are two routes we could take from Oklahoma City. One takes a bit longer, but it's more beautiful, passes through Amarillo, then over into New Mexico where the two lane desert highways extend out forever, then rise up off the basin onto the plateau. It's stunning, or at least I find it so. The other is faster by an hour, at least, and it's not quite as impressive, but it does have one other advantage—it passes through Pampa, where my story begins, or ends, depending on how you want to look at it. Getting arrested changed everything. It was the best worst day of my life.

Today I can't decide which way I want to go, so I'm letting the boys decide. They don't know that's what they're doing, of course. They think they're just picking where they want to eat. But if they choose the Big Texan in Amarillo, we'll bypass Pampa.

"Will you try to eat the seventy-two ounce steak?" TJ asks me.

I just look at him, like, 'no, of course not.'

"Can I?"

"Yeah, if you can pay for it when you don't finish."

The Big Texan has an enormous steak, that's free if you finish it in under an hour. It's a novelty I've never tried. And TJ is his father's son, sometimes bites off more than he can chew.

"I don't want to stop," Tyson says. "Let's just get to Taos." I look at TJ, and he nods. It's not quite like flipping a coin, but Pampa it is.

I don't allow myself to do it very often, and never for very long, because it's like looking into the void and sometimes it makes me shudder. But on an occasion like this when I'm passing through, I'll let myself wonder. What might've happened had I never met Officer Cunningham and his fine partner Jimmy? What calamity could've come along to stop me? Because from here, it's obvious—it was never going to be me. It took a power greater than me, which on that day was the law. And it took a secret so big that I'd never be able to keep it. As I pass by that stretch of highway, past the mile marker and the cornfield where I fell to my knees, I'm tempted to speed a little. Maybe the officers will top the hill in their black SUV, pull me over, offer to give me a warning. Because if I could, I'd like to say thanks. I know they wouldn't remember me, I'm just one of a dozen other clowns they probably pulled over that week, but I'd like them to see me with my boys, to see what they helped restore. The law wasn't enough to save me, but without it, how would I have ever found grace?

———————————

Tami isn't with us for two reasons. She hates the cold too much to ski, and also, we're divorced. When I first got back from treatment, things were still up in the air. Some days I'd be afraid that things weren't going to work out, and other times I'd be afraid that they would, and when I explained all this to my sponsor Ryan, he just said "sometimes when I don't know what to do, I don't do anything." It's not like he's a therapist, he doesn't have any credentials beyond his own experience, but when it comes to trying to sweep up the messes he's made, to take responsibility and fix what he can fix, he's more than qualified, and I took his suggestion to heart. I waited. I figured Tami waited on me for seven years or more, the least I could do was give her whatever time she needed. Turns out, what she needed was to get divorced, and that's okay.

As far as divorces go, I think it was as painless as possible, we'd been separated for so long it was more like ripping off a band-aid that was covering up a wound that wouldn't heal, and with the fresh air, it did. We'd been a sinking ship for quite some time, and in moments when we'd realize it but weren't quite ready to abandon ship, we sort of packed the lifeboats. Decided what was fair, what belonged where, and it's nice to be able to do that when you're not blinded by panic and fear. Or being told what you're entitled to by a lawyer. Maybe I'm a fool, a divorce attorney friend of mine rather bluntly suggested it, but his heart was in the right place, and it made me think, which was likely all he intended. But in the end, I just decided that I didn't need the legal system telling me what I ought to do, and I just did what I knew was right for me. Whether I like it or not, Tami is the most important person in my sons' lives. I might not have been the best husband, but I can be the best ex-one possible, and when it comes to raising TJ and Tyson, we are still partners.

347

That doesn't make it easy. Just like if our marriage hadn't ended, we have to work at it. I do my best to do what Ryan does, to clean up my own messes, and if I broke it, I try to fix it. But some of what got damaged can't be erased or replaced, only repaired, bit by bit, like trust. And early on, the way I decided to do that, was if Tami needed something done that I could do, the answer would be yes, and it would be honest. I'm welcome in their home, and just for myself, I decided that if I saw dirty dishes there, that I could wash them. I didn't do it just for her, to make life easier, I don't know if she even noticed. I did it for me, to remind myself that the clean up is continual. It has to be part of my life. The fact that Tami trusts me enough to let me take our children on a ski trip to Taos over Thanksgiving is evidence that it's working, and for that I am thankful.

———————

Speaking of partners, things went a little different with my work. We ended up getting back together. After I got back from treatment, I still had a few unresolved administrative loose ends with my severance, and I needed to get in touch to tie them up. People will surprise you. The managing partner at the time, a great guy named John, he's very buttoned-up, always has his shit together. He's a great doctor, and he's the kind of guy you don't want to disappoint, exactly the kind I wanted most to keep my secrets from. But when I told him where I'd been, far from being disappointed in me, he said he was *proud* of me. Said it must've been hard, and that he was rooting for me.

"So what are you going to do now?" John asked me, with just a slight hint of anticipation, although maybe I was imagining it.

"Well, I've got clearance to go back to work, I signed a five-year contract with the physicians health program, so I guess I'm going to start looking for a job."

He didn't even hesitate. "Well do you want to come back here?"

Dr. Hobaugh's advice echoed in my mind—ask for what you want. If the answer is no, then it wouldn't have worked out anyway. "Hell yeah, I do."

And three months later, I did. It wasn't just John, it seems the rest of my practice was rooting for me, too, and I could feel it when I first met with them to re-introduce myself—hey guys, I'm Tom, I'm an alcoholic and a drug addict. Well, I didn't do it exactly like *that*, it wasn't that kind of meeting, but that's essentially what I told them. Because I owed them honesty, and transparency, and the way I'd left six months or so before had been neither. I told them where I'd been and why, and what I intended to do about it in the future. I also told them about the welcome signs, and that although I hoped to find one from them, I'd understand if I didn't.

"It'll take a little accommodation on your part to bring me back," I told them. "I need an afternoon off once a month to get my Vivitrol shot, and some mornings I'll be notified that I have to take a urine drug screen, and somebody may have to cover my cases while I slip out to do that. And I get it if what you'd prefer is a regular partner with regular problems. It's ok. But if you liked working with me before, I'm pretty sure you're going to like the guy who comes back even better."

After the meeting, they voted, and John didn't wait until the next day to call me.

"Welcome back, Tom. Congratulations. Now get started on your hospital credentialing application ASAP." I could hear him smiling right through the phone. Them bringing me back like that, it says a whole lot more about my partners and the power of honesty than it does about me. I'm grateful to have my job back, and the fact that it was graciously given makes it all the more meaningful. More so than if I'd expected it, felt entitled to it, fought for it, demanded it. Even if pride would've worked, it wouldn't have been nearly as satisfying for my spirit. Humility, who knew?

My partners all had questions, of course, and in addition to telling them about the stop signs and welcome signs, I also shared with them the first lesson I'd learned from my psychiatrist—'*Now you know why I asked*'. Some of their questions might be designed to judge me, or perhaps just morbidly curious, even if they weren't fully aware of it. So I suggested that before they asked me anything, they first ask themselves, 'why do I want to know'? And it turns out, the most common question they had is "how can we help? How can we help you be safe and succeed?"

I can do anything I want, if I can do it without fear. I believe that can be true for anyone, but I wouldn't know for certain whether it was true for me until I walked back into the hospital and found out. My partners, they were asking healthy questions, and they suggested that for a week, why didn't I just put on some scrubs, come hang out in the OR, see what it feels like. Which sounds like a great idea I never could've conceived of on my own, I still had too much pride—Wouldn't that be embarrassing? Wouldn't everyone wonder what the hell I was doing there, if I'm not doing cases? But I do it, and it feels good. It feels like I am right where I belong. There are a few inevitable questions from the staff about where I've been, what's been going on, but for the most part, people are preoccupied with their own lives, just like I am, and simple answers satisfy. Sometimes it's a relief when the thing you've been expecting to happen, doesn't.

Which is exactly what happens when a week or so later, I handle my first vial of fentanyl—nothing. It is a sweet, silent, surprise that I would not have believed possible unless someone convinced me it could be. I'd swear, this shit used to be alive, it would glow, and seemed to have a sign on it saying "Eat Me", and the hungry ghost inside of me begged "Feed Me". But now, the vial is inert, I do not have to wrestle with it, because if it came to that, I would lose. It's just another medication, that can serve its purpose of soothing other people's pain. Mine is gone, and my hungry ghost is already satisfied.

——————————

It takes work to keep it that way, though. If I want to be physically fit, I have a lot of options. I can ride a bike, I can use the cardio machines, I could play some pickup basketball, if I were into that sort of thing. Hell, I could even just walk, it all works, anything to elevate my heart rate. The more I mix it up, the better. My body needs to stay uncomfortable to grow. And I might add in a little resistance exercise to build some muscle, lift some weights, or do some push ups. And of course, I've got to eat right. It's not easy, but it's simple, and if I do those things, my physical fitness will improve, as evidenced by increased stamina, greater strength, and lower resting heart rate. That is the fruit of my labor.

That might help keep me comfortable in my jeans, but if I want to be comfortable in my own skin, in the OR, or anywhere else, I have to treat my spirit the same way. It needs an exercise routine of its own, for spiritual fitness. The one I've chosen, it's a twelve step program, and if you know much about them, you've probably figured that out already. It's not the only path to sobriety, or the only way to strengthen your spirit, but it's one that works, and it has me doing all those things that Darren mentioned regularly. I don't have to do it all perfectly, the only thing that requires perfection is never taking a drug, and when I make an honest attempt at the rest of the work, it's remarkable how simple it is to do nothing.

Sometimes it seems *too* simple, it's kind of like elementary school spirituality, and I start thinking 'maybe I should add this', or 'maybe I could just drop that', but then I remember, if I want a specific result, I have to follow certain steps, and among other addicts is where I feel most myself being honest. There is fruit from this labor, too, and I've mentioned it before—it's peace, patience, kindness, and love. I may not be sure exactly what spirituality is, but I'm certain that's what it looks like.

Running for me, well it's somewhere in the middle. It's at the intersection of where exercising my body and my spirit meet, I guess. Even when I do it "wrong", it still works, even when I let my mind run, too, and it's off chasing rabbits. But when I do it right, it's like a silent prayer, it's a meditation through movement, and if anyone were to ask me how I make myself do it, the only thing I could come up with is 'how can you not?' Prayer is mostly that way for me now, silent like that. I'm not asking for much of anything. God doesn't need any ideas about what He should do from me, all He'd have to say is 'look what kind of a job you did running your own life, what are you trying to run the rest of the world for?' So I don't pray to try and change God's mind, I do it to change my own.

These intersections where life meets, they are balancing acts, and they are full of tension. Gravity pulls to either side. Between my flesh and spirit, pride and humility, heaven and hell, belief and unbelief, despair and hope. Science, and art. Between the law, and grace. A balancing act is no place to boast from. That happens when I'm down on the ground, where it feels more secure, with the certainty that things are black and white, having facts instead of faith. But there is little meaning, purpose, or satisfaction in this false security, and all you can do is poke and prod at the other side in smug self-righteousness convinced that I am right, and you are wrong. It is a debate that can only end in death, literally, and metaphysically. The only place of existence, of fully living, is on the thin gray line of the yin and yang, on the narrow road that leads to life, and few they are that find it. Or at least that's how I see it. It is where I go to be without fear. It is my recovery, and it is my salvation.

The boys and I, we had a great Thanksgiving. The snow wasn't great, it's usually not this early in the year, but that's not always the point. I'm just grateful we were able to go. On the way back, I don't ask the boys to decide the route. It's my turn to choose, and we're taking the long way back through the beauty of New Mexico. It's about the journey, rather than reaching our destination, which I didn't really understand until I was middle-aged, and my physical journey was over halfway through. It seems odd, but sometimes the hardest place to have peace and patience is at home, with these boys. But I know that it's just because I want the best for them, and sometimes I'm afraid. I know I need to teach them independence and self-reliance, to have a healthy pride and to work hard. But they also need to know what to do when those things fail them, and they will. Or at least I hope so. This story, it's for them, so that they can read it when they're older. It's no secret that addiction runs in families, but I try not to let that frighten me, and I certainly don't want it to frighten them. I pray it lets them know that whatever it is that brings them to their knees, it's only to put them right where they belong, where they may find a strength and wonder they would not have otherwise known existed.

I've often asked myself, if addiction is so awful, then why would God make people this way? Or if you like, why wouldn't evolution have weeded it out? Maybe it's like wondering what the world would be like with all of our tears wiped away, with no more sorrow, or pain. Not that I have an answer, but in retrospect, I wouldn't have it any other way. I'm not grateful despite my addiction, I'm grateful specifically because of it. It taught me in a way that nothing else could that I am a half-man, and that the only way to reach heaven, is to let go—"Ah, but a man's reach should exceed his grasp...or what's a heaven for."

———————

"So whaddya think, Big Texan this time?" I ask the boys as we reach the outskirts of Amarillo.

"Sure."

"Sure."

354

I have to shout because the boys have their headphones on, and they're not nearly as stoked about the scenic detour as I was. They're young, and they just want to get home. But then TJ, his eyes perk up. He sees the big yellow sign with the red letters.

"Oh dad, look! Denny's! We haven't been to Denny's in forever!" And it's true, we haven't.

I look at him. "You sure? You don't want to try to eat the seventy-two ounce steak? I heard an eleven year old kid did it. Even ate dessert after. I heard there was a woman that ate two."

"Nah." He pats his belly. "Wrestling season is starting. Gotta make weight, you know."

"Denny's it is, then. Tyson, you cool with that?"

"Yep. We love Denny's, don't we dad."

"Yes we do, son. Yes we do."

And what I get is the all-you-can-eat pancake special. It tastes like manna from heaven, like freedom, and home. I have a life I wouldn't trade for anything in the world. I'm Tom, an alcoholic and a drug addict. And I am grateful.

Printed in Great Britain
by Amazon